The Airline Business in the Twenty-first Century

Airlines spell glamour, high profits and big business. Television viewers watch airline programmes spellbound. The charismatic heads of certain airlines are known to everyone. But few know the real story. This book for the first time sets the record straight.

The Airline Business in the Twenty-first Century focuses on the major issues that will affect the airline industry as we enter a new millennium. It tells of an industry working on low margins, of cut-throat competition resulting from 'open skies'. It analyses the low-cost airlines, the impact of electronic commerce and fuels the debate on global airline alliances. In a particularly poignant chapter, the author – a former airline chairman and CEO – lays bare the perils and problems of privatising state-owned airlines.

Most importantly, the book carefully analyses the strategies that are needed for airlines to succeed in the twenty-first century.

This book is essential reading for anyone interested in aviation and a core text for those working in the industry.

Rigas Doganis is an airline and airport consultant. He is also Visiting Professor at the College of Aeronautics, Cranfield University and former Chairman/CEO of Olympic Airways in Athens. He is the author of *The Airport Business* and *Flying off Course*, also published by Routledge

The Airline Business in the Twenty-first Century

Rigas Doganis

Routledge
Taylor & Francis Group

LONDON AND NEW YORK

First published 2001
by Routledge
11 New Fetter Lane, London EC4P 4EE

Simultaneously published in the USA and Canada
by Routledge
29 West 35th Street, New York, NY 10001

Reprinted 2001 (twice), 2002 (twice), 2003

Routledge is an imprint of the Taylor & Francis Group

© 2001 Rigas Doganis

Typeset in Times by Florence Production Ltd, Stoodleigh, Devon.
Printed and bound in Great Britain by
MPG Books Ltd, Bodmin, Cornwall

British Library Cataloguing in Publication Data
A catalogue record for this book is available from the British Library

Library of Congress Cataloging in Publication Data
Doganis, Rigas.
    The airline business in the 21st century/Rigas Doganis.
       p.   cm.
    Includes bibliographical references.
    1. Airlines.   2. Airlines–Management.   I. Title.
    HE9762.D64 2000
    387.7′01′12–dc21   00-056137

ISBN 0–415–20882–3 (hbk)
ISBN 0–415–20883–1 (pbk)

Contents

Appendices   **227**

Figures and tables

Figures

Tables

Acknowledgements

To many, the international airline industry appears exciting, dynamic and forward-looking, operating at the frontiers of technological innovation. Few realise that despite its glamour, it is an industry whose long-term profitability is both marginal and very cyclical. Over the last three decades five to six years of reasonable profits have been followed by two to four years of declining profits and, in the case of many airlines, of losses. The airline industry is inherently unstable because it is an industry which is constantly buffeted by new developments and constraints – regulatory, operational and technological. This was particularly true at the end of the 1990s and the beginning of the new millennium.

In recent years, 'open skies', global alliances, low-cost, no frills carriers, electronic commerce and privatisation are just some of the crucial developments affecting the airline business. These changes in turn have required airlines to develop new policies and strategies for the twenty-first century. This is the focus of the present book. It sets out to examine the key factors affecting the airline industry and assesses alternative policies that can be used to respond to a dynamic and changing market place.

In writing this book I have been fortunate in two respects. First, from the beginning of 1995 till the late spring of 1996 as Chairman and Chief Executive Officer of Olympic Airways, the Greek national airline, I managed an airline which was buffeted by many of the same forces and developments described in this book. I also had to face up to similar policy issues. I was helped in this by many of Olympic's very capable managers, from all areas of the airline, who were unstinting in their help and advice. They are too many to name individually but I am indeed indebted to them all. Second, as Professor and Head of Air Transport at Cranfield University's College of Aeronautics, from 1991 to 1997 (except while I was at Olympic), I have been fortunate in working within an environment that provided a lively forum for discussing many aspects of the constantly changing airline business. I am particularly indebted to Peter Morrell, Dr Fariba Alamdari and Andrew Lobbenberg, now an aviation analyst with Flemings, for the many stimulating discussions and arguments we had over airline issues. Those discussions have undoubtedly influenced some of the chapters that follow.

I am also grateful for the help and support I received while at Cranfield and later from Ian Stockman and Conor Whelan. The latter has also been responsible for some of the better diagrams in this book. But I must also thank the numerous Cranfield postgraduate students in air transport who through their searching questions forced me constantly to re-examine my own views and thoughts regarding the airline business.

Finally a word of apology to my wife Sally for the many weekends I spent writing when we should have been walking on Hampstead Heath or playing tennis. Not once did she complain. I owe much to her support.

1 Recent trends and future prospects

1.1 The good, the bad and the indifferent

For the then Chairman of Air France, 1993 was an unhappy time. Every evening, as he left his office to go home, his airline had lost another US$4 million! This went on, day in day out, for a year or so. Of course, it was not quite like that. But by the end of that financial year, his airline had lost almost US$1.5 billion. Such figures graphically illustrate the depth of the crisis faced by the world's airlines in the early 1990s. This was a bad time for the airline business.

While the years 1987 to 1989 had been highly profitable, in the period 1990–93 the airline industry faced the worst crisis it had ever known. The crisis started early in 1990 as fuel prices began to rise in real terms while a worsening economic climate in several countries, notably the USA and Britain, began to depress demand in certain markets. The invasion of Kuwait on 2 August 1990 and the short war that followed in January 1991 turned crisis into disaster for many airlines. Eastern Airlines in the United States and the British airline Air Europe collapsed early in 1991 while Pan American and several smaller airlines such as Midway in the United States and TEA in Belgium had gone by the end of the year. The end of the Gulf War early in 1991 did not lead to any improvement in airline fortunes, since the underlying problem was the slowdown in several key economies, not the war. In many markets, such as the North Atlantic, liberalisation combined with inadequate traffic growth was resulting in overcapacity and falling yields as airlines fought for market share. Financial results in 1992 were worse than in 1991, and 1993 was little better. Of the world's twenty largest airlines, only British Airways, Cathay, SIA (Singapore Airlines) and Swissair made a net surplus in each of the three years 1991 to 1993. It was the North American carriers that posted the largest losses in this period. Conversely several Asian airlines continued to operate profitably.

A number of airlines required massive injections of capital to survive through the early 1990s, particularly Europe's state-owned airlines such as Air France. Those from member states of the European Union received

US$10.4 billion in 'state aid' in the period up to 1995. This was government funding provided after approval by the European Commission. Later in 1997 Alitalia was given $1.7 billion of state aid. In addition several airlines received government funds of various kinds totalling nearly $1.3 billion but not categorised by the European Commission as 'state aid'. Even privatised European airlines received capital injections from their shareholders through rights issues during this period (Chapter 8, Table 8.4). Outside Europe most state-owned airlines needed direct or indirect government subsidies to keep going.

After 1994 as the cost-cutting measures launched in the crisis years began to have an impact and as demand growth began to pick up, many airlines returned to profit. This improving trend continued in 1995, 1996 and 1997. Of the larger carriers two groups, the major Japanese carriers and the state-owned airlines of southern Europe, performed less well than their counterparts and several, such as Japan Airlines and Alitalia, continued to make losses. Overall, however, these were boom years for the airline industry. In absolute terms 1998 was the most profitable year ever.

The significant improvements in airline profit levels in the mid-1990s reflected the cyclical pattern that appears to characterise the airline industry (Figure 1.1). Four to six years of reasonable profits are followed by three or four years of marginal profits or losses. While the overall profits in the period 1994–97 appear to be higher than those of the corresponding period in the 1980s, the profit margins (i.e. profits as a percentage of revenues) are no better (Figure 1.2). However, even in the good years profit margins are low. The net profits, after interest and tax, rarely achieve even 2 per cent of revenues. In 1998, the best year in absolute terms, the net operating result was only 3 per cent. Clearly, the airline industry is not very profitable compared to other industries. Of course some airlines, as previously mentioned, performed much better than the average. But even they rarely achieved a 10 per cent operating margin.

Despite the overall improvement in airline financial performance after 1994, airlines had become increasingly indebted as they borrowed heavily to finance their losses or to pay for aircraft ordered in the good years of the late 1980s. As a result, during the 1990s interest payments rose alarmingly. Many airlines, while making an operating surplus, were pushed into the red as a result of their large interest payments. The total interest payments that had to be paid each year rose dramatically during this period and were an indication of the industry's growing indebtedness. Annual interest payments for the international operations of IATA's member airlines doubled from $1.8 billion in 1988 to $3.6 billion in 1992 and have remained at over $3 billion per annum since then. This is so despite the huge write-off of debts among many state-owned airlines in Europe who used their 'state aid' primarily to cancel some of their accumulated debts.

As the new millennium approached the airline industry was faced with conflicting signals. Early in 1998 the United States airlines announced that

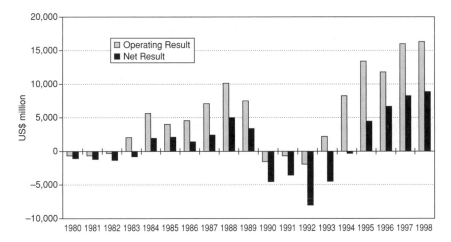

Figure 1.1 ICAO World airline financial results, 1980 to 1998 (US$).

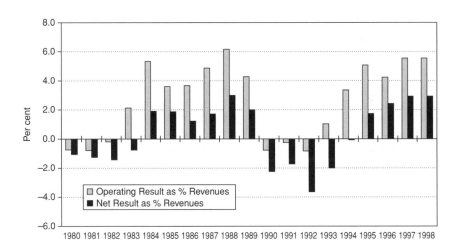

Figure 1.2 ICAO World airline financial results, 1980 to 1998 (as a percentage of revenues).

1997 had been their best year ever, with net profits reaching US$6 billion. Yet at the same time it was apparent that many Asian carriers were in dire straits. The economic crisis and meltdown that began to affect East Asia in the second half of 1997 hit Asian carriers hard. The economic downturn choked off the anticipated traffic growth. On many intra-Asian routes passenger and cargo traffic grew less rapidly than anticipated or even declined. At the same time, the dramatic devaluation of many airlines' home currencies significantly reduced the value of their foreign revenues while at the same time increasing those costs denominated in hard currencies. Fuel costs, interest charges and debt repayments rose sharply. Foreign currency denominated debts also rose.

By mid-1998 many East Asian airlines were posting large losses for the financial year 1997. Japan Airlines led the way with a net loss of US$513 million. Others' losses were not as high, but were still substantial. Asiana, the Korean airline, lost $425 million, Korean Airlines $424 million and Philippine Airlines $253 million. Only Thai Airways, Cathay Pacific and Singapore Airlines and some of the Chinese airlines bucked the trend, though the first two had significantly lower profits than in 1996.

For the East Asian airlines 1998 was even worse than 1997. While Japan Airlines and Korean managed to move from loss into profit, most carriers' financial performance deteriorated. Cathay Pacific nosedived into loss, its first ever. Philippine Airlines virtually collapsed in July 1998 after a disastrous pilots' strike. A very slimmed-down operation had to be resurrected twice through capital injections and financial restructuring in the months that followed. In Indonesia two large domestic airlines ceased operations while Garuda, the national carrier, teetered on the verge of collapse but kept flying. In 1999 both Philippine Airlines and Garuda brought in foreign managers to try and turn them round.

European and North American airlines were affected by the downturn in traffic on their routes to East Asia. In some cases, this forced them to close routes or switch some new capacity to other markets. Nevertheless, for these airlines, 1998 was as good or better in terms of profitability than 1997 had been. Results were helped by the fact that aviation fuel prices had dropped by nearly a third during 1998. Only a handful posted lower profits. British Airways, KLM and US Airways were among them. The first warning signs were appearing. Those American and European airlines which had performed so well in 1997 could see clouds gathering on the horizon. Yet they could still feel the pain of the deep economic crises they had suffered in the early 1990s.

The situation began to deteriorate further in 1999. Though in February 2000 the ten largest United States airlines as a group posted marginally higher net profits for 1999 than for the previous year, this was achieved through wide-ranging asset disposal. British Airways, which had maintained profitability throughout the crisis years of the early 1990s, was projecting losses for 1999. In fact, as the new millennium approached, many airline chairmen were issuing profit warnings.

Yet the major world economies were doing reasonably well and the forecasts were good. Even those Asian tiger economies which had gone into freefall in 1997, and Japan, where growth had slowed down, were on an upswing by the end of 1999. What were the causes of so much concern? Two major factors were affecting profits. First, overcapacity in many markets, especially on international routes as airlines fought for market share, was pushing down average yields. This trend was exacerbated in Europe and the United States by the pricing strategies of low-cost, no frills carriers. While yields were going down costs were starting to climb in real terms. During 1999 the OPEC countries had imposed production quotas so as to push up the price of oil. They succeeded in this. Prices for Brent crude oil rose from $10.28 per barrel in February 1999 to $28.14 a year later. Prices for jet fuel followed the same trend. Airlines which had not hedged their future fuel purchases were badly hit. The strengthening of the US dollar against many currencies, including the Euro, made matters worse.

Falling yields and rising costs suggests that the worsening climate for airlines, especially international airlines early in the new millennium appeared to be supply-led. This contrasts with the much deeper crisis in the early 1990s, which was demand-led in that it was caused primarily by a sharp drop in demand growth as major industrialised economies slowed down. The conundrum which had to be faced was whether the supply side problems would be sufficiently serious and unmanageable to bring about a major cyclical downturn in the airline industry some time in the period 2000 to 2003. History, as indicated in Figures 1.1 and 1.2, suggested that a downturn was due, or would airline managements take corrective action in time?

1.2 Past trends

To gain an insight into the airline industry's prospects and problems one must appreciate the market environment within which it has been operating and which has affected its development in recent years.

The most significant trend since the early 1980s has been the gradual *liberalisation of international air transport*. This has had profound effects both on market structure and on operating patterns. On the transatlantic and transpacific routes liberalisation started in the early 1980s as the United States, following domestic deregulation in 1978, began to renegotiate more open and less restrictive bilateral air services agreements (see Chapter 2). In Europe, the first liberal 'open market' bilateral was that between the UK and the Netherlands in 1984, which was followed in December 1987 by the first 'package' of liberalisation measures introduced by the European Community. In many parts of the world, governments influenced by the tide of liberalisation allowed the emergence of new domestic and/or international airlines able to compete directly with their established national carriers. Thus, in Japan, the domestic airline All Nippon Airways was allowed to operate on international routes for the first time in 1986. Elsewhere many new airlines emerged, EVA Air in Taiwan, Asiana in South Korea, Virgin Atlantic and Ryanair in Europe among them.

In Europe, the process of liberalisation culminated in the so-called 'third package' of measures, which came into force on 1 January 1993. These effectively ensured open and unrestricted market access to any routes within the European Union for airlines from any member state while at the same time removing all capacity and virtually all price controls. They also removed the ownership constraints. Henceforward, airlines within an EU member state could be owned by nationals or companies from any of the other member states. (Chapter 3 deals with these developments.)

In the mid- to late 1990s liberalisation in Europe facilitated the emergence of a new breed of low-cost low-fare airlines, such as easyJet, Debonair and Air One, which modelled themselves on Southwest in the United States (see Chapter 6).

At the same time, from 1992 onwards, the United States began to sign a series of 'open skies' bilateral air services agreements. They too effectively removed most market access or price controls on the air services between the countries concerned. But the ownership constraints remained. Airlines designated by each state had to be 'substantially owned and effectively controlled' by nationals of that state. The first 'open skies' agreement was with the Netherlands in 1992. Over forty such agreements had been negotiated by the United States by early 2000. (See Chapters 2 and 3 for an analysis of the deregulatory developments.)

This trend towards liberalisation of economic regulations significantly changed market conditions in those parts of the world where such liberalisation took place. In particular, it resulted in the emergence of new airlines on many international air routes. In some cases, these were newly created airlines such as EVA Air; in others they were established carriers entering particular international routes for the first time. Very powerful but hitherto largely domestic United States carriers such as United, Delta, American and Brannif, launched new international operations. They were joined in the early days by new entrant airlines such as People Express, Air Florida and others, though few of these survived for long. United and Delta launched their international networks beyond the Americas by respectively buying out and expanding the transpacific and transatlantic operations of Pan American.

A further consequence of liberalisation was that there was much less control of capacity and frequency on many routes while at the same time there was considerably greater pricing freedom. While published international fares continued to be established through the machinery of the International Air Transport Association (IATA), such agreed fares were frequently and openly flouted.

Another key factor which has had a major beneficial impact on the airline industry during the last ten years or so has been the *relatively low price of aviation fuel* and the general stability of the price level. This contrasts sharply with the high prices experienced in the late 1970s and early 1980s. The price of fuel shot up dramatically on two occasions as a result of crises in the Middle East: first in 1973–74 when it more than doubled in price and in 1979 when again the price doubled. The average

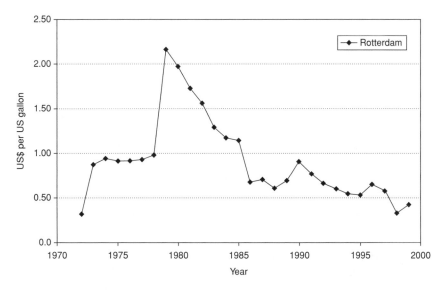

Figure 1.3 Fuel price trends 1972 to 1999 (Rotterdam spot prices at constant 1992 prices).

price of jet fuel rose from 32 US cents per gallon in 1972 (in 1997 US dollar values) to almost two dollars in 1980 (in 1997 US dollar values) (Figure 1.3). Fuel became the major airline cost for a time, representing 30 per cent to 33 per cent of total operating costs. These high fuel prices were one of the major causes of the losses incurred during the cyclical downturn of the early 1980s (Figure 1.1). But from 1981 onwards fuel prices began to decline gradually in real terms and dropped sharply in 1986. The sharp drop experienced in 1986 in turn partly explains the high profits achieved in the years 1986 to 1989.

What is more significant is that since 1986 the price of aviation fuel has stabilised at a value which in real terms is a little less than double the level prior to the two oil crises. But it is still substantially lower than the prices prevailing during the early 1980s. The price does fluctuate, but around a more or less constant level. Thus, while the 1990 Kuwait crisis and war of 1991 produced a sudden sharp hike in fuel prices, the prices were back close to their pre-crisis levels within a year (Figure 1.3). Again in late 1996 there was a sharp increase, but prices declined during 1997 to earlier levels. In fact, in 1998 jet fuel prices dropped even further to levels not experienced since 1972. Fuel prices did rise appreciably during 1999 and early 2000 as a result of OPEC cutbacks in petroleum output mentioned earlier. Average spot prices for jet fuel rose from around 32 US cents per gallon in February 1999 to almost 77 US cents in February 2000, an increase of 140 per cent or so. Despite this it is clear that fuel prices have tended to become less volatile in the long run because oil production is now much more dispersed geographically than it was in the 1970s. A crisis or shortfall in production in one area can more easily be met by increased production elsewhere. It is significant that low fuel prices prevailed in the late 1990s despite the fact that Iraq, previously the world's second-largest oil exporter, was no longer able to export oil as a result of a United Nations embargo on Iraqi exports. It is likely that in the medium term the high fuel prices of late 1999 and early 2000 will come down to levels prevailing in the mid-1990s, that is, 50 to 60 US cents per gallon. The decline and stabilisation in the price of aviation fuel means that the cost of fuel during most of the 1990s represented between 12 per cent and 15 per cent of airlines' total operating costs. Most forecasters predict that during the first decade of the new millennium fuel prices measured in constant values will either continue to be fairly stable, though with some sharp, short-term fluctuations, or at the very worst they may increase in real terms at a low rate of 1 or 2 per cent per annum.

The third trend underlying the development of air transport is that *traffic growth rates have been declining*. In the decade 1966–77 the world's air traffic measured in terms of passenger-kilometres grew at an annual rate of 11.6 per cent, effectively doubling every six or seven years. In the following decade up to 1987 annual growth was less but still high at 7.8 per cent. But during the period 1987 to 1997 the traffic growth declined further to around 4.8 per cent per annum. The average growth rate for the whole of the 1990s was expected to be a little below 5.0 per cent. Of course, in absolute traffic terms because of the much larger base a 5.0 per cent growth in the 1990s or today represents a huge jump in traffic compared to a 12 per cent rise in the late 1960s.

However, these global growth rates mask the fact that growth has been very uneven, with wide variations between different parts of the world and between different airlines. In particular, for the last twenty to twenty-five years, traffic to, from and between the countries of East Asia has been growing much faster than the world average.

The reasons for this are fairly clear. For more than twenty years, till late 1997, Japan and the tiger economies of South East Asia were developing much more rapidly than the traditional economies of Europe and North America. Their export-oriented economies generated considerable business travel while rising per capita incomes stimulated leisure and personal travel. At the same time countries such as Thailand, Singapore and Indonesia rapidly developed their tourism infrastructure, attracting growing numbers of tourists both from within and without the region. It should also not be forgotten that most of the countries and many of the major cities of East Asia are separated by large expanses of water. In many cases there is no alternative to air travel. Even when surface travel is possible, as between Kuala Lumpur and Bangkok, the infrastructure is poor and journey times are too slow. The 1970s and 1980s also saw the rapid growth of new Asian state-owned airlines such as SIA, Malaysia Airlines (MAS), Thai International, Garuda and the privately owned Cathay Pacific. Offering superior in-flight service and aggressive marketing, they both stimulated demand and captured a growing share of it.

As a consequence of above average traffic growth in East Asia and the dynamic expansion of Asian airlines, there has been a *dramatic restructuring* of the world's international airline industry away from the traditional United States and European international airlines and *in favour of the East Asian/Pacific airlines*. Whereas in 1972 the Asian and Pacific region airlines carried only 13 per cent of the world's international scheduled traffic, by the late 1990s their share was up to about one-third, around 31–2 per cent. In terms of tonne-kms carried on international services four of the world's top ten airlines are now Asian: Japan Airlines, SIA, Korean and Cathay. Conversely, the once dominant US and European airlines have lost market share. In 1972 airlines from these two regions carried three-quarters of the world's international traffic. Today their joint share is barely over 50 per cent though the United States airlines are currently slowly clawing back a greater market share.

Finally, a critical trend in recent years has been the gradual but *steady decline in the real value of airline yields* – that is the average revenue produced per passenger-km or tonne-km carried. Several factors have caused this. The liberalisation which, as mentioned earlier, has spread over more and more routes reduced or removed both capacity and price controls. New airlines emerged to compete with established carriers and in order to capture market share they reduced fares only to be matched in many cases by their competitors. Elsewhere competition focused on increased frequencies, but these extra frequencies had to be filled and fare reductions was one way of doing this. A widespread phenomenon in deregulated markets is that an ever-growing proportion of passengers is travelling on reduced or discounted fares while at the same time the fare reductions are cutting deeper and deeper into the scheduled fares. This first became evident on United States domestic air services during the 1980s following domestic deregulation in 1978.

The same trend is very evident within Europe. The average yield from promotional fares has gone down to less than half of the normal economy fare, whereas it was about 63 per cent in 1985. Yet the proportion of passengers travelling at these low fares has also risen from 57 per cent to 71 per cent of the total. The same pattern of more of the passengers flying at ever deeper discounts has been repeated in both the transatlantic and transpacific markets.

Fortunately, the fall in real yields has in many cases been matched by falling unit costs. This was made possible by the more widespread introduction of new-generation wide-bodied aircraft and by the great efforts made to reduce airline costs across the board during the crises years of the early 1990s. The fall in the real price of aviation fuel in the early to mid-1980s also helped. But, where average yields have fallen faster than unit costs airlines have been under great pressure to increase load factors to compensate for the lower yields.

1.3 Future developments in the operating environment

The long-term prospects for air transport look good. At the start of the new millennium, the decline in annual growth rates appeared to have been stemmed. Most long-term forecasts were modified downwards after the East Asian crisis of 1997–98, but they still predicted that growth rates for worldwide air traffic would average about 5 per cent over the first decade of the new millennium. But year to year, there will be fluctuations around this average figure. Despite the continuing economic problems in some European countries, and to a lesser extent in Japan, most forecasts prepared in 1998 and 1999 are optimistic. This optimism stems from the close link that has been established historically between the demand for air travel and world economic growth. The rate of growth of air traffic seems to follow closely developments in the world's gross domestic product (GDP). Though frequently there is a time lag before air traffic responds to changes in GDP, air traffic worldwide measured in terms of scheduled passenger-kms appears to have an income elasticity of around 2. This means that in general air traffic grows about twice as fast as the annual growth in the world's GDP. It is because economic forecasters early in 2000 were predicting medium-term growth in world GDP to average 2.5 to 3.0 per cent per annum that airline traffic is expected to grow annually at 5 per cent to 6 per cent.

Airbus Industrie, in their long-term forecasts presented in May 1999, predicted that airline traffic measured in terms of revenue passenger-kms would grow at an annual rate of 5.1 per cent in the ten years from 1999 to 2008. Growth would slow down to 4.9 per cent per annum in the decade after that. Boeing was forecasting somewhat lower annual growth of 4.7 per cent in the first decade to 2007. Both manufacturers were forecasting growth rates for the first decade of the new millennium which were close to those achieved in the 1990s. In other words, there would be no slowing down.

In the light of past trends, all air traffic forecasters, including Airbus and Boeing, expect much higher than average growth in particular markets, notably on routes to and from the East Asia and Pacific regions. Traffic growth to and from Latin America is also expected to be above the world average. On the other hand, traffic in two of the largest international markets, those of the North Atlantic or within Europe, will grow at or below the average world growth rate.

In a climate of long-term optimism but short-term uncertainty, the market environment for air transport during the first decade of the new millennium will be characterised by significant changes both in the regulatory regime and in market structures. The *trend towards a very liberal 'open skies' international regime is unstoppable*. Within Europe, the more or less total deregulation of intra-European air services that has already taken place within the European Union will increasingly spread eastwards to the former communist states. Ten states have been negotiating to adopt the 'third package' and the associated competition rules. They are expected to formally join the Common European Aviation Area during 2001, which already contains the fifteen member states of the European Union together with Norway and Sweden. This will create a vast single deregulated market for air transport covering most of Europe. Other states such as Switzerland or Cyprus are expected to join shortly, even before becoming full members of the European Union. Meanwhile, the removal since 1993 of any real distinctions between charters and scheduled services within the European Union will increasingly draw the two sectors closer together. New airlines will appear though several will collapse or be taken over including some of the weaker, state-owned carriers. The most dramatic impact on air transport in Europe will come from the rapid growth of low-cost, no frills airlines (Chapter 6).

In Asia and South America a number of states have already signed 'open skies' air services agreements with the United States while continuing to operate on the basis of traditional and more restrictive bilateral agreements with their own neighbouring states. Such an anomalous situation cannot continue for long. The emphasis in the near future will be on liberalising the economic regime between neighbouring states. This may be done on a bilateral basis, but is more likely to be implemented under the auspices of regional economic groupings such as ASEAN in South East Asia and ECOSUR in South America. In Africa the pressure to liberalise will not come from external sources but will arise from the dire financial position of most of the African state-owned airlines. Governments will liberalise both their domestic and international aviation regimes to ensure adequate air services in the event of the collapse of the state airline when government support is no longer forthcoming. In November 1999, African nations meeting in Yamoussoukro in the Ivory Coast signed an agreement aimed at achieving a single aviation market for the continent by 2002.

While liberalisation of market access will spread, another more controversial issue, namely that of airline ownership, will also need to be tackled. In one very important respect air transport is still treated quite differently from any other industry. The traditional and even the newer 'open skies' bilateral air services agreements require the airlines designated by each of the two states to be 'substantially owned' and 'effectively controlled' by nationals of the designating state. As other regulatory constraints on airlines' freedom of action in international operations are removed and as other industries become more internationalised in their ownership then the pressure to remove the nationality constraint on airlines will become overwhelming. It is inevitable that, during the first few years of the third millennium, more and more states will abandon this commercial constraint either through bilateral or multilateral agreements (Chapter 3, section 3.2). *Airline ownership will become increasingly multinational rather than national* as at present. Privatisation of hitherto government-owned airlines will facilitate this process. The airline business will become no different from any other multinational industry. The first decade of the new millennium will finally see the complete transformation of the airline industry from a protected, nationally owned industry into a true multinational business operating freely across frontiers.

This global airline business, however, will *become increasingly concentrated into a handful of worldwide airline alliances*. Experience in the United States domestic market during the 1980s showed that it was not the low-cost new entrants who were most likely to survive in a competitive environment but those large airlines which were successful in exploiting the marketing benefits of large scale and spread. It was the realisation of this that led to the growing concentration of the US airline industry through takeovers and mergers. As liberalisation spread to Europe in the late 1980s European carriers began to examine how they too could achieve the marketing benefits of large scale. They began to take over their smaller domestic competitors and looked to buying minority shares in European airlines outside their own countries.

By the early 1990s the process of concentration was internationalised. It was apparent that linking together the networks of airlines in different countries to create global networks could create not only marketing benefits for all the partner airlines but also help them in reducing distribution and sales costs. Thus, in the mid- and late 1990s one saw a host of airline alliances which took a variety of forms, from those that were little more than traditional commercial agreements, to code sharing, and share swaps between airlines or even outright mergers. (Chapter 4 deals with the growth of airline alliances.) A complex web of interlocking alliances was built up. Though it is true that many of these alliances had little logic and minimal commercial benefit to the alliance partners.

Many of the early alliances have not survived and collapsed after a few years as one or other of the partners sought new alliances. As part of its global network strategy British Airways bought 19.9 per cent of USAir in 1993 But in June 1996 it announced a new alliance with American Airlines, one of USAir's major domestic competitors, and was forced to sell its shareholding in USAir. Perhaps the first truly global alliance was that between Delta Airlines, Swissair and Singapore Airlines (SIA) launched in 1990 and involving a swapping of up to 5 per cent of shares between each of the partners. The share swap suggested long-term stability for this alliance. Yet seven years later the alliance suddenly collapsed when Singapore Airlines, in November 1997 unexpectedly signed a commercial agreement with Lufthansa which included code sharing and joint marketing. Then in November 1999 Delta announced it was in turn abandoning Swissair in favour of an alliance with Air France. The experience of the Delta-Swissair-SIA partners illustrates the marked instability of alliances in the second half of the 1990s as airlines jockeyed for position. Currently most alliances appear to be engagements rather than weddings. They can be broken relatively easily.

In the latter part of the 1990s alliance activity accelerated as, with a few exceptions most airline chief executives and chairmen felt alliances were a panacea that could solve many of their airlines' problems and create new market opportunities. Governments with loss-making state-owned airlines announced that what these airlines needed to be turned round was little more than a strategic partner (i.e. another airline) who would buy 15–30 per cent of their shares from the government. In 1998 the Greek, Irish, Portuguese, Thai and Jordanian governments among others all announced that strategic alliances for their airlines was one of the two cornerstones of their strategies for saving their national airlines. The other was *privatisation*.

During the next few years the global pattern of the major alliances will be rationalised through withdrawal of some partners and inclusion of others. A period of great instability will occur as soon as the nationality and ownership constraints are relaxed and cross-border acquisitions and mergers become possible. New alliance groupings are likely to emerge. At the same time competitive pressures will ensure that the commercial linkages between partners will be strengthened while commercial co-operation with non-partners will gradually diminish. The airline market will increasingly be dominated by a few global alliances or megacarriers, together with their partners and franchisees. Concentration will gradually give way to consolidation. Moreover, virtually all of the major airlines will be wholly or largely privatised and multinationally owned.

Growing consolidation within the airline business through the expansion and strengthening of alliances will raise the issue of market dominance and the possible abuse of that dominance when alliances operate as monopolists or duopolists in particular international markets. The risks of abuse will be greatest when and where an alliance dominates a major airport hub.

Despite greater industry concentration there will be a *strong downward trend in fare levels* and airline yields in real terms. A number of factors will create pressure to reduce fares. First, further liberalisation and more 'open skies' bilaterals will remove any vestiges of tariff controls while encouraging the launching of new airlines and the expansion of existing airlines onto new routes from which they were previously barred by the regulatory regime. Second, low-cost low-fare airlines will increasingly impact on international air routes, snapping at the heels of the established major carriers. Till the mid-1990s airlines identified as 'low cost', such as Southwest or the former Valujet, had been confined to United States domestic operations. They achieved much lower costs by introducing new operating practices and different service standards (see Chapter 6). From 1995 onwards several new European airlines, such as Ryanair or easyJet, adopted 'low cost' economies and entered European international markets. Offering much lower fares, their market share increased rapidly and before the end of the decade such established carriers as British Airways and KLM were launching their own 'low-cost' subsidiaries. The spread of 'low-cost' airlines to medium-haul international routes and possibly even long-haul will increase the downward pressure on fares. Third, during the early years of the new millennium there will almost certainly be over-capacity in many markets as the aircraft ordered in the good years from 1995 to 1998 are delivered and put into service. Despite the fact that in 1998 several Asian airlines, such as Philippine Airlines, Garuda and Thai Airways, cancelled or delayed the delivery of aircraft ordered a year or two earlier, the indications were that world-wide, the introduction of new capacity in the period 1999 to 2002 would aggravate overcapacity trends in several markets. But wherever overcapacity occurs there is a strong incentive for airlines to cut fares to fill up the empty seats. Finally, the devaluation in 1998 by 50 per cent or more of several East Asian curren-cies, the smaller devaluations in Latin America and the loss of value of around 10 per cent in the euro in 1999 would themselves reduce average revenues in real terms. Fares in devalued currencies cannot rapidly be adjusted sufficiently to compensate for the revenue dilution. Late in 1998 Airbus Industrie was predicting that average yields would decline in some markets by as much as 30 per cent in real terms over the following twenty years (Brown, 1998).

The downward pressure on yields will in turn make cost reduction a major priority for all airline managements. Cost cutting is no longer a short-term strategy to deal with short-term economic downturns in the airline business. *Cost reduction has become a continuous and long-term necessity for financial success.* The aim must be to continue to reduce unit costs. The long-term stability in the price of fuel mentioned earlier will help, but it is not enough. The focus of cost reduction strategies will inevitably be on reducing labour costs, which for most airlines represent 25 to 35 per cent of total operating costs. Labour is also a major cost differentiator between airlines competing in the same markets, since so many other input costs, such as fuel, landing fees, aircraft purchase and ground handling, will be broadly similar. Airlines will try to reduce labour costs first of all by improving labour productivity through reductions in staff numbers, by renegotiating work practices and by changing business and service processes (Chapter 5). This is unlikely to be enough. In order to cut labour costs more dramatically airlines will increasingly try to outsource what were, hitherto, in-house activities. They may even 'relo-cate' many key functions to low-wage economies or employ flight or cabin crews from these countries. The higher the wage levels in an airline's home country the greater will be the pressure to relocate labour-intensive activities to countries with low wage structures. The dramatic devaluation of several East Asian currencies in 1997–98 makes these countries very attractive as sources of labour for Japanese, European and United States airlines with high wage rates.

The strong pressures to reduce unit costs will also push airlines to re-examine another major cost area, that of sales and distribution. At the same time the industry will become more consumer-oriented and 'the customer will be king'. As part of this process there will be growing '*disintermediation*' of airline distribution systems, with airlines bypassing the traditional travel agent to deal directly with their customer. This will be done through use of the Internet, electronic ticketing, telephone sales and other direct sales methods. Ticketless, paperless travel will become normal. This is, after all, one of the lessons that can be learned from the low-cost airlines. The development and widespread use of so-called 'electronic commerce' will revolutionise the selling and distribution systems used within the airline business, while at the same time reducing the commissions paid to travel agents. Since agents' commissions may account for up to 12 per cent of total operating costs, the scope for cost reduction is substantial (Chapter 7).

In the early years of the new millennium, the airline industry will also have to face up to numerous problems arising from the *inadequacy of the aviation infrastructure* in several parts of the world. Continued growth at around 5 per cent per annum will put the existing aviation infrastructure, that is, the airports and the air traffic systems, under considerable pressure. In many parts of the world they may be unable to cope because of inadequate funds for investment, lack of political will or, in the case of airports in Europe and some other countries, through lack of suitable land available for the construction of additional runways. For many airports close to built-up areas the situation will be made worse by pressure from strong environmental lobbies opposed to further expansion and, in some cases, campaigning for a reduction in the current number of air traffic movements. Governments and airlines will increasingly have to look to developing satellite airports close to major conurbations either on what were previously secondary minor airports or airfields or even on military airfields no longer required by the armed forces.

Where airport capacity cannot be increased then access to runway slots will be at a premium. Airlines which through the existing grandfather rights control these slots will enjoy a major competitive advantage. This is particularly so at major hub airports where the base airline together with its alliance partners and franchisees may effectively control 60–70 per cent or more of the total available slots. For instance, at Schiphol, KLM and its partners have over 70 per cent of the scheduled slots and a very high proportion of the charter slots. The shortage of runway slots will reinforce the competitive strength of airline alliances. Attempts to open up the system of slot allocation by abandoning the grandfather rules are unlikely to be any more successful in generating real competition than they have been in the past. But more open and transparent slot auctions and/or secondary slot trading may be considered. How to ensure greater competition when slots are in short supply will be a key issue in the years to come.

In the case of air traffic control, the need to improve its efficiency, to find adequate funds for investment and to overcome interface problems between neighbouring states will push governments to privatise or partially privatise their air traffic services. The UK government was in the process of doing this in 2000 by selling off 46 per cent of the National Air Traffic Services (NATS). Once this happens and the implications are absorbed by other governments and service providers there will be a rush to further such privatisations. The privatisation of the British Airports Authority in the UK in 1987, the first airports to be privatised, was followed five years later by a deluge of such privatisations. The same will happen once NATS is privatised, but the follow-up will be more rapid.

The *environmental issues* pose a further and potentially an even greater threat to the airline industry. Moves are already under way within the European Commission to assess the feasibility of charging airlines for the pollution created by aircraft emissions as a way of inducing a reduction in engine emissions. While currently there are technical and political difficulties in imposing any such charges through a fuel tax, the concept of 'polluter pays' has been embraced. If during the first decade of the third millennium multinational agreement is reached on this issue, the consequences for airline costs will clearly be adverse.

1.4 The airline business in the twenty-first century

In summary, the foregoing analysis suggests that the following key developments and factors will underpin the growth of the international airline business in the first decade of the 21st century:

- While longer-term traffic growth over the years to 2010 as a whole will average close to 5 per cent per annum, growth rates will differ markedly between key markets.
- The period 2000–02 will be very difficult and critical for many airlines because of overcapacity, falling yields and relatively high fuel costs. All airlines will be adversely affected, but state-owned airlines in East Asia, Europe and the Third World will find it particularly difficult to survive. Already early in 2000 Canadian Airlines had to be rescued from collapse by Air Canada while Swissair bought a 34 per cent shareholding in Air Portugal in order to prevent its demise. Olympic Airways was looking to British Airways to save it by injecting desperately needed capital. Both Garuda and Philippine Airlines, like

Olympic, were being managed by foreign airline executives. More such rescues are likely to be needed. Many airlines operating in 2000 will no longer be flying in 2010 or will have been absorbed by larger carriers.

- The liberalisation of the existing regulatory constraints on the operation of international air services will spread to areas and markets hitherto unaffected. Restrictions on market access, on capacity, on pricing and even those on ownership of airlines will be progressively eroded. Real 'open skies' will be replaced by totally 'clear skies'. The airline industry will become a truly global business.
- Liberalisation in general, together with the abandonment of ownership restrictions and the privatisation of airlines hitherto government-owned, will accelerate the process of industrial concentration within global alliances. After some early instability, the alliances will become increasingly integrated and dominant. The three largest alliances will between them carry over 50 per cent and perhaps as much as 60 per cent of the world's air traffic and will totally dominate certain markets.
- Governments and regional authorities, such as the European Commission, will attempt to control possible abuses of such dominance. This will be done by trying to ensure that the competition rules of major regions or countries, such as those of the United States and the European Union, converge as much as possible.
- There will be strong downward pressure on fares and cargo tariffs. Average airline yields will continue to decline in real terms. The drop in yields will be most marked in the early years of the decade because of overcapacity resulting from over-ordering in the mid-1990s and from 'open skies'. New 'low-cost' carriers will also help erode fare levels, especially in Europe and later in other regions such as South East Asia.
- Falling yields will reinforce pressure to cut unit costs. Cost reduction will become a long-term and continuous prerequisite for financial success. Airlines will be helped in this by the projected stability in the real price of fuel. The main emphasis will be in reducing the cost of labour through staff reductions, improved work practices and outsourcing, not only of functions such as catering but even the actual flying, to lower-cost operators. Airlines will also increasingly relocate certain activities and employees to low-wage economies.
- In order both to reduce costs and to improve service to customers, airlines will increasingly use electronic commerce not only to sell and distribute their products, but also in their business-to-business relationships. E-commerce will in turn revolutionise the customer–airline relationship and put traditional travel agents and freight forwarders under pressure to adapt to a new reality.
- The continued growth of air traffic at about 5 per cent per annum will place airport and air traffic control systems under tremendous pressure,

especially as current capacity is already inadequate in many airports and flight regions. Problems will be aggravated by pressure from environmentalists for the reduction both of airport noise and aircraft emissions. To ensure adequate airport capacity is available where new runways cannot be built at existing airports greater use will be made of satellite airports, many of which will be on former military airfields. New ways will be explored for allocating runway slots between airlines where demand exceeds supply. The privatisation of air traffic control in the United Kingdom in order to ensure adequate investment will lead to further such privatisations in other countries.

The chapters which follow deal in detail with most, though not all, of the key developments highlighted here. The focus is on those strategic and managerial aspects which are essentially internal to the airline industry. While recognising that inadequate infrastructure and future environmental constraints are crucial issues affecting the future of air transport, they are perhaps better dealt with in a separate book.

2 Towards 'open skies'

Nothing like the system of government imposed impediments to economic decision-making exists in any other sector of international trade . . .

(Jeffrey Shane, 1992)

2.1 Traditional bilateralism under pressure

In January 1977 Jimmy Carter, a peanut farmer from Georgia, became President of the United States. The Carter administration set off a chain of events that were to transform international air transport from a closeted and highly protected industry into a business that is more truly competitive and open. The transformation is not complete but the process of change should be finalised in the early years of the 21st century. The international airline industry can be understood only in the context of the changing regulatory environment within which it operates.

The airline industry is a paradox. In terms of its operations it is the most international of industries, yet in terms of ownership and control it is almost exclusively national. It has also been very highly regulated, beset by a complex web of economic regulations. These constrained airlines' market access, pricing policy and output decisions and, as a result, competition itself. While each country and government tightly controlled its own domestic air services, the traditional regulatory framework affecting international air transport operations was based essentially on bilateralism and emerged in the aftermath of the Second World War.

At an intergovernmental conference in Chicago in 1944 an attempt had been made, spearheaded by the United States, to create a competitive regime for international air transport with minimal regulation. The attempt failed. While the Chicago Convention did establish the technical and legal framework for the operation of international air services, it did not deal with economic regulation. To resolve economic issues, three separate but interlinked elements of international regulation rapidly emerged and provided the basic regulatory framework for the airline business USAir until the early 1980s. These are the bilateral air services agreements (ASAs), the inter-airline commercial or pooling agreements and the tariff-fixing machinery of the International Air Transport Association (IATA).

Bilateral air services agreements between pairs of countries have had as their prime purpose the control of market access (points served and traffic rights) and of market entry (designation of airlines), though in many cases they also controlled capacity and frequencies. Such bilateral agreements became and remain the fundamental core of the regulatory regime. This bilateralism was reinforced till the 1980s by the IATA system for controlling tariffs and by inter-airline pooling agreements.

Air services agreements contain both administrative and economic provisions. Most of the administrative articles of such agreements deal with so-called 'soft rights' aimed at facilitating the operation of air services, such as taxation issues, exemption from customs duties on imports of aircraft parts, airport charges, transfer abroad of airline funds, and so on. The economic provisions are those that deal with the 'hard rights', namely the number of designated airlines, the regulation of tariffs, and capacity and traffic rights, that is, access to routes. The bilateral will specify whether one or more airlines can be designated by each country to fly on the agreed routes. In most traditional agreements only one airline (i.e. single designation) was to be designated. Irrespective of the number of airlines to be designated, all had to be 'substantially owned and effectively controlled' by nationals of the designating state. This nationality clause was to prove the biggest obstacle to the normalisation of the international airline business.

Two key articles dealing with 'hard rights' concern the regulation of tariffs and capacity. Most traditional bilaterals specify that passenger fares and cargo tariffs should be agreed by the designated airlines, but these were encouraged to use the tariff-fixing machinery of the International Air Transport Association (IATA) to agree such tariffs. However, both governments must approve such fares and tariffs. This is the so-called 'double approval' regime. In other words, ultimate control on tariffs rests with individual governments. On capacity, some bilaterals require very strict control and sharing of capacity by the airlines of the two countries whereas others have minimal control.

The second part of the bilateral is the annex containing the 'schedule of routes'. It is here that the remaining 'hard rights' – the actual traffic rights granted to each of the two states – are made explicit. The schedule specifies the routes to be operated by the designated airline(s) of each state. These are the Third and Fourth Freedom rights (see Appendix A for fuller description). The points (towns) to be served by each designated airline are listed, or (less often) a general right may be granted for instance from or to 'any point' in one or both of the signatory states. The schedule will also indicate whether the designated airlines have been granted rights to pick up traffic in other countries on services to or from points lying between or beyond the two signatory states. These are the Fifth Freedom rights. They cannot be used, however, unless the third countries involved also agree.

Table 2.1 Key features of traditional air services agreements*

	Bermuda/liberal type	*Predetermination type*
Market access	Only specified and limited number of points/routes to be operated by each airline.	
	Several Fifth Freedoms granted, but total capacity related to end-to-end (i.e. Third/Fourth Freedom) demand on route.	Few Fifth Freedoms granted.
	Charter traffic rights *not* included.	
Designation	Generally single but some double or multiple.	Single designation.
	Airlines must be under substantial ownership and effective control of nationals of designating state.	
Capacity	No frequency or capacity control: but capacity review if one airline too adversely affected.	Capacity to be agreed or fifty-fifty split.
		Inter-airline revenue pool required (by some bilaterals).
Tariffs	Tariffs related to cost plus profit.	
	Approval of both governments needed (i.e. double approval).	
	If possible, airlines should use IATA procedures.	

Note
* Despite subsequent liberalisation of many United States and West European bilaterals with third countries, most of the world's current ASAs in 2000 were still of the traditional types shown above.

Until 1978, all air services agreements were more or less restrictive in terms of market access, that is, points to be served, and capacity and price controls. They were broadly of two kinds (Table 2.1). The more liberal bilaterals, frequently referred to as the Bermuda type, differed from the more restrictive predetermination type of agreements in two respects: first, Fifth Freedom rights were more widely available; second, there was no control of frequency or capacity on the routes between the two countries concerned. Bermuda-type agreements became widespread, but their impact is not as liberal as their terms might suggest. This is because they do not preclude airline pooling agreements (which effectively restrict capacity competition) or indeed subsequent capacity restrictions imposed arbitrarily by governments.

The main purpose of *inter-airline pooling agreements* was to enable airlines to share the revenues generated on the routes they served in common in proportion to the seat capacity they each offered in that market. The mechanism whereby revenues were shared was complex and varied. Some agreements were open-ended, allowing unlimited transfer of funds from one carrier to the other, so as to ensure that each airline's final revenue equated with its capacity share, which was normally 50 per cent. Where this was the case there was little incentive to compete. But most agreements limited the proportion of the total revenues earned that could be transferred and thereby encouraged some competition (see Doganis, 1991 for details).

Thus, though revenue sharing was the prime objective, it could only be effective with control of capacity on a bilateral basis by the two airlines concerned. Many airlines espousing deregulation and multilateralism, as Singapore Airlines did in the 1980s, nevertheless entered into many bilateral revenue-pooling agreements. However, pooling agreements were never entered into on routes to the United States, as they breached US anti-trust legislation. While they sometimes involved more than two airlines, such revenue-sharing agreements were essentially bilateral in nature and could only be effective when entry of additional Third and Fourth Freedom airlines was controlled by the bilateral air services agreement (see Appendix A). Where airlines had not been granted Fifth Freedom rights under existing bilateral agreements they were sometimes able to purchase such rights by paying royalties to the airline of the country from/to which they wanted to operate on a Fifth Freedom basis. Such royalty or 'revenue compensation' agreements were and still are a further feature of bilateralism.

The International Air Transport Association (IATA), an association of international airline companies, provided the third element of an essentially bilateral regulatory regime. In the 1946 Air Services Agreement signed with the United Kingdom in Bermuda, the United States made a major concession. It agreed to approve tariffs fixed by IATA, an association of producers (i.e. the international airlines), even though such price-fixing was illegal under United States anti-trust legislation. In essence, IATA tariff decisions were exempted from the provisions of such legislation. Subsequently, the tariffs article of most early bilaterals, including the predetermination types, included wording to the effect that tariff agreements should 'where possible be reached by the use of the procedures of the International Air Transport Association for the working out of tariffs'. It was only in the 1980s that this wording began to be dropped when bilateral air services agreements were renegotiated. Even states such as Singapore or Malaysia, whose national airlines were not members of IATA, agreed in their early bilaterals to approve where possible IATA tariffs. Thus, approval for the IATA tariffs procedures was enshrined in the majority of bilateral agreements. This is what gave the IATA tariffs machinery such force until deregulation set in from 1978 onwards.

In the twenty-five years or so after the Second World War bilateralism was at its peak. However, during the 1970s it came under growing pressure from several directions. Within Western Europe and on the North Atlantic, charter or non-scheduled services had grown dramatically by offering much lower fares than the scheduled IATA tariffs. On the North Atlantic routes, governments tried to impose all kinds of regulatory and operational constraints to protect scheduled carriers. Despite these constraints, by 1977 nearly one-third (29 per cent) of air passengers across the Atlantic were using charter or non-scheduled services. At the same time, new Asian airlines not belonging to IATA entered the routes between Europe and East Asia and captured a growing market by ignoring IATA rules on service standards and offering much better in-flight service than IATA carriers, often at lower tariffs. As a result of these competitive pressures, it was becoming increasingly difficult to enforce IATA tariffs and conditions of service. Some IATA members were themselves forced to break the rules. The public, the press and consumer groups in particular increasingly attacked the restrictive nature of bilateralism which prevented lower-cost airlines entering new markets and which appeared to protect high-cost airlines and the high fares they imposed. There was growing public pressure to break out of the confines of bilateralism.

As a result of these pressures, the traditional bilateral regulatory regime became increasingly shaky. Thus, when the United States began to push for liberalisation it found support in several countries. Two distinct phases of change emerged. The first was that of partial liberalisation and the opening up of markets in the period up to 1992. The second phase which followed was that of 'open skies'.

However, despite the liberalisation of many bilateral ASAs in the period after 1978, it should not be forgotten that at the start of the new millennium the majority of the world's bilaterals are still of the traditional types described in Table 2.1.

2.2 Liberalisation and 'open markets' 1978–91

The initial impetus for change came from the strong public pressure for deregulation of domestic air services in the United States culminating in the 1978 Deregulation Act, and was reinforced by the inauguration of the Carter administration in January 1977. Up to then, the United States had acquiesced in the three-pronged structure of economic regulation of air transport described earlier. The Carter administration set out to reduce regulatory controls to a minimum. One of its election pledges had been to support the interests of consumers. In air transport, as in other industries, this meant less regulation and more choice. The US government was initially supported in this by several other governments, especially those of the Netherlands and Singapore, though later other governments, including that of the United Kingdom, also adopted a deregulatory stance.

In the summer of 1978 a statement on 'International Air Transport Negotiations' was signed by President Carter (Presidential Documents,

1978). This stated that the US aim was to provide 'maximum consumer benefits . . . through the preservation and extension of competition between airlines in a fair market place'. This was to be achieved through the negotiation or renegotiation of bilateral air services agreements with the aim of achieving the following:

- greater opportunities for innovative and competitive pricing;
- elimination of restrictions on capacity, frequency and route operating rights;
- elimination of discrimination and unfair competitive practices faced by US airlines abroad;
- flexibility for multiple designation of US airlines;
- authorisation of more US cities as international gateways;
- liberalisation of rules regarding charter flights;
- more competitive air cargo services.

In a series of negotiations, the United States offered foreign states a small number of additional gateway points for their airlines in exchange for all or most of the above objectives. It was the United States-Netherlands agreement, signed in March 1978, which was to become the trendsetter for subsequent US bilaterals. Since the Netherlands was starting from a viewpoint very similar to that of the United States, it was inevitable that their bilateral agreement would be a particularly liberal one. Both sides set out to reduce the role of the government in matters of capacity, frequency and tariffs, and in the setting of market conditions.

Meanwhile negotiations had already been opened between the United States and Belgium and Germany for a revision of their bilaterals. Because of the geographical proximity of these two countries to the Netherlands, their negotiators realised that they could not afford to be less liberal on either scheduled or charter rights than the Dutch had been; otherwise, considerable German transatlantic air traffic would be diverted via Amsterdam. As a result, the United States-Germany and United States-Belgium bilaterals that concluded at the end of 1978 were very similar to the earlier United States-Netherlands agreement. There were variations, but the pattern was set. Other countries in the European area were under pressure to follow suit in their own negotiations with the United States. In time several did so. But not the United Kingdom, which was the largest transatlantic market. It had signed a new bilateral with the United States in July 1977 but it did not go far enough in liberalising this market.

Deregulation through bilateral renegotiation was also being pursued by the United States in other international markets. The most important after the North Atlantic was perhaps the North and mid-Pacific market where the United States negotiated several key bilaterals between 1978 and 1980 with Singapore, Thailand and Korea, and with the Philippines and other states later. These bilaterals followed the same pattern as those in Europe: the

Table 2.2 Typical features of post-1978 US-type 'open market' bilaterals*

	US airlines	*Foreign airlines*
Market access	Any point in United States to specified points in foreign country.	Access only to limited number of US points.
	Extensive Fifth Freedom rights granted, but generally more for US carriers.	
	Unlimited charter rights included.	
Designation	Multiple.	
	Airlines must be under substantial ownership and effective control of nationals of designating state.	
Capacity	No frequency or capacity control.	
	'Break-of-gauge' permitted in some ASAs.[†]	
Tariffs	Double disapproval (i.e. filed tariffs become operative unless *both* governments disapprove)	
	or	
	Country of origin rules (less frequent).	

Notes
* Examples include United States-Netherlands, United States-Singapore and United States-Germany.
† Allows airline to switch to smaller aircraft on flights beyond the other state.

countries were offered a handful of gateway points in the United States, usually less than five, in exchange for most if not all of the US objectives previously outlined. (For more details on US air services agreements after 1977, see Doganis, 1991.) But here, too, the largest transpacific market, that between the US and Japan, escaped the liberalisation process for the Japanese government held out against agreeing to a new 'open market' bilateral.

The key features of the post-1977 US bilaterals are shown in Table 2.2, but it should be borne in mind that there is greater variation in the detail of these newer bilaterals than in those they replaced. In particular, some of the newer bilaterals were not quite as open as Table 2.2 would suggest. However, the bilaterals between, for example, the United States and the Netherlands, Singapore or Germany did encompass virtually all the features outlined in the table. In some cases, traditional Bermuda-type bilaterals have been modified by subsequent memoranda of understanding or diplomatic exchanges of notes to such an extent that they resemble the newer open market agreements.

It is clear that the 'open market' bilaterals offered more to United States carriers than to European or Asian carriers. Only the former could fly from any point in the USA, which was the largest traffic generator, and benefit from multiple designation, since most other countries only had one international airline. The US carriers were also better placed to take advantage of Fifth Freedom rights. But in the early 1980s, the unbalanced nature of the 'open market' agreements was not too scary for other countries to accept because at that time the main US international carriers, Pan American and TWA, were not very aggressive.

Though it lagged behind the US, Europe too began to move away from the traditional bilaterals. As support for liberalisation policies spread, the more liberal and free-market attitudes prevailing in the United Kingdom pushed that country to renegotiate most of its key European bilaterals in the period from 1984 onwards. This was ironic given that the UK continued to hold on to a rather restrictive bilateral with the United States.

The first major breakthrough in Europe was in June 1984, when a new air services agreement was negotiated between the UK and the Netherlands – another country set on liberalisation. This agreement, together with further modification in 1985, effectively deregulated air services between the two countries. Free entry of new carriers, open route access by designated airlines to any point in either country, no capacity controls and a double disapproval regime for fares were the key elements introduced. These features, similar to those in the revised United States bilaterals discussed earlier, represented a clear break with the traditional European bilaterals which had prevailed until then. However, the more liberal of the European bilaterals went a step further than those of the United States by allowing open route access, that is, they removed any controls on the points that could be served in each country by the other country's airlines. In this respect they offered a more equal balance of opportunities to the airlines of each country. On the other hand, the intra-European agreements granted significantly fewer Fifth Freedom rights, if any. However, under the first two liberalisation packages agreed by the European Council of Ministers, in December 1987 and June 1990 more extensive Fifth Freedom rights on intra-Community services did become available.

The United Kingdom-Netherlands agreement set the pattern for the renegotiation of other European bilaterals. Later in 1984, the United Kingdom signed a new air services agreement with Germany; the following year, agreements were concluded with Luxembourg, France, Belgium, Switzerland and Ireland. Not all of these went as far as the United Kingdom-Netherlands agreement in removing constraints on competition, but all of them allowed for multiple designation of airlines by each state, and several also removed capacity restrictions and introduced double disapproval of tariffs. Some UK bilaterals went through a two-stage process. An initial agreement brought partial liberalisation, and was followed by a more radical second agreement. This happened with the United Kingdom-Ireland bilateral. A revised agreement in 1985 was superseded

Table 2.3 Traditional and post-1985 'open market' European bilaterals

	Traditional (pre-1984)	*New 'open market' bilaterals**
Market access	Only to points specified.	Open route access – airlines can fly on any route between two states.
	Very limited Fifth Freedoms sometimes granted.	
	(Charter rights secured under 1956 ECAC agreement.)	
Designation	Generally single – but double/multiple in some bilaterals.	Multiple.
	Airlines must be under substantial ownership and effective control of nationals of designating state.	
Capacity	Shared fifty-fifty.	No capacity control.
Tariffs	Double approval.	Double disapproval.

Note
* Examples include United Kingdom-Netherlands and United Kingdom-Ireland.

by a further agreement in 1988 which allowed for multiple designation, open route access, no capacity restrictions and double disapproval of fares.

While the United Kingdom set the pace, other European states also began to renegotiate their bilaterals in this period. Usually they did not adopt all the features of the United Kingdom-Netherlands agreement in one go; the aim of the negotiations was to introduce gradual liberalisation. These developments were paralleled by the two liberalisation packages of the European Community previously mentioned.

Two agreements, that between the United Kingdom and the Netherlands and that with Ireland, are good examples of the most open of the new-style bilaterals. Their key features are contrasted in Table 2.3 with those of the more traditional European bilaterals. It is evident in comparing the two columns in Table 2.3 that the open market bilaterals cleared away many of the earlier constraints on market access, capacity or frequency, and on tariffs.

The effect of these new liberal agreements on fares, number of carriers and traffic growth was dramatic. Where new airlines entered routes previously operated by only two carriers, normally one from each country, fares dropped significantly. The lower fares and the new entrants in turn stimulated traffic growth. In 1983, prior to the revision of the UK-Netherlands bilateral, the cheapest London–Amsterdam fare was an advance purchase fare of £82 return and only three other reduced fares were available. Within two years of the new bilateral, fifteen different discount fares were available and the lowest was £55 return. New airlines began to impact on this route in 1986 and over the next two years average fares paid by passengers fell by about 15 per cent. The most dramatic impact of liberalisation was evident on the London–Dublin route. In May 1986 a new start-up airline, Ryanair, launched a Dublin service from Luton, an airport 50 km north of London, offering very low unrestricted fares. Ryanair and other new entrants, such as Virgin Atlantic, forced Aer Lingus and British Airways to introduce a host of lower but restricted fares. Average passenger yields dropped by a third in three years. Traffic boomed. There had been very little growth in passenger traffic between London and Dublin between 1980 and 1985, but it doubled in the next three years, that is, by 1988.

A few European states also began to negotiate liberalised air services agreements with non-European countries which were like-minded. Thus, in July 1989 the revised bilateral between the United Kingdom and Singapore introduced multiple designation and double disapproval on tariffs. It granted Singapore's designated airlines full Fifth Freedom rights between European points and Britain but no such rights beyond London to North America. Frequencies between the two countries were increased gradually but only to a maximum of twenty-one flights a week by airlines of each state. So some capacity control remained.

By the late 1980s, as certain countries and airlines felt more at ease with the impact of the 'open market' bilaterals they had signed at the beginning of the decade, they began to revise them. A case in point was the revised US-Singapore air services agreement signed in December 1990. This increased the gateways on the US Pacific Coast served by Singaporean airlines from six to eight, it added four Atlantic Coast points including New York and granted Singapore Fifth Freedom rights to Mexico, Chile and from Europe. But Singapore was still restricted to only seven weekly Japan–US services.

It is apparent, from the UK-Singapore and the 1990 US-Singapore bilaterals as well as from many others that the new 'open market' bilaterals, whether of United States or European type, failed fully to liberalise aviation markets in several respects. The first was in relation to market access in each country's territory. In most bilaterals the points to be served by the designated airlines were still listed and limited in number. Second, while Fifth Freedom rights were granted fairly liberally, in many cases they could not be used because the third countries involved were not prepared to give away such rights. Third, domestic 'cabotage', that is, the right of foreign carriers to operate domestic services in another country, was excluded from the new bilaterals, though some limited domestic cabotage rights had been granted within the European Union. Also, none of the new bilaterals granted the so-called Seventh Freedom, that is, the right of an airline to carry traffic between two states on services that do not start in its own country. Finally, the requirement to designate only airlines which were 'substantially owned and effectively controlled' by nationals of the designated state remained as an essential feature of the new bilaterals. In all these respects the international air transport industry continued to be treated, and to operate, with severe restrictions, quite unlike most other international industries.

On the other hand, the 1980s saw gradual liberalisation of air services *within* many countries. This was in part a response to public pressure and in part a response to changing political attitudes and a view that greater competition was in the public interest. Also, it did not make much sense for states to sign 'open market' bilaterals encouraging greater international competition while maintaining only one national flag carrier designated to fly internationally. In many countries during this period airlines that had previously been wholly domestic or charter operators were designated to enter scheduled international markets. For instance, Japan Airlines' virtual monopoly on Japanese international routes was broken in 1986 when All Nippon Airlines were allowed to operate internationally. In several countries new airlines were launched during the period and many of them were designated to fly on international routes. EVA Air in Taiwan, Asiana in Korea, Ryanair in Ireland and Lauda Air in Austria were among them.

At the same time, that is, from the early 1980s onwards, the introduction of multiple designation in the new 'open market' US bilaterals allowed many US airlines, previously wholly or largely domestic, to inaugurate services to Europe, Asia or Latin America in direct competition with the traditional US flag carriers such as Pan American and TWA. National, People Express, Frontier, Braniff, Eastern and Piedmont were among new entrants on the North Atlantic, though most did not survive long. Of greater significance was the impact of major domestic airlines, United, American and Delta, who were able to launch and develop very significant international networks for the first time. Thus, United started transpacific services in 1983 while American and Delta entered this market in 1987. In some cases, these majors expanded rapidly by taking over parts of networks previously operated by the traditional US flag carriers, more especially those of Pan American and TWA, who were having difficulties coping with the more competitive environment. In 1986 United bought Pan Am's Pacific routes. Delta later did the same with Pan Am's German services. In some cases, this change-over was costly. Thus, in 1991 when United and American took over Pan American's and TWA's services to London they had to negotiate access to Heathrow, for which they were not themselves designated from the UK authorities. The UK, while still not willing to accept a full 'open market' agreement, did squeeze two important concessions out of the Americans in return for access to Heathrow for the new carriers. First, almost unlimited code sharing between UK and US airlines on routes to and from the United States. Second, UK airlines were granted rights (Seventh Freedom) to fly direct from Belgium, Germany or the Netherlands to the United States. These rights have yet to be used.

While the international aviation business was not fully liberalised by 1992 and was still constrained in several respects, many international markets had been opened up to new airlines. Even on many routes without new entrants, one saw greater competition between airlines in terms of frequency, service standards and often price.

2.3 Towards 'open skies' – 1992 onwards

By the early 1990s it was clear that international liberalisation and the 'open market' bilaterals which characterised it had not gone far enough. The need for further liberalisation became increasingly apparent as a result of several developments.

First, there was a growing body of expert opinion that the airline industry should be normalised; that is, it should be allowed to operate as any other major international industry. It is true that most governments willingly accepted the bilateral system and a smaller number grudgingly acquiesced to it while wishing to modify it more or less radically. Wide acceptance of the system, despite its apparent shortcomings, suggests that most countries considered the perceived benefits to their own airlines and consumers to be greater than any costs. But there was a strong counter-argument, namely, that the airline industry was no longer different from other industries and should not be treated any differently. This theme was echoed in different ways by some of the speakers at the April 1992 ICAO Air Transport Colloquium in Montreal. For instance, Mr Jeffrey Shane, at that time Assistant Secretary for Policy and International Affairs in the US Department of Transportation, argued that the debate was not about liberalisation but 'really about normalisation – applying the rules that normally govern trade, to trade in international air services' and that 'nothing like the system of government imposed impediments to economic decision-making exists in any other sector of international trade' (Shane, 1992). The view that aviation should be treated no differently from other industries gained ground both among aviation specialists and government officials in several key countries, even though it did not prevail at the 1992 Montreal Colloquium.

A second and perhaps stronger argument against bilateralism was that the system, though world-wide, was and is inherently restrictive. This is because even when countries signed the more liberal open market bilaterals, the market opportunities opened up tended to be those considered acceptable by the least liberal of the two countries. Speaking at the same ICAO Air Transport Colloquium in Montreal, the Director of Corporate Affairs of Singapore Airlines highlighted the problem: 'Generally, bilateralism tends to trade restrictions rather than opportunities. The bartering process of bilateralism tends to reduce the opportunities available to the level considered acceptable by the most restrictive party.' (Samuel, 1992). The frequent occurrence of disputes between countries over the application and interpretation of their bilateral agreements suggests that too often, one of the two countries has felt disadvantaged in some way. Disputes in 1991–92 between Thailand and the United States, Canada and Singapore or between the United States and both France and Germany showed that this happened with the new liberal open market bilaterals as much as, if not more so, than with the more traditional and restrictive agreements.

The third factor pushing towards further liberalisation was that the airline industry had matured during the previous decade. It had undergone structural changes which made it progressively more difficult for airlines to operate within the confines of the bilateral system. Structural changes had been brought on by the following trends:

- growing concentration within the US airline industry and the emergence of the US domestic majors as big players in international markets;
- the search by many international airlines for the marketing benefits of very large-scale operations through mergers with other airlines in their own country and minority share purchases or strong marketing alliances with airlines in other countries (see Chapter 4 on alliances);
- a loosening of government ties with and support for national airlines as a result of partial or full privatisation (the UK Government set the trend here with the successful privatisation of British Airways in 1987);
- increased emphasis on reducing government direct and indirect support to airlines and pressure for financial self-sufficiency among airlines in turn meant less protectionism domestically and in international markets.

All these trends created a critical need for successful airlines, whether private or state-owned, to be able to operate more easily outside the narrow confines of their own national markets, while freed from the remaining constraints imposed by bilateralism.

Again the initial motor for change was the United States. At first in the early 1980s the US carriers had lost market shares on the North Atlantic and the transpacific routes as more dynamic European and new Asian carriers entered new routes and competed against the rather slow and unresponsive traditional US airlines such as Pan Am and TWA. But as the latter were progressively replaced by the powerful and very large domestic majors such as American, Delta and United the market share of United States airlines began to rise. These carriers benefited from having huge domestic networks to feed their international services and enjoyed great marketing power from their sheer size. In some markets they reinforced their marketing strength by setting up hubs in foreign destination countries such as Delta's hub in Frankfurt and Northwest's in Tokyo. They could outsell the competition on selected routes by high frequencies and innovative pricing made possible by lower unit costs. But many of the existing bilaterals, even if of the 'open market' type, still limited their scope and freedom of action. American, United and Delta among others pushed for further liberalisation for two basic reasons. As major domestic carriers relatively new to large-scale international operations they saw that the long-term opportunities for expansion were much greater in international markets than within the more mature US domestic market. At the same time they felt that in a fully liberalised 'open skies' environment they would do better than their foreign competitors because of the traffic feed that they as US majors would obtain from their huge domestic networks and from their sheer size. In addition, they had lower unit operating costs than most of their foreign competitors, especially in Europe, and they were also more commercially oriented. The State Department and the Department of Transportation also felt that 'open skies' would benefit both American consumers and their airlines. At the same time, developments within the European Community, later to become the European Union, were also pushing inexorably towards 'open skies'.

In the case of the United States bilaterals, the first key breakthrough came in 1992 in negotiations with the Netherlands, whose government and airline, KLM, were also keen to adopt 'open skies'. KLM had done well under the earlier 1978 'open market' agreement with the United States and by the mid-1980s its market share on the US–Amsterdam routes was over 80 per cent. Much of this traffic was travelling to other points in Europe through KLM's well-operated hub at Amsterdam's Schiphol airport. KLM was anxious to reinforce its position while its government felt that as a small country the Netherlands had much to gain from further liberalisation of international air services, especially if it was the first in Europe to do so.

In September 1992 the Dutch and United States' governments signed what was effectively the first 'open skies' agreement and inaugurated a new phase of international deregulation. In brief the key elements of this bilateral are as follows:

- open route access – airlines from either country can fly to any point in the other with full traffic rights;
- unlimited Fifth Freedom rights;
- open access for charters;
- multiple designation of airlines;
- no frequency or capacity control;
- break of gauge permitted;
- no tariff controls (except if tariffs too high or too low);
- airlines free to code share or make other commercial agreements.

But the new US-Netherlands bilateral coincided with the worst financial crisis the airline industry had ever experienced (see Chapter 1). There was growing concern about the future of the industry. After three years of record losses, numerous bankruptcies and the demise of such well-known airlines as Pan American and Eastern, the United States Congress in May 1993 established the National Commission to Ensure a Strong Competitive Airline Industry. Three months later, and after numerous public hearings, the Commission reported its findings and made more than sixty recommendations. These were grouped into three broad areas. First, technological and institutional changes to enhance efficiency. These dealt largely with improvements in air traffic control management and operations. Second, measures to improve the financial performance of airlines primarily through reductions in user fees, and taxes, and reduced government interference. Third, the Commission recommended measures to expand access to global markets for US airlines and passengers. In particular, it suggested that the US government should renegotiate its bilateral air services agreements to achieve an open and liberal market environment in which US airlines could operate without restriction or discrimination. The Commission even went so far as to recommend that foreign ownership of up to 49 per cent of US airlines should be permitted under certain circumstances (Kasper, 1994).

Spurred on by the findings of the National Commission, the Clinton administration shortly afterwards undertook its own review of aviation policy and in April 1995 Secretary of Transportation, Federico Pena, issued the first formal statement of international air transportation policy in 17 years. This came three years after the 1992 'open skies' agreement with the Netherlands and shortly after a broadly similar but phased agreement with Canada. The policy statement encapsulated the thinking that went into these earlier agreements and clarified US objectives for the agreements that followed, of which there were several in 1995. According to Secretary Pena the Clinton administration was taking steps to 'ensure that global marketing and services will lead to improved services for travellers and shippers' while it was also seeking to 'find ways to help strengthen the US airline industry so that it may continue its leadership role in international air services' (Pena, 1995).

To achieve these twin objectives, the US government clearly saw the urgent need to create open aviation markets with unrestricted access for the airlines of the countries concerned. According to the policy statement the continuing rapid growth of demand for international air transport and the changing nature of that demand, with greater emphasis on long-haul travel, was leading to structural changes in the airline industry. In order to provide the service products required by the travelling public airlines were having to develop global networks. These were of two kinds, *sole-carrier systems*, where the same airlines provided end-to-end services either on direct flights or online through its hubs, or *joint carrier systems* where the required services were offered by connecting flights of two or more airlines under code-share arrangements. Both needed to be encouraged and facilitated. The former required substantial access and traffic rights not only to key hub cities overseas but also through and beyond them to numerous other cities, mostly in third countries. The joint carrier systems also required increased market access but in addition they needed to provide code-sharing arrangements designed to 'address the preference of passengers and shippers for on-line service from beginning to end through co-ordinated scheduling, baggage- and cargo-handling and other elements of single-carrier service' (Pena, 1995).

Explicitly allowing code sharing on international air services was a major change in US policy since otherwise code-share arrangements might be deemed anti-competitive. This ability to grant anti-trust immunity for code share or other commercial agreements was to become a major negotiating asset in subsequent bilateral discussions. But markets could only function efficiently if consumers made choices based on full information. So the new policy also required airlines to give consumers clear information to enable them to distinguish between code-shared and other services.

In the light of developments in the international air transport industry, the key US government objectives were henceforward to be as follows, though there were others too (US government, 1995):

- To increase the variety of price and service options available to consumers.
- To enhance the access of US cities to international air transport.
- To provide carriers with unrestricted opportunities to develop types of services required by the market place. This means:
  - carriers' freedom to develop carriers' own direct services or indirect services through commercial agreements with other carriers,
  - no frequency or capacity restrictions,
  - unrestricted pricing freedom,
  - all to apply to charters and cargo services too.
- Elimination of government subsidies, ground handling or other monopolies and unequal access to infrastructure facilities etc., so as to ensure fair competition.
- Reduction of barriers to the creation of global aviation systems, such as limitations on cross-border investments.

These objectives were to be achieved primarily by entering into 'open skies' aviation agreements initially with like-minded states and later with other less liberal states. The US government was also prepared to agree to phased removal of restrictions and liberalisation of the air service market. But for those countries not willing to advance market liberalisation the threat of US counter-measures was explicit in the policy statement. The US could limit those countries' airlines' access to the US market and restrict commercial relations with US carriers. In other words, foreign airlines should not expect code-sharing arrangements with US airlines to be approved and be given anti-trust immunity if their states did not agree to 'open skies' bilaterals.

As previously mentioned, prior to the 1995 policy statement, the United States had already negotiated 'open skies' agreements with the Netherlands and with Canada. Shortly after the 'open skies' agreement with the United States, KLM applied for and obtained anti-trust immunity from the US authorities to enable it to exploit more fully the potential benefits from its partnership with Northwest, an airline in which it had bought an almost 20 per cent share three years earlier. Both airlines wanted to code share on many of their flights, not just those between the US and Amsterdam but also on services beyond each other's gateways. For instance, Northwest wished to put its code on KLM flights beyond Amsterdam to points in Germany so as to capture and carry German traffic across the Atlantic without actually flying there.

Immunity provided KLM-Northwest with considerable freedom jointly to plan their code shares, schedules and pricing policy. European airlines negotiating commercial alliances with US carriers appreciated the potential benefits which anti-trust immunity could provide. The US government grabbed the opportunity. In the 1980s it had offered access to more US gateway points in order to persuade countries to sign up to 'open market' bilaterals. Now it offered an even more enticing exchange – anti-trust immunity for alliance partners in return for agreement on new 'open skies' bilaterals.

In 1995 the United States signed such bilaterals with a group of nine of the smaller West European countries. But the big prizes – the UK, Germany and France, together representing over 60 per cent of the transatlantic passenger market – eluded it. There had been a transitional agreement with Germany in 1994 but the breakthrough came in 1996 when pressure from Lufthansa and United Airlines pushed the German government to bring forward the implementation of a full 'open skies' agreement. Interestingly it refused to sign the bilateral until *after* anti-trust immunity had been granted.

By early 2000 around thirty-five new agreements had been signed by the United States. These were with most of its major aviation partners except the United Kingdom and Japan, which are the two largest markets. All these agreements, such as the one with Singapore signed in 1997, were very similar to the US-Netherlands agreement detailed above. Some countries, reluctant to jump to a full 'open skies' agreement in one step – often to protect their own airlines – signed phased bilaterals. In these the full 'open skies' features were introduced gradually over a two-year period. The US-Italy agreement signed in November 1998 was such a phased agreement, whose aim was to allow for anti-trust immunity to be granted for the imminent link-up between Alitalia and Northwest. The US-France agreement signed earlier that year also had anti-trust immunity as an objective. One or two other states also signed their own 'open skies' agreements, as did Singapore with New Zealand in 1997.

In January 1998 the United States and Japan did sign a new bilateral which went much of the way towards 'open skies', especially for incumbent carriers. It also allowed code sharing for the first time on the very busy US–Japan market. But non-incumbent carriers (Delta, Continental, American) still faced a ceiling on the total weekly flights that could be operated. The agreement also foresaw the opening of talks within three years on a fully liberalised 'open skies' bilateral. Later in October 1998 and again in 1999 US–UK bilateral negotiations broke down when the UK balked at US demands for an immediate 'open skies' agreement as opposed to one with a phasing-in period such as the French had signed. The UK was also unhappy at the US demand for more or less unlimited access to Heathrow slots for US carriers wishing to mount new services. The US were also making their approval of the proposed alliance between British Airways and American Airlines conditional on obtaining a full 'open skies' agreement. This emphasised once more the linkage between anti-trust immunity and 'open skies' bilaterals which became a feature of the late 1990s.

'Open skies' policies have also been adopted and actively pursued by a few other states. New Zealand, which signed an 'open skies' bilateral with the United States, had secured similar deals with Singapore, Malaysia, Brunei, the UAE and Chile by the end of 1999. This was in addition to the single aviation market pact concluded earlier with Australia. The latter country plans to pursue its own 'open skies' agreements and signed the first one with the UAE. This represented a major policy shift. Australia was prepared to offer not only all the key features of US-style 'open skies' agreements but was also willing to consider granting Seventh Freedom rights for stand-alone air services between the bilateral partner and a third country on a case-by-case basis. Domestic cabotage, however, was not negotiable. On the other hand it relaxed its ownership rules to allow foreign interests or airlines to own up to 100 per cent of Australian domestic airlines.

The 'open skies' agreements, generally very similar to the US–Netherlands agreement described earlier, were a significant improvement on the 'open market' agreements they replaced in several respects, most notably in relation to market access and tariff regulation (Table 2.4). They opened route access to any point in either country whereas the earlier bilaterals had tended to limit the number of points that could be served by foreign carriers in the United States. Also mutual Fifth Freedom rights were granted without restraint compared to the more limited Fifth Freedom in earlier bilaterals. On tariffs, double disapproval or the country of origin rule were replaced by a clear decision that governments should not meddle in tariffs except *in extremis* to prevent discriminatory practices, to protect consumers from unreasonably high or restrictive prices or to protect airlines from artificially low fares due to government subsidies or support. This was already the actual position on many routes to or from the United States, but the new agreements made this explicit.

Table 2.4 US 'open market' and post-1991 'open skies' air services agreements

	1978–91 'open market' bilaterals	*Post-1991 'open skies' bilaterals*
Market access	Named number of points in each state – more limited for non-US carriers	Unlimited.
	Generally unlimited Fifth Freedom.	Unlimited Fifth Freedom.
	Domestic cabotage not allowed.	
	Seventh Freedom not granted.	
	Open charter access.	
Designation	Multiple.	
	Substantial ownership and effective control by nationals of designating state.	
Capacity	No frequency or capacity control.	
Tariffs	Double disapproval or country of origin rules.	Free pricing.
Code sharing	Not part of bilateral.	Code sharing permitted.*

Note
* Co-operative arrangements, e.g. code sharing, blocked space or leasing allowed between airlines of signatory states or within airline(s) of third states if they permit reciprocal arrangements.

A further innovation was the inclusion of an article dealing specifically with inter-airline commercial agreements such as code sharing (this is when airlines add their partner's code to their own flight number) and block space or leasing agreements. This was critically important. Such close-knit commercial agreements, which went further than simple code sharing on routes between the two countries, risked falling foul of US anti-trust legislation. As mentioned earlier, this new article in the 1992 'open skies' bilateral effectively granted KLM and Northwest immunity from prosecution for a commercial agreement which might otherwise be considered anti-competitive.

The final innovation, explicitly foreseen in the 1995 US policy statement, has been the inclusion in the bilaterals of an annex adopting principles of non-discrimination on the data bases and visual displays of the global computer reservation systems and ensuring open access and free competition among CRS providers in each country.

2.4 The single European market

In parallel to the United States, Europe was also moving towards 'open skies' but the approach was structurally quite different. The US strategy was essentially bilateral. The implementation of 'open skies' was being promoted by one country through a series of bilateral air services agreements. In contrast to this the development of a single open aviation market in Europe was to be achieved through a comprehensive multilateral agreement by, initially, the member states of the European Union. This multilateral approach to opening up the skies enabled the Europeans to go further in pursuit of deregulation than was possible under US bilateralism.

Within the European Union (previously known as the European Community) the push towards multilateral liberalisation of air transport among the member states was driven by two complementary lines of approach. The Directorate General for Transport (DG VII) espoused airline liberalisation early and had been trying since about 1975 to push various proposals through the Council of Ministers. The second driver for change was the Directorate General for Competition (DG IV), which was trying to ensure that competition between producers and service providers within the Community was not distorted by uncompetitive practices imposed by governments or introduced by the industries themselves.

The twin objectives of air transport liberalisation and fair and open competition were achieved in stages. While some liberalisation was taking place in Europe as a result of the revised air services agreements which followed the new UK-Netherlands agreement of 1984, and some limited Community-wide measures, it was not till December 1987 that the first important breakthrough came at a Community level. This was the so-called 'December 1987 package' of measures agreed by the Council of Ministers. It introduced a more liberal fares regime. It forced the abandonment of the equal sharing of capacity on routes served by airlines of the two states at either end of such routes and it facilitated the entry of new airlines by opening up market access (CEC, 1987a). The 1987 measures also explicitly acknowledged that the competition articles of the Treaty of Rome, articles 81 to 90, did apply to air transport, reinforcing an earlier 1986 decision of the European Court of Justice to the same effect (CEC, 1987b). Many of the inter-airline agreements then in existence between European carriers would be anti-competitive and illegal unless specific exemptions were granted. Such exemptions, but with demanding conditions attached, were published by the European Commission in August 1988 covering any agreements between Community airlines relating to capacity co-ordination, revenue pooling, tariffs, runway slot allocation and scheduling, computer reservations systems and passenger and cargo handling (CEC, 1988). In June 1990 a new 'second package' of liberalisation measures was agreed by Community ministers.

These further loosened constraints on pricing, on capacity restrictions and on market access. They allowed multiple designation of airlines on routes above a certain traffic density as well as opening up Third and Fourth Freedom rights on most inter-Community routes.

The gradual steps towards air transport deregulation can only be understood within the wider political context of European integration and the creation of a single internal market covering the twelve member states of the European Community (later to become fifteen). In a series of meetings during the 1980s the heads of state of member governments had pledged themselves to the completion of the internal market as the Community's first priority. The agreed date for the single market to come into existence was 1 January 1993. This meant that by the end of 1992 immigration and customs controls between the twelve were to be abolished, so that to all intents and purposes the European Community would become a single 'domestic' market open to the free movement of goods, services and people. The European Commission, in effect the administrative arm of the Community, acting through the Council of Ministers, took steps in all areas of economic activity to ensure that the movement of goods and services within the internal market was not distorted by artificial barriers to trade. Liberalisation of air transport was only one of the Commission's many initiatives. It was achieved through the so-called 'third package' of aviation measures, which came into force on 1 January 1993 (CEC, 1992).

The third package consists of three inter-linked regulations which have effectively created an 'open skies' regime for air services within the European Union. There is open market access. Airlines from member states can operate with full traffic rights on any route within the EU and without capacity restrictions even on routes outside their own country (EU Regulation 2408/92). Domestic air services to the Greek islands and in the Azores were exempted from competition for a five-year period, but this has since expired. Governments may impose restrictions only on environmental, infrastructure capacity, regional development or public service grounds, but any restrictions would have to be justified. There are no price controls. Airlines have complete freedom to determine their fares and cargo tariffs but there are some limited safeguards to prevent predatory or excessive pricing (EU Regulation 2409/92). The third regulation harmonises the criteria for granting of operating licences and air operators' certificates by EU member states (EU Regulation 2407/92). Apart from technical and financial criteria which have to be met, the airline must be majority owned and controlled by any of the member states or their nationals, or companies, but not necessarily nationals or companies of the state in which the airline is registered. Henceforward, all regulations apply equally to scheduled and charter services with no distinction being drawn between them.

The third package went further than the 'open skies' bilaterals in two important respects. First, it was a multilateral agreement to open up the skies covering not just pairs of states but a whole region, the fifteen eventual member states of the European Union plus Norway and Iceland, who adopted the package of measures without joining the EU. Second, whereas the 'open skies' bilaterals did not change the nationality rule at all, the third package for the first time explicitly allowed cross-border majority ownership. It gave the right to EU nationals or companies from any member state to set up and operate an airline in any other EU member state or to buy such an airline. This has enabled British Airways to own and manage Deutsche BA in Germany or KLM to buy and operate a British airline previously known as Air UK. However, this so-called right of establishment is restrictive in one important sense. While Deutsche BA can operate freely within the area of the European Union it cannot, as a British-owned airline, operate international services from Germany to, say, Moscow, because the Germany–Russia air services agreement contains the traditional article regarding substantial ownership and effective control by nationals of the designating state.

In parallel with the liberalisation of air transport regulations, the European Commission felt that greater freedom for airlines had to be accompanied by the effective application and implementation to air transport of the European Union's so-called 'competition rules'. These were designed to prevent monopolistic practices or behaviour which was anti-competitive or which distorted competition to the detriment of consumers. The competition rules cover three broad areas, namely, cartels and restrictive agreements, monopolies and mergers and state aid or subsidies to producers.

The basic principles were originally laid down in articles 85 to 94 of the Treaty of Rome and the separate Council Regulation on Mergers of 1989 (Regulation No. 4056/89). Article 85, renumbered in 1998 as 81, prohibits all inter-company agreements which have as their object or effect the restriction or distortion of competition within the EU and which may affect trade between member states. It was this article which necessitated the publication of specific exemptions in 1988 for a number of inter-airline agreements. For its part, article 86 (now 82) prohibits abuse of a dominant position in a way which may affect trade between Member States. A series of decisions by the European Court of Justice and the Commission have attempted to clarify both what constitutes dominance and abuse of that dominance (Soames, 1999). For instance, in allowing an alliance between Lufthansa and SAS in 1996, which would have a major impact on air services between Germany and Scandinavia, the Commission imposed a number of conditions. These aimed to facilitate the entry of new carriers on the routes operated by the alliance partners since such routes would henceforth be monopolies. The effect of such decisions has been to make airlines quite circumspect.

The 1987 liberalisation package did not give the Commission power to apply articles 81 and 82 to airline agreements covering air routes between the European Union and third countries even when such agreements have a major impact on trade within the Union. However, the Commission has used articles 88 and 89 (now 84 and 85) which relate to transitional measures to take action on air transport between the EU and third countries and in particular on the alliances between European airlines and major US carriers. In its decisions on both the proposed American Airlines–British Airways alliance, which has not progressed and the Lufthansa–SAS–United alliance, the Commission required the partners to give up substantial numbers of runway slots at their European hubs to competitors so as to ensure effective competition (See Chapter 4, section 4.9).

The subsidisation of airlines by central or local government clearly distorts competition. Articles 92 to 94 (now 88 and 89) of the Treaty of Rome specifically prohibit 'state aid' of any kind. Yet during the 1980s and early 1990s most of Europe's numerous state-owned airlines were being heavily subsidised by their governments. To overcome this contradiction, the European commission in a series of decisions between 1991 and 1997 approved major injections of state aid to a number of airlines but with strict conditions whose purpose was to ensure their transformation into profitable enterprises (see Chapter 8, section 8.5).

The state aid had to be used for financial and operational restructuring of the airline through debt repayment, early retirement of staff, and so on. It could not be used to support increased competition against other European carriers. A specific sum was authorised by the Commission on the basis of a very detailed restructuring plan whose whole progress was monitored annually by the Commission's consultants. The state aid was approved on the basis of a 'one time, last time' principle. In other words, no further requests for approval of additional state aid would be considered. However, the legal basis for this was uncertain. With the exception of the authorised state aid schemes no direct or indirect subsidisation of any kind by governments or their airlines is permitted within the European Union. For example, governments can no longer guarantee airline borrowings or reduce airport charges. Governments can offer support for the operation of air services to meet social service needs but in a manner which is transparent.

The final element of the competition rules is the EU's regulation on mergers first agreed in 1989 and subsequently modified. It extended the powers of the European Commission so that it could effectively monitor mergers, acquisitions or full-function joint ventures above a certain predetermined size. The threshold levels were reduced in 1997 (Regulation 1310/97). Any mergers or acquisitions which exceed the stated threshold in terms of turnover must be first notified to the Commission. It will only give its approval if the transaction does not lead to the strengthening or creation of a dominant position. To ensure that this does not happen the Commission may impose demanding conditions. Thus, when Air France took over the French independent long-haul airline UTA in 1990 and thereby also obtained a majority share in the domestic airline Air Inter, the Commission forced Air France to divest itself of its shareholding in TAT, the second largest domestic carrier in France. This enabled British Airways subsequently to take over TAT.

The merger regulations even enable the Commission to examine mergers between non-EU companies which are deemed to have the potential to restrict or distort competition within the EU. It was on this basis that in 1996 the Commission assessed the merger between the Boeing Aircraft Company and McDonnell Douglas. Thus there is even here an extra-territorial dimension to the EU competition rules. This was evident more recently in October 1999 when the Commission launched an investigation into the proposed merger of Air Canada and the Canadian Airlines on the grounds that it would reduce competition on services between London and Canada.

In addition to its decisions arising directly out of the application of the competition rules, the European commission, acting through the Council of Ministers, has passed various directives, regulations or codes of conduct both to ensure greater competition in areas where competition was previously limited and to ensure that competition is not distorted through unfair practices. Both the code of conduct for slot allocation at airports (Council Regulation 95/93) and the directive on ground handling services (Council Directive 96/97) were aimed at ensuring greater competition. On the other hand, the code of conduct for computer reservation systems aimed at avoiding unfair practices (Council Regulations 3089/93 and 323/1999). Such directives and regulations were in addition to the numerous measures introduced to protect consumers directly, to ensure safety of aircraft and so on.

If the aim of transport deregulation and 'open skies' is to encourage much greater competition, then competition rules appear to be necessary to ensure that the increased competition is effective and is not undermined by anti-competitive practices or the abuse of dominant market positions. Hence the parallel development in the European Union of an 'open skies' regime and a raft of competition rules. At the beginning of 2000 this regime prevailed in the fifteen member states, plus Norway and Iceland. But negotiations for a multilateral arrangement with ten Central European countries to allow them to adhere to the EU's air transport regime were close to completion. It was expected that the agreement would be ratified by the various EU institutions and the governments of the ten states during 2001. Effectively these ten states would eventually adopt the third package and the competition rules, but there would be varying transitional arrangements for a gradual opening up of their markets to the full force of competition. Before moving from the transitional phase to the final EU regime there would be a qualitative assessment by the Commission. A separate transport agreement has also been reached with Switzerland. This includes the accession of Switzerland to the EU's aviation regime and should be ratified during 2000 or 2001. By the end of 2001 a European

Common Aviation Area with an 'open skies' regime would be in place covering twenty-seven or twenty-eight countries, that is, most of Europe.

By the start of the new millennium, the pursuit of 'open skies' bilaterals by the United States and the creation of 'open skies' within the European Common Aviation Area had gone much of the way towards normalising the economic and regulatory framework for international and domestic air transport in certain major markets. But the process of normalisation was not complete. Clouds were still visible within the 'open skies'. The final step required is to move from 'open skies' to 'clear skies'. This is the new challenge for governments and regulators.

3   Beyond 'open skies'

A Transatlantic Common Aviation Area ... would also set the stage for negotiating beyond the classic five "freedoms", and comprise a shared and completely open market environment.

(Loyola de Palacio, Vice President of the European Commission, Chicago, 1999)

3.1 Clouds in the 'open skies'

The creation of a single European Common Aviation Area has been a major breakthrough. But while creating an open sky for air transport within much of Europe, it has had little impact on air/services between Europe and third countries. Such services are still regulated by bilateral air services agreements between individual European countries and states outside Europe. Except, of course, for the 'open skies' bilaterals with the United States and a handful of others, most of the existing agreements are quite traditional and protectionist.

Outside Europe, the thirty or so US-style 'open skies' agreements, while representing a significant leap forward, have not in fact resulted in total economic deregulation of international air services. Nor have they 'normalised' the air transport industry. While much more liberal and open than anything that preceded them, they still contain certain restrictive features. To start with, not all traffic rights are freely exchanged. Two types of services in particular are still excluded in virtually all cases. The first is the right of an airline to carry domestic traffic between two airports within the territory of the other signatory country to the bilateral agreement. This would normally be on an extension of international flights within that country. This is referred to as 'cabotage'. In the case of the United States it is claimed that a change in legislation is required to grant such rights and that it is unlikely that Congress would agree. Another right which has not been yet given away is the so-called 'Seventh Freedom'. This is the right to carry passengers between points in two foreign countries by an airline operating entirely outside its home country, though the UK did get some Seventh Freedom rights from Belgium, Germany and the Netherlands in the 1991 round of negotiations with the US. Perhaps the most glaring anomaly is the continued restriction on foreign ownership of airlines. Airlines still have to be 'substantially owned and effectively controlled' by their own nationals even though minority ownership by foreign individuals or companies may be permitted. In the United States the position is still that only up to 25 per cent of foreign ownership of its airlines may be allowed, despite the recommendation of the 1993 National Commission to go to 49 per cent. Clearly, even the most free enterprise economy, the United States, feels that the national ownership of its airlines needs to be protected.

In other respects too, the new 'open skies' bilaterals were not as open as one might imagine. In fact they continued to be blatantly protective of US carriers in several respects. Under the so-called 'fly America' policy, officials or others travelling on behalf of the US government were and still are required to fly on US airlines or on US carrier code shared flights operated by foreign airlines. International airmail contracts by the US Post Office are also effectively limited to US carriers, even though the latter can bid for UK or other mail contracts. Also, while US airlines cannot lease in foreign aircraft and crews, they can offer their own aircraft on wet leases to foreign carriers. For instance most of Atlas Air's thirty or so Boeing 747 freighters are wet leased to European and Asian carriers. Finally, cargo generated as a result of US government contracts also has to 'fly America'.

Both in terms of traffic rights and ownership the 1993 European so-called 'third package' of liberalisation measures went further than the US style 'open skies' bilaterals, but only in respect of intra-European air services. As we have seen, airlines of the member states were granted unlimited traffic rights on routes to, from and within any of the other member states. This included 'Seventh Freedom' rights and domestic cabotage. At the same time ownership and nationality constraints on airlines registered in any member state were also removed, provided the owners or purchasers were from another EU member state. Ownership by nationals or companies from non-member states is still limited in theory to 49 per cent. However, this totally 'open skies' regime is in respect only of intra-European Union air services. Any services or routes to points outside the European Union are still governed by the air services agreements that each individual EU state has with third countries. Thus, while a British owned airline, Virgin Express, can be based in Brussels and operate flights from Brussels to other points within the European Union, or, as it did in 2000, from Madrid to Rome, it cannot fly to, say, Moscow or Tunis. This is because the bilaterals between these two countries and Belgium specifically require that the designated airlines in each case should be substantially owned and effectively controlled by nationals of their own country.

The European Commission has been very critical of the 'open skies' agreements signed by some member states with the United States on several grounds. First, by giving away extensive Fifth Freedom rights to United States airlines on routes that were essentially 'domestic' routes between member states of the European Union, the Commission feels that signatory states were granting rights that were no longer at their discretion because they affected trade within the single European market. Second, by making separate agreements with the United States, such countries were undermining the negotiating strength of the Commission to obtain greater concessions from the United States in any future bloc negotiations. Moreover, the Commission and many European airlines felt that 'open skies' bilaterals created an asymmetry and an imbalance of opportunities. While US carriers can fly from any airport in the United States to a wide range of airports in the EU, European airlines can only operate to the United States from their own country. Consequently they cannot exploit fully the whole EU market of 360 million passengers to compete more effectively with their transatlantic competitors. In addition, US carriers obtained and in many cases used extensive Fifth Freedom rights between European points which are now essentially domestic sectors within the European Union. Yet European airlines cannot enjoy the equivalent rights to serve domestic city pairs in the United States.

The Commission has felt that 'open skies' bilaterals constituted a major distortion of the single internal market created by the third package of EU liberalisation measures since they granted Fifth Freedom rights within the EU to United States carriers while discriminating between Community carriers on the grounds of nationality (European Commission, 1999). In fact, in the autumn of 1998 the European Commission claimed, in a legal case launched in the European Court of Justice under article 226 of the Treaty of Rome, that the 'open skies' agreements signed by eight EU member states with the United States were contrary to EU regulations and should be suspended.

3.2 The nationality rules: an anomaly in the global economy

It is clear from the preceding analysis that at the start of the new millennium three major changes are needed before the international airline industry can operate as freely in a global market as any other truly international industry. The first would be to allow airline(s) from one country to operate domestic services without restriction within another country. The second would be to allow a country of one nationality to operate air services between two other countries entirely independently of the country of nationality. This so-called 'Seventh Freedom' has rarely been granted. But without it 'open skies' are not fully open. The final and most significant change would be to remove the existing constraints on airline ownership by foreign nationals.

In the first decade of the third millennium it is the ownership and investment rules that are the most likely to be liberalised. For it is on this issue that the economic and political pressures for change are greatest. This is because while there are strong economic forces pushing the airline industry towards concentration and the creation of competing global alliances, the existing bilateral regime clearly constrains airlines' freedom of action and their ability to maximise the potential benefits of scale and of global networks. Moreover, relaxing the ownership rules would also make it unnecessary any longer to safeguard domestic or Seventh Freedom rights. Once airlines are no longer owned by nationals of a particular state there is little point in that state protecting its air traffic rights as assiduously as in the past.

The bilateral system evolved in order to protect the interests of smaller countries. There are three key elements in traditional air services agreements which enable states to safeguard their sovereignty and their traffic rights. Governments have the right to designate the airline(s) which will exercise/exploit their country's traffic rights; such designated carriers must be 'substantially owned' by nationals or companies of the designating state, and these carriers must also be 'effectively managed' by such nationals or companies. Thus, there are severe constraints as to which airlines can be designated to operate the traffic rights that have been negotiated. However, in the past there have been important exceptions:

(i)   Where airlines have multinational ownership (usually involving ownership by several governments) they may be designated as the 'national' carrier by a number of states and accepted as such by countries with which they have bilaterals (e.g. Gulf Air, Air Afrique, SAS, and LIAT, the Eastern Caribbean airline).

(ii) The Assembly of the International Civil Aviation Organisation (ICAO) has accepted (Resolution A24–12) the 'Community of Interest' concept which urges contracting states to accept the designation by one developing state of an airline substantially owned and effectively controlled by another state within the same regional economic grouping (e.g. USA, Canada and Germany have allowed Barbados to designate BWIA as its carrier even though it was substantially owned by the Trinidad and Tobago government).

(iii) Both Britannia and Monarch, large charter airlines, whose beneficial ownership ultimately resided in Canada and Switzerland respectively, have long been accepted as UK-designated airlines by other states. Several European Union Regulations and Directives have specifically mentioned that these airlines are considered to be EU airlines despite the fact that their beneficial ownership was not from within the EU. In fact, in 1998 the Thomson Travel Group, including Britannia Airways, was separated from its parent company and floated on the London Stock Exchange in part to ensure that problems in relation to its nationality did not arise in the future.

(iv) In the past Cathay Pacific was an airline that was 'substantially owned and effectively controlled' by British rather than Hong Kong or Chinese interests. For some years prior to July 1997, when the colony was returned to China, the Hong Kong Government had negotiated its own air services agreement independently of the UK Government. To get around the fact that Cathay was not Hong Kong owned, air services agreements signed by Hong Kong required its designated airline(s) to be incorporated and have their principal place of business in Hong Kong. This was accepted by States signing bilaterals with Hong Kong. So 'substantial ownership and effective control' was replaced by 'principal place of business' as the key criterion for designation of airlines.

(v) When in 1991 Iberia bought a majority shareholding (85 per cent) in Aerolineas Argentinas, the ailing state-owned airline with the aim of turning it around, Argentina's bilateral partners continued to accept Aerolineas as the Argentinean designated airline. They did this despite the fact that effective control had switched to Spain. But the United States only agreed to accept such designation on condition that frequency or capacity limitations on US airlines flying into Buenos Aires were lifted. Similarly, Air New Zealand bought a 50 per cent share of Ansett in Australia, yet governments continued to accept its designation as an Australian carrier. Since the early 1990s the ownership of Aerolineas Argentinas has become even more complex and problematical. By early 2000, SEPI, a Spanish Government holding company, together with two US banks, Merill Lynch and Bankers Trust, held 68 per cent of the shares. American Airlines held a further 8.5 per cent and had taken over the management from Iberia in 1997. Yet Aerolineas continued to be accepted as an Argentinean designated airline.

These numerous exceptions show that where two signatory states mutually agree to ignore the ownership and/or control principle they can do so even though the relevant article remains in their air services agreement.

Since January 1993 the European Union's 'third package' allows airlines within the EU to be owned by nationals or companies from any member state. Thus, British Airways was able in July 1996 to take a majority share in the French airline TAT. However, ownership of an EU airline by non-EU nationals/companies is limited to 49 per cent. In 1996 Swissair only was able to purchase 49.5 per cent of Sabena, the Belgian airline, because Switzerland, unlike Belgium, was not within the European Union.

Hitherto it has been generally assumed that 'substantial ownership' ensured 'effective control'. The United States, Australia and many other countries adopted the view that if foreign ownership was no more than 25 per cent then effective control remained in the hands of their own nationals. In 1991, in a case regarding the Northwest-KLM alliance, the

US Department of Transportation made a distinction between voting and non-voting interests. It would henceforth allow up to 49 per cent foreign shareholding as long as foreign equity did not exceed 25 per cent of voting shares. This was made explicit when British Airways bought a 19.6 per cent shareholding in USAir early in 1993, but with an option to increase it to 33 per cent. But the US position is contradictory. While it restricts foreign ownership of US airlines to 25 per cent of voting shares, it is prepared to accept the designation of foreign airlines by their respective governments even though 49 per cent of their voting shares are owned by non-nationals of the designating state. For example, the US Government accepts Sabena as the Belgian designated airline even though 49.5 per cent is owned by Swissair. Nor did it raise objections early in 2000 when Singapore Airlines announced its purchase of 49 per cent of Virgin Atlantic, the British airline, which has numerous routes to the United States.

The issue of effective control cannot be resolved purely in terms of a particular ownership share. When SAS was bidding for 24.9 per cent of British Caledonian in 1988, the then UK Secretary of State for Transport deemed that the financial arrangements being proposed to save B. Cal gave SAS 'effective control' even with less than 25 per cent shareholding. As a result B. Cal could no longer be designated as a UK carrier, and the SAS bid collapsed. In 1992 the European Commission decided that Air France had effective control of Sabena even though it had acquired only 37.5 per cent of the shares, and imposed strict conditions on competition grounds before granting approval (Official Journal No. C272, 21 October 1992). In 1996, when Swissair bought 49.5 per cent of Sabena, it had effective control and appointed one of its own senior managers as Chief Executive of Sabena. But in this case the issue of effective control was overlooked because Swissair held only a minority shareholding, the majority of board members were Belgian and Switzerland was seen, at that time, as a possible new member of the European Union.

Privatisation also means that ownership is becoming more diffuse, further complicating the issue. Already around 30 per cent of BA shares are owned by a vast number of non-EU nationals or companies, mainly American or Japanese. But share ownership is so diffuse that there is no threat to the company's effective control staying British. If a single non-EU shareholder built up a significant shareholding, the articles of association allow the board of directors to ask the UK government to intervene.

It appears that the spread of liberalisation and privatisation has made 'effective control' the crucial determinant rather than 'substantial ownership'. This is why the Council Regulation No. 2407/92 on licensing of air carriers, which is part of the EU's 'third package' separates the two and for the first time clarifies the meaning of 'effective control'. It requires a majority of the board to be representatives of EU states or nationals. The same must be true of any undertaking that has a controlling shareholding in an EU airline. Moving from ownership criteria to placing the emphasis only on effective control would be a step forward. An example was the Singapore-New Zealand bilateral signed in October 1997. This abandoned limits on foreign ownership of each country's airlines but required that 'effective control' should remain with nationals of the respective country and the head office must be in the home country.

The advantages of the current ownership rules are clear-cut. First, all states view aviation as vital to their national economic interests and consequently feel a need to support and sustain their own airlines whether they own them or not. Both the US 'National Commission to Ensure a Strong Competitive Industry' and the European 'Comité des Sages' emphasised the importance of the aviation industries in their respective economies. The Comité stated that 'a genuine European Air Transport Industry is a key industry for the overall economic welfare of Europe' (Comité des Sages, 1994). It would seem that the ownership rules afford protection for an economic activity which may be vital to most economies. Clearly, the need to support air transport industries applies just as much to large as to small states.

Second, the ownership rules have allowed a number of states, which thirty to thirty-five years ago did not have an air transport industry, to develop successful and financially strong airlines. The highly profitable Singapore Airlines, protagonists today of 'open skies', only survived their infancy in the early 1970s because of the protection they were afforded by the bilateral system. A more recent successful example has been Air Mauritius. Even today, the ownership rules may facilitate the emergence of new and potentially viable flag carriers.

Finally, the ownership articles in bilaterals can prevent the emergency of flags of convenience in air transport. This was highlighted by IATA in its Working Paper (WP/18) to the November 1994 ICAO Air Transport Conference:

> Taking a whole airline to another country for the sake of economically better conditions is the extreme case of using location advantages in air transport. Such a concept, at present, is obviously avoided by national ownership and effective control clauses, which will at least keep the majority of airline capital and management in the country designating the airline. Once these clauses were removed, the way for a 'flag of convenience' airline structure would in principle be open.

On the other hand, there are some adverse consequences arising from the ownership rules. The requirement to designate a 'nationally' owned airline effectively encouraged all states to set up their own airlines irrespective of their traffic potential. These were usually government owned and in many cases they were unprofitable for long periods. Many became a serious drain on the national economy, especially in smaller or poorer developing countries. Moreover, they may not have served their national air transport interests particularly well. States without an international airline of their own have been unable to designate an airline from another country to exploit their traffic rights with third countries (though some exceptions, such as those mentioned above, do exist).

US airlines operating domestically, in the world's largest single air transport market, have been able through mergers and acquisitions, to become very large and gain very substantial scale benefits. With their huge domestic network and marketing spread as a base they have become very powerful in many international markets, often reinforcing their market power through commercial alliances aimed at building global networks. European, Asian or Latin American airlines are at a distinct disadvantage. The ownership rules prevent them from building the large 'home' base they require to ensure the same scale benefits as those enjoyed by US carriers. Even within the EU this is not possible since the ownership rules have not been relaxed in bilaterals with non-EU countries, including the United States. The potential for European carriers to build up through mergers a large 'domestic' market base in Europe comparable to that of their US competitors, is limited, since they must meet the current nationality rule.

Perhaps the most significant criticism of the ownership rules is that they distort the airline industry's structure by treating it differently from any other industry. The UK government has allowed its motor car industry to be entirely foreign-owned, as is much of its computer industry and its media. Why should the rules that govern trade in air services be different from those that govern trade in most other goods and services? To get around the ownership rules airlines resort to complex share ownership arrangements, such as that between KLM and Northwest, or to code-sharing alliances which are constrained by anti-trust or competition rules and confuse or mislead consumers. Relaxing or removing the ownership and nationality rules would do more than any other measure to create an open global airline industry. In the era of globalisation the existing rules are an outdated anomaly.

3.3 Towards clear skies

Mounting pressure for further liberalisation of air services together with the strong trend towards large-scale global airlines mean that the owner-ship rules are under strain. They are increasingly seen by many governments, by airline managements and by consumers as imposing unac-ceptable restrictions on the development of the industry. On the other hand, many governments and a large number of smaller airlines see these rules as an essential safeguard against the threat of being swamped by a few megacarriers. Yet the pressures for change are such that three possible alternatives to the current ownership criteria for designation might be considered:

(i)   The first and least radical approach would be for individual states to decide to allow their own airlines to be owned up to 49 per cent by non-nationals. This is the criterion already adopted within the EU; also in the case of the United States but with regard to non-voting equity only. But this would not in itself be sufficient to meet most of the objections to the current regime.

(ii)   A second approach would be for like-minded states to sign a multi-lateral agreement under which a state could designate any carrier which is substantially owned or effectively controlled by nationals of any state(s) that is (are) party to that common multilateral market access agreement. This would be similar to the ICAO 'community of interest' concept described earlier except that signatories to such an agreement need not be developing countries nor necessarily from the same geographical region.

(iii) A more far-reaching approach would be to abandon the ownership criteria in favour of basing designation on an airline's principal place of business. A state could designate any airline whose headquarters, administration or principal place of business is in the designating state regardless of who are the beneficial owners. Such owners may be from states which are not signatories to any collective agreement. This is similar to the Cathay Pacific or Monarch Airlines exceptions mentioned above. De facto this is what has also happened with Aerolineas Argentinas. The essential requirement would be that the designated carrier must be legally established in the designating state and subject to its laws.

Whatever the approach adopted, airlines designated would still have to comply with all other aspects of the bilateral agreements entered into by the designating states. So many constraints would remain. But this approach would allow for cross-border acquisitions.

The two more radical proposals above, if adopted, would represent a major shift away from the existing legal regime and from current practice. The advantages of the proposed arrangements for states which adopted them can be summarised as follows:

- They would give states a wider choice of carriers which they could designate to use their traffic rights.
- States without airlines could designate a non-national carrier and thus participate more effectively in international air transport. Alternatively, they could attract a foreign airline to set up a subsidiary with headquarters within their own territory.
- Airlines would have the potential to enter many more markets.
- Inward investment by foreign airlines to establish new carriers or buy into an existing one would be encouraged. This might provide much-needed capital and management expertise for smaller carriers.

- Development of new services and air links would be facilitated.
- The issue of airline ownership would become more open and less narrowly national.

Relaxing the current ownership and nationality rules is the first major challenge for international air transport in the new millennium. This alone would only be a partial response to the pressures for real 'open skies'. It would not necessarily create unlimited traffic rights or ensure open market access. The development of an 'open skies' regime within the European Union and its extension to a wider European Common Aviation Area during 2001, as described earlier, shows that it is possibly to make real progress through multilateral agreement. However, three inter-governmental conferences organised by the International Civil Aviation Organisation (ICAO) in Montreal in 1992, 1994 and 1997 also underlined how difficult it is to reconcile the conflicting views of governments on the future of international regulation. World-wide agreement on the abandonment of the bilateral system in favour of a more open multilateral system is not realisable. Moving forward through ICAO seems unlikely.

A possible alternative approach would be to use the new round of negotiations starting in 2000 on the extension of the General Agreement on Trade and Services, the so-called GATS/2000, to introduce much greater liberalisation of air services. The aim of GATS is, after all, the progressive removal of barriers to trade in all services. However, there are two difficulties in using GATS to further liberalisation of air transport. The first is that there are some very specific issues relating to air transport, particularly in relation to the commercial traffic rights, that is, the Third, Fourth and Fifth Freedoms, that cannot be dealt with satisfactorily as part of a comprehensive agreement covering all sectors. It is best if they continue to be considered within a specific sectoral basis. The second problem is that because of divergent government views a global agreement through GATS on these so-called hard rights would be unlikely. The best that GATS/2000 could achieve would be agreement on some of the softer issues such as ensuring that all countries, and in particular those that have not ratified the 1944 Air Services Transit Agreement, grant the non-commercial transit rights, namely, the First and Second Freedoms. Other issues that could be dealt with through GATS might include the right of airlines to do their own ground handling at foreign airports, sound charging policies for airport and en-route charges or removal of national restrictions on wet leasing of aircraft.

Rather than a multilateral solution, perhaps the easier way forward would be through a plurilateral agreement between like-minded states. The United States government has raised the possibility of interlocking 'open skies' bilateral agreements. This would involve a group of states signing similar 'open skies' bilaterals with each other. However, this would not overcome the shortcomings and gaps previously identified in such agreements such as the exclusion of domestic cabotage or Seventh Freedom rights.

The successful development of an open aviation market within the European Union and the imminent creation of the European Common Aviation Area (ECAA) covering twenty-seven or more countries suggests that a regional approach may be the most practical way to move forward. For some years it has been obvious that the next logical step should be to bring together the European Union and the United States and Canada into a common aviation area. Europe and North America represent two of the three largest air transport markets in the world. Scheduled passenger air transport within and between these two regions generates around 52 per cent of the world's passenger-kilometres. This share increases to nearly 80 per cent if one includes all traffic to and from North America and Europe. Clearly, the successful conclusion of an agreement between these two regions, which others could subsequently join, would be a major first step in laying the foundations for a world-wide 'open skies', or, better still, 'clear skies' regime to replace the current complex maze of bilateral agreements.

3.4 A Transatlantic Common Aviation Area

The European Commission, as pointed out earlier, has for some time felt that the existing web of bilaterals between the United States and EU member states created an unequal balance of rights and market opportunities that favoured US airlines. The Commission has long wanted to obtain domestic cabotage rights for European airlines within the United States in exchange for those already enjoyed by American airlines within the European Union. The Commission felt that the way forward, in order to resolve the anomalies created by the United States negotiating separately with each of the fifteen member states of the European Union, would be for the latter to negotiate as a single block with the US. The aim would be to establish a common aviation area covering the European Union and the United States within which key market issues such as anti-trust and competition rules, ownership restrictions, code sharing and dispute settlement would be harmonised. In June 1996 the Council of Ministers by qualified majority (the United Kingdom voted against) authorised the Commission to open negotiations with the United States. However, this mandate was not a full mandate. It did not and does not include market access, that is, traffic rights issues.

Attempts by the European Commission to move forward and exert some authority over external aviation negotiations have had mixed success. The Commission has successfully negotiated the accession of the ten Central European states to the European Common Aviation Area. On relations with the United States and in pursuit of its June 1996 mandate, the Commission appeared at first to be less successful, partly because of policy disagreements among the EU member states and partly because the European airlines themselves were lukewarm towards the concept. When Mrs Loyola de Palacio took over as the new Transport and Energy Commissioner in September 1999 she made no secret of her intention to set about creating a new aviation regime by negotiating a transatlantic agreement. At the same time, Europe's airlines, which had previously appeared uncertain as to their policies on this question, issued a major policy statement through the Association of European Airlines in support of a Transatlantic Common Aviation Area. This would be open to other states as well and its overall objective would 'to replace the current fragmented regulatory regime by a unified system that on the one hand gives airlines full commercial opportunities on an equal basis and on the other hand ensures that their activities will be governed by a common body of aviation rules, avoiding any unnecessary regulation' (AEA, 1999).

In December 1999 the US Transportation Secretary Rodney Slater hosted an inter-ministerial meeting in Chicago on the theme 'Beyond Open Skies'. For the US government this was an opportunity to open up discussion on the final push towards free trade in the air – in other words, on how to go beyond 'open skies' bilaterals. The Europeans surprised everyone by stating that they were ready to open negotiations and move forward. The European Union's position on this was made very clear by the Commissioner for Transport and Energy, Mrs de Palacio. She strongly advocated the creation of a Transatlantic Common Aviation Area (TCAA) whose aim would be to bring together the US concept of 'open skies' and the European concept of an open internal market.

> A TCAA between the US and the EU would not simply comprise the standard exchange of rights under "open skies". It would also set the stage for negotiating beyond the classic five freedoms, and comprise a shared and completely open market environment.
>
> (de Palacio, 1999)

Inevitably, no agreement was reached at Chicago on concrete proposals or what should be the next steps forward. It is for this reason that the AEA Policy Statement is significant because it does clarify what needs to be done and the issues that need to be resolved, with detailed proposals on each.

It is clearly the case that establishing a Transatlantic Common Aviation Area through negotiations between the EU and the United States would be an easier step than trying to reach a single multilateral agreement between a large number of individual governments. On the other hand it will be a long and laborious process to achieve convergence between the EU and the United States on several contentious issues. However, the establishment of a TCAA need not wait until all issues have been resolved and all details have been agreed. One could initially establish the TCAA by agreeing to those issues on which there is already common ground or on which agreement is not far off. During the lengthy preparatory and negotiating phases existing bilateral air services agreements would need to remain in force and could be amended further.

A TCAA or any other similar regional agreement on clear skies would need to address four key issues. The first would be that of open market access within the common aviation area itself. Airlines of the signatory states should be free to operate between any two points, including domestic sectors, without capacity or price controls. Nor would there be any form of discrimination between airlines. In effect the so-called Seventh Freedom would also be available. So a British airline would be able to operate services between, say, Copenhagen and New York without such services originating or stopping in the United Kingdom. But open market access would only apply to services within the TCAA. Services between states within the TCAA and third countries would continue to be governed by the conventional bilateral system. The main difficulty in achieving full open market access is likely to be US reluctance to grant domestic cabotage rights to foreign carriers.

The second issue is that of the nationality or ownership rules and the right of establishment. As has been argued previously, fundamental change is required here in view of the economic pressures towards industrial concentration within the airline industry, which is currently being distorted by restrictions on ownership. The simplest and first step would be to allow ownership of TCAA airlines by nationals or companies from any of the states within the TCAA. This would be similar to the current regime within the European Union. Once this is agreed it would be possible for a US airline to buy Eurowings in Germany or for Lufthansa to buy a majority share of America West, since these are airlines operating wholly within the TCAA. In other words, some cross-border mergers and acquisitions would become possible. But air services to countries outside the TCAA would still be governed by the conventional bilateral agreements with the traditional nationality requirement. Airlines operating such services could not be taken over by airlines or companies from states other than their own even if they were from other states within the TCAA. Thus, for most major international airlines within the TCAA little would have changed. They would still need to be 'substantially owned' and effectively controlled by nationals of their own state. To open up and normalise the industry, the next logical step would be for the TCAA member states when renegotiating their own bilaterals with third countries to insist that designated airlines should have their principal place of business in the designating states and that the traditional ownership rule should be abandoned. Given the importance of the larger countries within the TCAA as international markets it would be difficult for third countries to resist pressure to change the current nationality rule in favour of designating airlines on the basis of their 'principal place of business'. Or the TCAA member states could as a group go even further and insist on their right to designate any airline from within the TCAA to exercise their traffic rights with third countries. Few of the latter would relish taking on the combined might of Europe and the United States in a dispute about designation.

A key requirement within any regional aviation area is to ensure that competition is open, fair and safeguarded. Therefore a third issue to resolve in creating a TCAA would be to try and harmonise competition policy. The EU competition rules (Chapter 2, section 2.4) and US anti-trust legislation both have the same basic principles and objectives. But in applying them the EU and the US often reach different conclusions. A case in point is that of transatlantic airline alliances. The US permits such alliances provided they are with European airlines whose states have signed 'open skies' bilaterals with the United States allowing the free entry of new airlines on the relevant markets. This is considered sufficient to safeguard competition. The European Commission, on the other hand, is much more proscriptive. After analysing what it considers to be the relevant markets it normally requires the partner airlines to give up runway slots to prospective competitors while reducing their own frequencies (Chapter 4, section 4.9). Clearly, it would be impractical to try and have the same competition rules on either side of the Atlantic, given the differing legislative frameworks. The aim should be, however, to try and ensure that in their application of these competition rules the relevant authorities converge as much as possible (Soames, 2000). This would minimise the possibility of conflicting decisions and would remove the current uncertainty and delay that distorts airline decisions on alliances and co-operative agreements. Clearly, the focus of discussions between the European Union and the United States should be on convergence rather than harmonisation.

Finally, linked to the issue of competition policy, one would need to establish a common approach and convergence on a range of regulatory issues on which there are still a few remaining differences on either side of the Atlantic. The most critical of these are slot allocation rules at congested airports, bankruptcy protection regulations and the leasing in of foreign registered aircraft. Issues on which convergence would be easier include government subsidies or state aid, cargo and mail preference rules and codes of conduct for computer reservation systems.

The large number of issues that need to be covered in moving towards a Transatlantic Common Aviation Area highlights the difficulties involved. It is clear that progress will be slow. The creation of the TCAA will be phased and in steps as agreement is reached on policy and convergence in different areas. Transitional arrangements may also be necessary on particular issues or for specific markets.

Plurilateral agreements between like-minded states, which could lead to the creation of common aviation areas such as that proposed between the European Union and the United States, appear to be the way to achieve clear skies. Or, at least clearer skies. Other regions of the world are moving towards the plurilateral model. In the Far East, the Asia-Pacific Economic Co-operation (APEC) forum has been examining whether groups of like-minded states from within this region could agree to a common set of principles. The African states have actually moved a step further. Meeting in November 1999 in the Ivory Coast, they adopted a new policy frame-work, the so-called Yamoussoukro II agreement, for the liberalisation of the continent's air transport industry. Though awaiting ratification by the Assembly of the Organisation of African Unity and individual states, the agreement aims to liberalise market access by the year 2002 in order to create a single African aviation market. The agreement is far-reaching. Signatory states would grant each other unlimited Third, Fourth and Fifth Freedom rights. There would be no control of capacity of frequencies operated or of tariffs, though the number of designated airlines might be limited. The agreement proposes to abandon the traditional nationality rule in favour of allowing states to designate airlines having their headquar-ters, central administration and principal place of business in the designating state, and being 'effectively controlled' from within that state. A state would also be able to designate an airline from another state to operate on its behalf (*African Aviation*, December 1999). If ratified and implemented, even by a limited number of states, Yamoussoukro II would show one way towards achieving clear skies.

For the international airline industry as a whole, the creation of a Transatlantic Common Aviation Market would clearly be of much greater significance because of the sheer size of the markets involved. A break-through here will have far-reaching consequences for the whole air transport industry. There appears to be a political will both in the United States and the European Union to move forward on creating a common aviation area. Developments on the TCAA will be the key regulatory issue for international air transport in the early years of the new millennium. After a slow start it is to be hoped that progress will accelerate and that other countries will join.

4   Alliances

A response to uncertainty or an economic necessity?

Alliances are a tool for extending or reinforcing competitive advantage, but rarely a sustainable means for creating it.

(Michael Porter, *The Competitive Advantage of Nations*)

4.1 Alliance frenzy

In the second half of the 1990s the airline industry was characterised by a frenzy for inter-airline alliances of various kinds. The most frenetic period of alliance making was triggered by the deteriorating financial performance of international airlines as they were hit first by the crisis in the tiger economies of East Asia from late 1997, then by the slowdown in some European states in 1998 followed by the rapid escalation of fuel prices in 1999. *Airline Business* in June 1998 recorded 502 separate inter-airline alliances, 32 per cent more than a year earlier. As new alliances were being formed old ones were being broken up. The most notable divorce occurred in June 1999 when Delta abandoned its partner Swissair and its partner of ten years, the Atlantic Quality alliance. A few months later Austrian Airlines deserted the same alliance and announced its adhesion to the rival Star grouping. Equally dramatic was the sudden collapse in May 2000 of the relatively young but troubled alliance between KLM and Alitalia.

Some years earlier Michael Porter (1990) referring to industries in general, had written: 'Alliances are frequently transitional devices. They proliferate in industries undergoing structural change or escalating competition, where managers fear that they cannot cope. They are a response to uncertainty, and provide comfort that the firm is taking action.' To what extent was this true of the frenzy for international airline alliances in the 1990s? Were these alliances merely transitional devices reflecting managers' inability to cope with liberalisation and the intensified competition which followed or are airline alliances and industry concentration an inevitable response to the economic characteristics of airline operations once regulatory constraints are removed?

Airline industry concentration through mergers and commercial alliances is not new. Restructuring of the United States airline industry was one of the major consequences of airline deregulation in that country. While the Airline Deregulation Act was signed into law in October 1978 it was not till five or six years later that a wave of mergers and acquisitions led to greater concentration. The initial response to deregulation had been a proliferation of new start-up airlines, some of which were initially more successful than others. In addition, some existing smaller intra-state carriers took advantage of deregulation to expand outside their own states. As international air routes were liberalised under the Carter administration (see Chapter 2, section 2.3) some new entrants such as People Express and Air Florida also launched international services. While there were some mergers in the early 1980s, such as that between Pan American and National in 1980, it was not till the mid-1980s that a real shake-out began.

The early 1980s had been difficult years for the airline industry. But more significant was the fact that some of the established majors such as American, United and Delta were successfully beating off the challenge of lower-cost new entrants. Their success in doing this was attributed to the marketing advantages of large size and network scope. As a result of the perceived benefits of larger size, some financially stronger carriers bought weaker airlines, especially where this would extend their geographical and market spread. The purchase of Air Florida by Midway in July 1985 was an example. In other instances two or more weak carriers came together through acquisitions and mergers in an attempt to achieve the larger size and scope which they felt essential for survival. This was the rationale for the merger of Continental, People Express and New York Air in April 1987. But alliances should reinforce a competitive advantage – they can rarely create one. Thus combining two weak airlines is unlikely to create a strong competitor. This is why most alliances or mergers of weak partners failed in the longer term.

The mid-1980s were the peak years for mergers, acquisitions and alliances within the United States domestic airline industry. Between April 1985 and the end of 1987 over twenty significant acquisitions and mergers took place. As a result by 1987, ten years after deregulation, the level of concentration had increased markedly. While in 1978 the top six airlines generated 72 per cent of US domestic passenger-miles, by 1987 the six largest airlines' share had risen to 83 per cent (US Congressional Budget Office quoted in *Avmark*, 1988).

Clearly, the primary goal of the larger US airlines in the 1980s, once they had the freedom to expand and grow, was to achieve critical mass within the United States domestic market. Having done this, their attention, towards the end of the decade, turned to capitalising on the growth potential of international markets once these had been opened up for new entrants and in terms of new destinations. For the larger US carriers growth in international markets could be achieved in several ways – through gradual development of their existing networks, by purchasing routes from those US airlines in decline and as a result of cross-border alliances. Delta Airlines exemplified this trend. Delta had consolidated its domestic position by acquiring Western Airlines at the beginning of 1987. Meanwhile, in the period up to 1991, Delta developed a limited international network across both the Atlantic and the Pacific by establishing new routes to more liberal-minded countries such as Germany, France, Korea or Thailand. The next major step was the purchase in August 1991 of ailing Pan American's North Atlantic operations out of New York. Earlier in 1985, Pan American had sold its Pacific operations to United. Delta's acquisition of Pan Am routes enabled it to set up a hub in Frankfurt serving and linking nine US airports with eleven cities in Central and Eastern Europe, the Middle East and India. This acquisition was seen by Delta as a key step in ensuring that Delta would be a major player within the future air transport industry (Callison, 1992). Another key step was to create a global network through cross-border alliances with airlines in the world's two largest markets outside North America, namely Europe and East Asia. The alliance between Delta, Swissair and Singapore Airlines was launched in 1989 and focused primarily on joint marketing (e.g. joint frequent flyer schemes, shared ticket offices, round-the-world fares, through check-in, joint airport handling, and so on). Though it was to break up about ten years later, this was the forerunner of other global alliances.

Developments among European airlines lagged behind those in the United States because liberalisation did not start until the mid-1980s and progressed more gradually than the almost overnight domestic deregulation which had occurred in the United States in 1978. Moreover, European airlines' actions were distorted by the constraints imposed on them by the nationality rules (see Chapter 3, section 3.2) and the need to operate within relatively small domestic markets. Nevertheless, starting a decade or so later, the larger European carriers began to implement a threefold growth strategy very similar in essence to that of the United States' airlines described above. First, they set out to dominate as far as possible their own home markets through acquisitions, franchising or other commercial agreements. Second, they attempted to establish a foothold in the larger European markets outside their own. The three largest were the United Kingdom, Germany and France. The strategy here was to buy into existing airlines already operating within these other countries and whenever possible to rebrand them. The third growth strategy was, as in the case of US airlines, to develop a global marketing spread through one or more alliances with airlines in North America or the East Asia-Pacific region, the two largest markets outside Europe. This was to be done through marketing and code-share agreements or even share purchases.

Of the larger European airlines, KLM, Lufthansa, Swissair and SAS all followed similar three-pronged strategies during the late 1980s and the 1990s. But British Airways (BA) was the first to develop most clearly a growth strategy based on these three key objectives – dominate your home market, ensure a presence in the other major European markets and establish a global spread through alliances with US and Asian/Pacific carriers.

In 1987 BA bought a 40 per cent share in Brymon Airways, a small regional turbo-prop operator in the South West of Britain, buying it outright in 1993. Also, at the end of 1987 and only after the UK government had blocked an SAS rescue package, BA took over British Caledonian. This was then the UK's second-largest airline with an extensive domestic and international network radiating from London's Gatwick airport. With effect from November 1992, BA also acquired the principal European and domestic scheduled routes of Dan-Air, another Gatwick-based airline. In 1993 BA entered into franchise agreements with Maersk Air, operating out of Birmingham, and with City Flyer Express which flew a range of feeder services out of Gatwick. Franchise agreements with other small UK airlines followed and in 1999 BA bought City Flyer Express outright. By 1995 the only significant UK scheduled airlines outside BA's control or influence were British Midland, where SAS had bought a 24.9 per cent share following its earlier failure to buy into British Caledonian, Air UK where KLM had acquired a 14.9 per cent share in 1987 and Virgin Pacific a niche long-haul carrier. Both SAS and KLM had clearly established a foothold in the UK, Europe's largest market. Subsequently KLM took over all Air UK's shares and SAS's share of British Midland was increased to 40 per cent, though early in 2000 it sold half of this to Lufthansa.

When, after 1995, low-cost new entrants such as easyJet and Ryanair created a new challenge to BA's very strong position in the UK scheduled market, BA set up its own low-cost, no-frills airline, Go, which launched operations from London's Stansted airport in May 1998.

The second part of BA's strategy was to establish a presence in the largest European markets outside the UK, namely, Germany and France. During 1992 Delta Air, a domestic German airline, was acquired by BA (49 per cent) and a consortium of German banks. BA exercised its option to acquire the remaining 51 per cent in 1997. In January 1993 BA invested £15 million in buying 49.9 per cent of TAT, France's largest independent domestic airline, again with an option to move to 100 per cent ownership in 1997. Late in 1996 BA was successful in its joint bid with the Rivaud Group to purchase Air Liberté, another French domestic airline which joined the BA Group in January 1997. During that year TAT and Air Liberté were merged under the single name Air Liberté with BA eventually retaining an 84 per cent shareholding. Early in 2000 its own deteriorating performance forced BA to sell off Air Liberté at a loss.

In achieving its third strategic objective, that of creating a global network, BA has had some setbacks. In 1987 BA and United Airlines announced a world-wide marketing partnership, one of the very first. But this somehow failed to gel and it was suspended in December 1989. In 1992 BA, keen to find a United States partner, began negotiations with

USAir, then the sixth-largest US airline and the fourth largest in terms of passenger kilometres. In that year USAir lost US$601 million before tax and looked at the BA proposals as a lifeline. By early 1993 BA had acquired a 24.6 per cent shareholding in USAir with the right to increase this to 40.7 per cent, though with voting rights limited to 25 per cent because of restrictions on foreign ownership of United States airlines. Also in early 1993 BA paid A$665 million for a 25 per cent stake in Qantas shortly after the latter had acquired Australian Airlines, Australia's largest domestic carrier. Paradoxically, earlier in 1988, Qantas had bought a 19.4 per cent share in Air New Zealand to prevent BA taking a major share in this airline. (Qantas subsequently sold this 19.4 per cent stake early in 1997.) With the purchase of shareholdings in both USAir and Qantas, BA's global strategy appeared to be in place. But USAir was not a major operator on the North Atlantic compared to American, United or Delta, and was much smaller than these carriers domestically. After United concluded an extensive code-share alliance with Lufthansa in 1995 BA felt threatened. In June 1996 much to USAir's surprise and annoyance, BA announced a far-reaching alliance with American. The partnership with USAir was effectively destroyed and in May 1997 BA sold its investment in this airline. However, the new alliance with American fell foul of the regulators, both in Europe, the UK and the United States and could not be consummated in its original form. More of this later.

As a result of the regulatory barriers to the original BA/American alliance, a weaker marketing alliance was launched in 1998 under the 'Oneworld' banner bringing together five airlines, American, BA, Canadian Airlines, Qantas and Cathay Pacific, though others were to join later.

British Airways' alliance activity was mirrored during the late 1990s by most of the larger European carriers, though some lagged behind and were slow to develop and implement a coherent alliance strategy. Alitalia, Iberia and, most notably, Air France were among these. In North America it was American Airlines that had been the last to enter into global alliances and when it did in June 1996 with British Airways it found this alliance effectively blocked by the long delays while waiting for approval from the European Commission and the US Government. In Asia, most airlines had been hesitant of entering comprehensive strategic alliances, though they had accepted more limited commercial agreements. The economic crisis which hit several East Asian countries in 1997 and 1998 changed all that. Suddenly airlines such as Cathay Pacific, which had traditionally been hostile to alliances, fell over themselves in their rush to find alliance partners.

4.2 Diversity of airline alliances

The discussion so far has focused largely on airline alliances involving equity participation, mergers or marketing co-operation through code sharing or joint operations. In practice, over the years a very wide range of complex inter-airline agreements has grown up to meet specific airline needs. Many such agreements pre-date the period of 'alliances' and were primarily aimed at facilitating the operation or marketing of international air services by airlines that were national in character. Agreements were sometimes purely technical and might, for instance, involve provision of engineering back-up by two airlines at each other's home base or even joint maintenance of specific aircraft types in their fleets. In Europe, for instance, within the long-established KSS consortium KLM provided heavy maintenance for Boeing 747s and CF6 engines for all three airlines in the consortium, while Swissair maintained MD-11, DC-10 and Airbus A310 aircraft and SAS maintained JT9D engines. Many agreements concern the joint operation of cargo or passenger flights or the operation by one airline of such services on behalf of two or more partners. An example is the scheduled freighter service between Singapore and London operated jointly by BA and Singapore Airlines. The majority of inter-airline agreements are, however, essentially commercial in character and are primarily concerned with marketing and selling of passenger and/or cargo services. At the simplest level, they may be little more than a *pro-rate agreement* which fixes the revenue that one airline will pay the other for carrying the latter's ticketed passenger on a particular part of the former's network. Or they may be more complex agreements for *sharing codes* on a particular flight or on several flights with or without *block space* agreements whereby one partner will purchase an agreed number of seats from the other on the code-shared flights. Airlines may also jointly own *computer reservation systems* or have *joint sales offices* or *telephone call centres*.

Each airline has over time built up a complex web of interlocking agreements with other airlines covering various aspects of its operations and in different geographical areas. It would be difficult to argue that all such agreements represent an alliance. Especially as many agreements clearly cut across what appear to be the accepted global alliance groupings. Thus, British Airways in 1998 was joined with American Airlines in the Oneworld Alliance but was at that time also in partnership with United as major shareholders in Galileo, the major computer reservation system. (BA subsequently sold its Galileo shares in June 1999.) BA handled KLM at London-Heathrow despite KLM being in a separate alliance. Members of BA's Executive Club could earn air miles (frequent flyer points) on Singapore Airline flights even though the latter belonged to a different FFP group and was linked to the Star Alliance. BA also operated, as mentioned, a joint freighter service with SIA. One of BA's earliest domestic franchisees was Loganair (later British Regional), at that time a subsidiary of BA's major domestic competitor, British Midland, itself 40 per cent owned by SAS, which was in alliance with Lufthansa. Conversely, Cathay Pacific, another Oneworld member, in 1999 had a cargo co-operation agreement with Lufthansa. Cathay and SIA, though in different global groupings, are both shareholders in Taeco a maintenance joint venture in China, and in a catering joint venture. Such apparent anomalies abound. However, it is evident that gradually over time the linkages with declared alliance partners will strengthen and be reinforced while those with non-alliance airlines will, where possible, be replaced or will fade away.

To make some sense out of the complexity of inter-airline agreements one should distinguish between those that are primarily commercial and those that are more strategic. A *strategic alliance* is one where the partners co-mingle their assets in order to pursue a single or joint set of business objectives. Co-mingled assets may be terminal facilities, maintenance bases, aircraft, staff, traffic rights or capital resources. If two or more airlines offer a common brand and a uniform service standard then that means they are co-mingling their assets and have moved into a strategic alliance. Many franchise agreements are of this kind. The franchise partners also have a joint objective which is to profit from the common passenger traffic generated as a result of the franchise. Thus, despite the fact that one partner may be much smaller than the other, many franchise agreements are truly strategic. Conversely, many code-share agreements, joint frequent flyer programmes and even some block space agreements are essentially *marketing alliances*. They are not strategic because the partners continue to operate and use their assets independently, each pursuing his own objectives.

Inter-airline agreements fall along a spectrum, as illustrated in Figure 4.1, which starts with a very straightforward marketing alliance, which may be little more than an interline agreement or a joint frequent flyer programme. Partners stay very much at arm's length. As the agreements involve greater integration and co-mingling of assets they move from being purely commercial to being increasingly strategic in character. Towards the end of the spectrum are joint ventures where airlines come together to operate a business activity jointly. Thus, when the KLM and Alitalia alliance was announced in November 1998, an explicit aim was to operate their passenger and cargo services as two integrated joint ventures. This would be achieved during 1999–2000 and would create a truly strategic alliance. The ultimate strategic alliance is a full merger of the airlines involved. Conversely, share purchases or mutual share swaps do not necessarily indicate a strategic alliance if the partners continue to pursue their own particular objectives. This was the case with the earliest global alliance created in 1989, that between Swissair, Delta and SIA, where each held a small shareholding in the other. They joined up for different reasons and pursued differing objectives. As a result it was not a truly strategic alliance but purely a commercial agreement concerned with frequent flyer programmes, joint ground handling, pro-rate revenue agreements and inter-lining. SIA withdrew in 1998 after ten years, precisely because it was not a strategic alliance pursuing common objectives. As Dr Cheong Choon

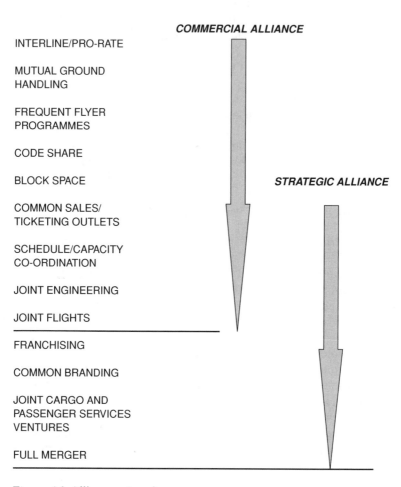

Figure 4.1 Alliance categories.

Kong, Deputy Chairman and CEO of Singapore Airlines put it: 'We tried moving in harmony with one another but each of us was dancing to a different tune' (Cheong, 1998).

Alliances also have a spatial dimension. Whether commercial or strategic they can also be categorised according to their geographical spread and importance. The simplest and by far the most numerous are *route-specific* alliances covering one route or a limited number of city pairs. There is a wide variety of such alliances. However, the simplest will involve either special pro-rate agreements for interline traffic or code sharing or both. (Pro-rates are the prices or tariffs airlines agree to charge for carrying each other's passengers on their own aircraft.) Sometimes both airlines will fly the route(s) but all flights will carry the codes of both carriers. But frequently, on thinner routes, one of the partner airlines may operate the service on behalf of both. Thus, in 2000 Cyprus Airways operated a daily Larnaca–Amsterdam service which also carried a KLM flight number. The service was scheduled to link in both directions with one of KLM's 'banks' of departing and arriving flights so as to maximise the potential for online passenger feed. Where only one airline operates the service some kind of revenue allocation agreement has to be entered into to establish the number of seats the non-operating airline will buy from the operator and the price to be paid. Such agreements may be more or less complex. A simple formula is a block space agreement where one airline buys a specified number of seats from the other, irrespective of whether they are filled, at a specified price.

Regional alliances are on a much wider scale and are generally of two kinds. The first and more widespread is a commercial agreement covering many routes, though usually to and from a particular geographical region or country. Such agreements will normally involve code-shared flights, joint marketing and sales, some capacity co-ordination, use of each other's business lounges and so on.

During 1999 Malaysian Airlines and Thai Airways had a regional alliance covering code sharing on several routes between their two countries. Similarly SIA, Air New Zealand and Ansett had an alliance covering routes between South East Asia and Australasia as well as some domestic routes within Australia. The second kind of regional alliance is a franchise agreement between a larger carrier and a regional or feeder operator. The latter adopts the livery, brand and service standards of the franchiser and normally only carries the latter's flight code. In 1999 British Airways had nine franchisee partners, of which seven were UK airlines operating both domestic and international services, one was the Danish airline Sun Air and one a South African domestic operator. They added seventy-four destinations to the BA network. The most significant of these franchise agreements was with City Flyer Express entered into in July 1993. This was an airline with a relatively extensive network of domestic and some short-haul international services radiating from London's Gatwick airport. These provided excellent domestic feed to BA's own international services from Gatwick. When at the beginning of 1999 City Flyer Express was put up for sale BA bought it but only after receiving approval from the UK Monopolies and Mergers Commission.

The most significant alliances in terms of network expansion are clearly those with a *global* scope. Here the prime purpose is to achieve all the marketing benefits of scope and the cost economies from any synergies

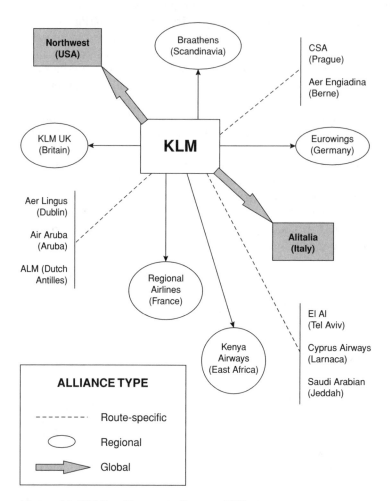

Figure 4.2 KLM's alliances in January 2000.

through linking two or more large airlines operating geographically distinct markets, ideally in different continents. Global alliances would normally involve code sharing on a very large number of routes, but ideally they aim to go much further. They may include schedule co-ordination, joint sales offices and ground handling, combined frequent flyer programmes, joint maintenance activities, and so on. Such alliances may include mutual equity stakes. They may be largely commercial in character, such as the Oneworld Alliance when it was launched in the autumn of 1998, or more strategic, like the Northwest-KLM alliance. The individual members of a global partnership may each have a large number of route-specific and a small number of regional alliances. Thus, the network spread and influence of a global alliance may be much wider than is at first apparent. The aim of a *global alliance* is effectively linking airlines in a different geographical area so as to provide world-wide network coverage and the benefits of large size and scope. KLM's route-specific, regional and global alliances as they were early in 2000 are shown in Figure 4.2.

On the basis of the above categorisation, alliances such as that between Swissair and Austrian or Lufthansa and SAS, at least when originally launched, were essentially regional in character. They linked airlines in the same region, in fact in adjacent countries. However, these regional alliances became part of or were subsumed within wider global alliances.

Growing awareness during 1999 that the airline industry's financial performance was beginning to falter heightened the alliance frenzy. New and, in some cases, unexpected partnerships emerged and old ones disintegrated. The major casualty was the 'Atlantic Excellence' alliance linking Swissair, Sabena, Austrian Airlines and Delta. In June 1999 Delta announced it was leaving to set up a new global alliance with Air France, an airline which had hitherto stayed aloof from major groupings. Shortly afterwards Austrian Airlines announced it was also abandoning a forty-four-year relationship with Swissair in order to join the Star Alliance. The latter, whose major partners were United Airlines, Lufthansa and SAS, was busy signing up new members and by early 2000 had increased its membership to thirteen airlines. In 2000, UAL, United's parent company, announced it was buying US Airways, the sixth-largest airline in the United States. This deal, due to be finalised early in 2001, was subject to regulatory approval. The other major grouping under the 'Oneworld' banner had also been actively pursuing new members. However, its two major partners, British Airways and American continued to face difficulties in obtaining anti-trust immunity from the United States authorities because of the repeated failure of the UK Government to agree to a full 'open skies' bilateral with the US. This alliance also found itself in the anomalous position of finding one of its members, Canadian Airlines, being bought in January 2000 by Air Canada, an airline belonging to the Star Alliance.

There was a fourth grouping based around the KLM-Northwest alliance. This was created as a result of Alitalia entering into an alliance with KLM at the end of 1998 and formally joining the KLM-Northwest alliance in May 1999. In November 1998 Northwest had bought a controlling interest in Continental in defiance of a Department of Justice lawsuit. Continental was expected to join Northwest's alliance grouping but by the end of 1999 the outcome of the lawsuit was not yet settled. The exact composition and name of this alliance was still uncertain, though it was likely to be called 'Wings'. This grouping was thrown into disarray in May 2000 when the KLM-Alitalia partnership suddenly collapsed.

The profiles of the four alliances based on their membership early in 2000 but using 1999 annual data, which was then available, are shown in Table 4.1. There are clearly two larger alliances, that is, Star and

Table 4.1 Profile of the major global alliances in July 2000

Alliance members (April 2000)	Key data*				
	Gross revenue (US$ billion)	Number of aircraft	Employees	Pass. carried (millions)	Share of world scheduled Pass.-kms (%)
Star Alliance United Airlines Lufthansa SAS Air Canada Thai Airways Varig Air New Zealand Ansett All Nippon Singapore Airways Mexicana Austrian British Midland	70	1,885	262,000	293	21.3
Oneworld American British Airways Qantas Cathay Pacific Iberia Finnair Lan Chile Aer Lingus	50	1,460	232,000	199	16.4
Wings† Northwest KLM Continental	25	924	127,000	117	9.8
Delta/Air France Delta Air France Aeromexico	23	864	132,000	151	9.7
TOTAL FOUR ALLIANCES	168				57.2

Note
* Key data is for the year 1999. Staff numbers in some cases do not include staff in aviation-related separate subsidiaries, e.g. in maintenance companies.
† The KLM-Alitalia alliance broke up in May 2000 leaving the Wings grouping reduced in size.

Oneworld and two smaller ones, the Delta/Air France and Wings group-ings. The latter two are about half the size of the Star Alliance in terms of all the key data analysed. While both Star and Oneworld each generate around one-fifth of the world's scheduled passenger traffic they both contain a large number of very diverse airlines. Star alone has thirteen formal members, each of which has other regional partners, generating over US$70 billion in gross revenues from operating close to 1,900 aircraft with over 260,000 employees. Perhaps the smaller alliances may find it easier to mould their partners' operations into a cohesive and seamless product offering a consistent service quality.

Between them the member airlines of these four alliances generated about 57 per cent of the world's passenger-kms in 1998. However, most of these airlines also had separate or regional alliances with individual airlines with which they had code-share or franchisee agreements, but which were not formally within their global alliance. Some of these regional partners were also their subsidiaries as in the case of KLM UK owned by KLM or Deutsche BA and Air Liberté owned by British Airways. If one adds the traffic of such regional partners to that of the core members of each global alliance the potential market power of the latter becomes evident. The four alliance groupings together account for over two-thirds of the world's scheduled traffic, domestic plus international, whether measured in passenger-kilometres or revenue tonne-kilometres. This growing level of concentration may be a cause for concern. At the very least it is an issue which must be watched and monitored.

But what is driving this search for alliances? Four major factors appear to be behind the push towards transnational industry concentration: a search for the marketing benefits of large size and scope; a desire to reduce costs; the need to reduce competition wherever possible as the international airline industry becomes more liberalised and competitive; and finally the 'nationality rules' which make cross-border acquisitions and mergers virtu-ally impossible.

4.3 The marketing benefits of large scale and scope

In the decade or so after deregulation in the United States it became apparent that cost economies of scale in airline operations were limited. In other words, the very large US airlines, the so-called 'majors', were unable to achieve lower unit operating costs than much smaller airlines merely because of their enormous size. In fact, the opposite was often the case. Their unit costs were actually higher than that of their smaller competitors who initially blossomed after deregulation. Yet while most of the majors survived and prospered, most low-cost low-fare new entrants eventually collapsed. It was the distinct marketing advantages enjoyed by the majors that enabled them to survive. These marketing advantages can be summarised as follows:

- attraction of widespread and interconnected network offering 'all' destinations;
- market dominance at several hubs;
- ability to squeeze competitors through rescheduling, frequency increases and/or price cuts;
- traffic connecting through hubs supports high-frequency services;
- more powerful distribution system through access to numerous travel agents in several markets;
- ability to maximise benefits of large advertising spend;
- ability to ensure consistently high service standard through world-wide network despite change of aircraft/airline;
- extensive network creates much more attractive customer loyalty scheme (FFP).

These advantages stemmed essentially from the very large scale of their operations and the wide spread of their networks. On the other hand, smaller airlines or new entrants were focused on niche markets or particular geographical areas. This made the former very attractive to potential passengers because they knew that these major carriers would almost certainly serve the destination or destinations they wished to fly to. The majors developed hub and spoke operations through their hub airport(s), thereby providing good online transfer connections to most points passengers would wish to travel to. Effective hubbing also ensured higher frequencies than could be achieved by competitors' point-to-point services, and they often compensated for the need to change aircraft by offering lower fares. The majors' dominance at two or more hub airports, in terms of the number of departures, made it very difficult for other airlines effectively to compete on the thicker and more lucrative routes from those hubs. Moreover, new entrants might have great difficulty obtaining sufficient runway slots or terminal gates to mount effective competition.

If and when new entrant airlines tried to enter such routes the airline operating that particular hub could 'squeeze' new competitors through frequency increases, by rescheduling their own flights to leave shortly before those of competitors and, where necessary, through fare reductions. The larger airlines also had better and more effective distribution systems. Because of their very size they had access to more travel agencies in more markets. In the 1980s they were also the first to develop and effectively exploit computerised reservation systems such as United's 'Apollo' (later 'Galileo') and American Airlines' 'Sabre' system, though this initial advantage has since disappeared. Large size also produced benefits in terms of advertising spend. A given amount of expenditure could promote more destinations/services because the network was so wide. With a much wider network and greater geographical spread through the use of one or more large hubs, the majors could ensure consistently high service and handling standards even when passengers had to change aircraft. Smaller airlines with more limited networks often needed to transfer passengers on to other carriers in order for the latter to reach their final destination. As a result they could not ensure consistency of service quality. Finally, airlines with very extensive networks have much more attractive frequent flyer programmes (FFP) because they offer many more opportunities both to earn points and to spend them. As such loyalty schemes became more popular, the attractiveness of those airlines with widespread networks was reinforced.

It would appear from the above analysis that the marketing benefits described arise primarily from large scope, that is, geographical spread, rather than from size per se, though the two are clearly linked. It was these clearly perceived advantages of larger scope that were one of the major drivers for the frenzy of acquisitions and mergers in the United States in the mid-1980s described earlier. The majors were able in this way to increase the scale of their operations and their market power. Only a handful of the US low-cost carriers have survived, most notably Southwest (see Chapter 6).

The rationale and justification for the expansion and strengthening of domestic networks, seen so clearly in the case of the United States, applies equally strongly to international air services. Through code sharing and other forms of commercial alliances with foreign airlines, US airlines could reach into new markets and thereby dramatically increase their network spread and market power at little additional cost. It is not surprising that the first two US majors to enter into cross-border global alliances in 1989 were Northwest and Delta, airlines with the weakest international networks, especially on the North Atlantic.

International alliances offered two additional marketing advantages. They enabled airlines to expand their existing markets through the extra traffic generated by the feed to and from the foreign airline partner and to do this at little extra cost. But, in addition, such cross-border alliances enabled airlines to expand into and develop new markets previously inaccessible to them. Thus, the alliance between United and Lufthansa, initially launched in October 1993, has enabled United to access and develop new markets in Eastern Europe via Lufthansa's Frankfurt hub which were previously either unavailable in terms of traffic rights or non-viable in terms of direct flights. On the United Airlines/Lufthansa trunk route between Chicago and Frankfurt, traffic transferring at either or both ends has more than tripled as a result of the connections available at either end. Between 1993 and 1998 daily online transfer passengers rose from a little over 200 to over 600, while local point-to-point traffic has increased only slowly. It was the rapid growth of transfer traffic that enabled United/Lufthansa to increase their daily code-shared frequencies from two in 1996 to four in summer 1998. Alliances are seen as a way of both developing existing markets and expanding into new ones.

A good example of how alliances can increase market power is provided by KLM and its regional partners. KLM traditionally a long-haul carrier, had a much weaker European network than other large European airlines. In the early 1990s KLM's share of scheduled intra-European international and domestic traffic was less than 4 per cent even when one included traffic of airlines in which it had a shareholding. This contrasted with market shares of well over 10 per cent for Air France, British Airways, Iberia or Lufthansa (Doganis, 1994). With growing liberalisation, KLM needed to support its long-haul operations at Amsterdam and the three daily complexes of arriving and departing flights that it was planning. To do this KLM set about expanding its European services in the three years after 1995, but also, most importantly, it developed key regional alliance partnerships. In July 1997 it increased its 45 per cent shareholding in Air UK, the third-largest domestic and short-haul international carrier in the UK to 100 per cent and in 1998 rebranded the airline as KLM UK. This airline provides high frequency services from more than thirteen regional airports in the United Kingdom to Amsterdam. As a result, it operates the second-largest number of slots at Schiphol after KLM. In order to access the German market more effectively KLM entered into a partnership with Eurowings, the second largest German domestic airline. Eurowings flights from several German regional airports, such as Munster, Stuttgart or Nuremberg to Amsterdam, subsequently carried a KLM flight code. As with other regional partners these flights were scheduled to connect with KLM's intercontinental flights Towards the end of 1997 KLM bought a 30 per cent shareholding in the Norwegian airline Braathens, which had earlier bought into the two Swedish airlines Transwede and Malmo Aviation. Finally, KLM tied up a code-share partnership with Regional Airlines, a French airline with an extensive third-level operation and with some international flights from French regional airports to nearer European points. Through these regional partnerships, which involve code shares, schedule co-ordination, some joint branding, participation in the KLM 'Flying Dutchman' loyalty programme and other areas of mutual support, KLM has been able to tie in closely with its own operations at Amsterdam four large European markets – those of the United Kingdom, Germany, France and Scandinavia (Figure 4.2). It continued to operate its own services to these countries as well. However, as a result of these alliances the number of seats offered at Amsterdam on partner airlines with KLM codes increased by 42 per cent in 1997 and 34 per cent on 1998. By 1999 almost half the seats on KLM European flights out of Amsterdam were on code-shared services operated by these four airlines and other smaller partners. This in turn meant much more online transfer traffic for KLM's medium- and long-haul flights.

The increased market power of alliance partners, especially on long-haul routes dependent on feed from both ends, is well illustrated by American Airlines' experience on several North Atlantic routes. In the

Table 4.2 Impact of US-European alliances on market share of passengers on selected transatlantic routes

Market	1994 (%)	1995 (%)	1996 (%)	1997 (%)	1998 (%)
Chicago–Dusseldorf					
American	100	100	0	0	0
United/Lufthansa	0	0	100	100	100
Miami–Frankfurt					
American	0	32	36	15	0
United/Lufthansa	95	68	64	85	100
New York (JFK)–Zurich					
American	38	29	28	2	0
Delta/Swissair	62	71	72	98	100
New York (JFK)–Brussels					
American	43	44	27	18	0
Delta/Sabena	45	49	61	71	87
Others	12	7	12	11	13

Source: Merrill Lynch (1999).

mid-1990s it was competing effectively on Chicago–Dusseldorf, Miami–Frankfurt and on New York to Zurich and Brussels. But once it had to face competition on these routes from US and European airlines in an alliance its market share collapsed and by 1998 it had withdrawn from all these markets (Table 4.2).

To summarise: alliances have a twofold beneficial impact. By increasing each airline's scope and network spread they produce marketing benefits which ultimately mean more passengers and freight. But at the same time the alliance itself extends each airline's total market by extending its geographical reach, and it does this with little extra cost. The potential benefits are substantial. It was claimed by Lufthansa in October 1997 that its marketing alliances with United, SAS, Thai Airways, South African Airways and VARIG were producing benefits of DM 250–70 million a year. And that was even before the Star Alliance was formally set up. An earlier study by the US General Accounting Office stated that in 1994 KLM had increased its traffic by 150,000 passengers as a result of its alliance with Northwest, while its revenue had gone up about US$100 million. The benefits to Northwest were estimated at 200,000 passengers and US$125–75 million in revenue. For British Airways, its alliance with USAir had generated 68,000 extra passengers and US$100 million additional revenue (GAO, 1995). At the regional alliance level BA's nine franchisees made an important contribution to its revenues. In the financial year 1997/98 they provided almost 400,000 connecting passengers and £71.5 million in additional revenue (Scard, 1998). SAS has stated that its aim is to generate 5 per cent of its airline operating income from the Star Alliance (Reitan, 1999). Clearly, if this was achieved at relatively little additional cost, then its impact on profitability would be considerable.

It is because the primary benefits of alliances are deemed to be in marketing and extending an airline's reach, that most alliances are based initially at least on marketing agreements. Co-operating with other airlines through franchises, code shares, block space agreements, frequent flyer programmes and so on is seen as a way of extending an airline's domestic, regional and global reach. Moreover, the better scheduling which alliances make possible results in alliance flights being placed higher on computer reservation system screens, making bookings more likely.

A senior Delta executive in 1999 summed up the key role of marketing benefits in alliance formation as follows:

> The reason that alliances are so critical is simple – they allow carriers to place more of their products on more shelves, to expand the scope and reach of networks more efficiently. But we are also in the business to make money and alliances allow us to generate additional revenue with minimal capital outlay.
>
> (Lobbenberg, 1999)

4.4 Cost synergies and reductions

Larger size and scope do not in themselves necessarily lead to lower unit costs. In the airline industry there are cost economies of scale, but only at the lower end of the size range. As airlines increase in size from two or three aircraft to about fifteen to twenty, the unit costs tend to decline as certain fixed and overhead costs are spread over more units of output. This is particularly true if the fleet is composed of a single aircraft type. But as airline size increases beyond fifteen to twenty aircraft there are no further significant cost economies arising purely from greater size. Other factors, such as size of aircraft used, average length of sectors flown, the level of wages, and so on, become the key cost drivers (Doganis, 1991).

While increased market power rather than cost reduction was and continues to be the major driver for alliance formation, there is now little doubt that alliances can have a beneficial impact on costs in four ways. First, because the increased market power created by an alliance will generate higher traffic volumes. These in turn can produce economies of traffic density. In other words, the ability of alliances to build up traffic levels on many routes more rapidly than would otherwise be the case, means that there is scope for reducing unit costs through higher load factors, switching to larger aircraft and higher utilisation of fixed assets such as terminal facilities, sales offices, and so on.

Second, cost economies may arise from possible synergies between the alliance partners. The synergies in operations or marketing enable alliance members to share some costs or reduce costs through route rationalisation.

Partner airlines can share sales offices, airport facilities such as dedicated passenger lounges and reservations/ticketing staff. Swissair and Austrian were the first successfully to establish joint ticketing and sales offices in many parts of the world, thereby reducing the number of offices and total staff required. As a result of their own alliance, SAS no longer has sales or ground staff in Germany while Lufthansa has no such staff in Scandinavia. They each sell for and handle the other in their own home markets. More importantly, by co-ordinating schedules and aircraft they can reduce their fleet requirements. Following BA's acquisition of 25 per cent of Qantas in 1993, they joined together to co-ordinate their UK–Australia services. In time, they were able to reduce their aircraft requirements on this trunk route by one Boeing 747 each and still provide a better service. In late 1998, following the Asian crisis, Qantas cut its five-times weekly Sydney–Kuala Lumpur service which was replaced by extending three of BA's London–Kuala Lumpur services to Sydney. Fleet standardisation can also produce lower costs through interchange of aircraft and crews, centralised or common maintenance facilities, standardised handling equipment, and so on. With one exception: all the eight airlines in The Qualiflyer Group in Europe led by Swissair have decided to have all-Airbus fleets based on the Airbus A319, A320 and A340 aircraft for their European and long-haul fleets. As alliances become more strategic rather than purely commercial the scope for cost sharing and reduction increases as airlines begin to co-mingle their assets. The greatest potential for cost savings can come from joint procurement of externally supplied goods and services such as ground handling, catering, maintenance and fuel.

Third, alliances can enable one airline, usually the major partner, to benefit from the smaller partner's lower operating costs. A major factor affecting airline unit costs is the cost of labour, which can vary significantly between neighbouring countries and also between airlines in the same country if some are highly unionised and other airlines are not (see Chapter 5). Some smaller airlines with lower wage rates reinforced this cost advantage by having low administrative and overhead costs and also in some cases by judicial outsourcing of key functions such as maintenance or catering. Substantial unit cost differences between airlines has meant that while many alliances aimed at marketing benefits as a primary objective, a further objective in many cases was to take advantage of the partner airline's lower operating costs. This was particularly true of many route-specific or regional alliances. Thus, KLM's code-share and block space agreement with Cyprus Airways whereby the latter operates a daily Larnaca–Amsterdam return service was partly motivated by the fact that Cyprus Airways' costs on this route were substantially lower than those of KLM. In Switzerland, Crossair, an independent airline founded in 1975 and based in Basel, developed a network of short-haul services from Basel, Zurich or Geneva, many operated by turbo-prop aircraft. Crossair's unit costs are high because of the nature of its operations, but they are significantly lower than the Swiss national carrier Swissair could achieve, especially on thinner routes requiring smaller aircraft. Crossair could do this by paying lower salaries, by having less restrictive work practices and through less costly overheads. Swissair eventually forged an alliance with Crossair and initially bought a small shareholding which by 1999 had increased to 70.9 per cent. Swissair now uses its regional partner Crossair to operate a wide range of short-haul domestic and international services from several Swiss airports in order to benefit from Crossair lower unit costs. Similarly British Airways' franchising of City Flyer Express and American Airlines purchase of Reno Air in December 1998 were also motivated in part by a desire to take advantage of the smaller airlines' lower operating costs.

Finally, alliances offer scope for cost reduction through joint purchasing in many areas. The Star airline members purchase about US$15 billion of goods and services each year. It is estimated that joint purchasing could reduce the prices paid by 5 to 7 per cent or so, cutting the total bill by up to US$1 billion each year. Late in 1996, Swissair, Sabena and Austrian announced a joint US$1 billion order for Airbus A330 aircraft. By buying in bulk they achieved a better price per aircraft than if each had ordered separately, as they had done previously.

The increased competition in international markets as a result of liberalisation has resulted in a decade of declining average yields in real terms. This has emphasised the need for alliances to focus on cost reduction as well as on increasing market spread.

In some cases alliances may be driven by the need to share the high fixed costs of major investments, especially in advanced and expensive technologies. Such alliances have tended to be involved either in joint maintenance facilities or for the joint development of computer reservation systems. In the late 1960s groups of European airlines set up two consortia to share and co-ordinate expensive maintenance facilities. By the 1990s these consortia had been discontinued or changed, but other maintenance consortia emerged. Lufthansa and Swissair, for example, set up a joint engineering facility, Shannon Aerospace in Ireland. The area where airline co-operation was most essential was in financing the enormous cost of the major computer reservation systems (CRS) developed in the mid- to late 1980s. Multiple ownership was essential since such high investments could not be financed by individual airlines. Airlines had to group together to share high development costs as well as their existing sales outlets in order to achieve the sufficiently wide distribution system required to justify the initial investment. European airlines set up two competing CRS systems in 1987, Galileo and Amadeus. British Airways, KLM, Swissair and Alitalia were the major shareholders in Galileo, though other airlines such as Olympic Airways had smaller shares. At the end of 1987 Galileo merged with Covia, United Airlines' CRS. Subsequently both USAir and Air Canada joined Galileo. The few global CRS systems that emerged virtually all required multiple airline consortia. As the marketing alliances spread in the late 1990s, many airlines that were partners in the same CRS found themselves in competing global alliances. Only American Airlines bucked the trend towards joint funding by developing the Sabre CRS very much on its own. More recently the focus for cost reduction has switched to jointly funding and developing common IT platforms. In 1999 airlines such as British Airways and KLM began to sell their shareholdings in the CRSs in order to benefit from the appreciation of their original investment.

However, alliances may have a downside too. Costs may actually rise through increased overheads or greater redemption of frequent flyer points. The costs of the integration necessary to achieve the hoped-for synergies may be higher than anticipated; for instance, the cost of IT integration. Decisions may be slowed down by the need to reach a joint agreement between different airlines. Union problems may spread from one member of an alliance to its partners. Poor customer performance by one partner may dilute the brand strength of the others. To reduce or mitigate the impact of such risks alliance partners need to set up a strong and powerful central co-ordinating unit to ensure operational and commercial integration. This is crucial especially as they want to move towards creating a true strategic alliance.

4.5 Reducing competition

While rarely stated publicly as an objective when airline alliances are formed, there can be little doubt that airline executives see alliances, especially when they involve code sharing and capacity rationalisation as a way of reducing or limiting competition. The reduction of effective competition is likely to be most marked in route-specific or regional alliances and least clear-cut in global alliances where routings via competitors' hubs may be a feasible alternative for long-haul passengers.

In the United States, alliances or mergers were most effective in reducing competition when the partners served the same hub airport. A case in point was the 1986 merger of Northwest and Republic. Both airlines used Minneapolis-St. Paul as their main hub and competed on many routes, even though Northwest was primarily making medium- and long-haul flights and Republic's network focused on medium- and short-haul routes. Because of the complementarity of their networks and the scope for some efficiency gains from the synergies available, the US Department of Transportation, at that time responsible for airline mergers, approved the merger. But the Department of Justice recommended that it should not be approved on the grounds that it was anti-competitive. In fact, as a result of the merger not only was competition eliminated from many duopolistic routes but the new Northwest became totally dominant at its hub. By June

1998, together with its regional code-share partners, it accounted for 80.7 per cent of departures and 81.3 per cent of seats available each week out of Minneapolis-St. Paul.

The most marked and adverse effect on competition is where, as a result of an alliance, two carriers previously competing on a route on which there is no third carrier decide that only one of the alliance partners should operate the route. Examples abound. Following the purchase in 1996 of 49.5 per cent of Sabena by Swissair, services between Switzerland and Belgium were rationalised. By the summer of 1999 Sabena was alone in operating six times daily on Geneva–Brussels following the withdrawal of Swissair services. Swissair flew five times daily on its own between Zurich and Brussels and only Crossair, a Swissair subsidiary, served Basel–Brussels five times a day. All flights had both partners' codes. But there was no other operator on any of these three key routes. Effectively routes where there had been duopolistic competition had been turned into monopolies. By eliminating competition, capacity growth could be held back and fares kept high.

The impact of alliances is less visible when both partners continue to operate on route(s) between their two countries but share codes on these flights. This is what happened on the six busiest routes between Germany and Scandinavia following the alliance between SAS and Lufthansa in 1995. Competing services offered by the two airlines were replaced by services operated as a 50/50 joint venture, with each of the airlines operating some of the joint flights (Table 4.3). The European Commission, in approving the proposed arrangement in 1996, imposed some conditions to ensure that new entrants would have an opportunity to enter these markets. In particular, the two carriers were required to freeze their frequencies until 31 October 2002 and to give up runway slots if new entrants could not obtain the required slots through the normal slot allocation procedures (Official Journal, 1996). In practice the ability of the two airlines to maintain their frequencies at existing levels has discouraged other airlines from entering these markets. Once again competition has given way to monopoly. But with both airlines flying on the denser routes consumers may think there is some competition. With frequencies frozen by the European Commission there will be little incentive to reduce fares as passenger demand builds up.

The SAS/Lufthansa example illustrates another way in which competition is reduced. By code sharing their flights on a route, by co-ordinating their frequencies and timings and through joint selling, alliance partners may become so powerful on a given route that potential competitors will hesitate to enter point-to-point markets. This has clearly happened on the six densest routes between Germany and Scandinavia. To compete effectively with an alliance monopoly on denser short- or medium-haul routes new entrants must either offer high frequencies, which means a high 'initial' investment and possibly overcapacity in the market, or they must

Table 4.3 Impact of SAS-Lufthansa 1995 alliance on major routes to Germany
and Scandinavia

	Competing daily departures, July 1995		*Joint venture code shared daily departures, June 2000*
FRA–Copenhagen	LH 4	SK 3	LH/SK 7
FRA–Stockholm	LH 3	SK 2	LH/SK 6
FRA–Oslo	LH 1	SK 1	LH/SK 5
DUS–Copenhagen	LH 2	SK 2	LH/SK 4
DUS–Stockholm	LH 2	SK 1	LH/SK 2
DUS–Oslo		SK 1	LH/SK 3

Notes
No new entrants competing by summer 2000
LH = Lufthansa
SK = SAS.

offer low-cost, low-fare services where frequency is less important. Yet
even on thin routes alliance partners are in a position to deter competitors. By building up their own traffic and frequencies with connecting
transfer passengers the alliance carriers may make it very difficult or
impossible for other carriers to compete against them on such routes.

The market power of airlines at their own hubs is reinforced as they
enter into alliances with partners operating into those hubs. The case of
British Airways at London's Gatwick airport illustrates this clearly. BA's
traditional base and hub in London was Heathrow. In 1987 it had only
10 per cent of the weekday scheduled departures at London-Gatwick.
When in 1987 it took over British Caledonian it was required by the
European Commission to give up some scheduled slots to allow new
entrants to start up new competing services. Air Europe was one of these.
But it collapsed and its scheduled services were inherited by Dan Air. In
due course Dan Air was itself in trouble and sold to BA for £1. As a
result of this merger and of further expansion, BA's share of scheduled
departures at Gatwick had risen by Summer 1998 to 36 per cent. But its
subsidiaries, such as TAT and Deutsche BA, and its franchisees, such as
Cityflyer Express and GB Airways, accounted for a further 30 per cent,
making the British Airways alliance share 66 per cent. There are, of course,
many charter services from Gatwick, but the BA grouping dominates
scheduled departures and the grandfathered scheduled slots. The same has
happened at Amsterdam as a result of the build-up of KLM's alliances
described earlier (see section 4.3). In June 1998 KLM had 41.8 per cent
of scheduled flights operated each week at Amsterdam (Table 4.4). Its
regional partners, KLM UK, Eurowings, Regional Airlines and Braathens,
had a further 21.2 per cent of flights between them. Its global partners
Northwest and Alitalia produced 2.6 per cent of flights. KLM's charter

Table 4.4   Impact of alliances on KLM's share of scheduled departures from Amsterdam, June 1998

	Total seats (%)	Total frequencies (%)
KLM	44.4	41.8
KLM's Dutch subsidiaries:		
Transavia	3.0	2.5
Martinair	1.5	0.7
Regional partners:		
KLM UK	9.3	12.3
Eurowings (Germany)	2.9	7.2
Regional Airlines (France)	0.3	1.1
Braathens (Scandinavia)	0.6	0.6
Sub-total	13.1	21.2
Global alliance partners:		
Northwest	4.0	1.6
Alitalia	1.2	1.0
Route-specific partners:		
Aer Lingus, Cyprus Airways, El Al etc.	1.9	2.1
Total for KLM and partners	69.1%	70.9%

Source: Compiled by author using *OAG World Airways Guide.*

subsidiaries Transavia and Martinair generated 3.2 per cent of scheduled frequencies as well as a high proportion of non-scheduled departures. Finally airlines such as Cyprus Airways, with whom KLM had route-specific alliances, accounted for a total of 2.1 per cent of frequencies. If one adds the frequencies of all these alliance partners to KLM's share of scheduled frequencies its share jumps from 41.8 per cent to 70.9 per cent. KLM and its partners are in a very powerful market position in Amsterdam because they control more than two-thirds of departures. This also gives them considerable flexibility to swap runway slots to maximise connecting opportunities, to improve timings or to undermine particular competitors through better schedules.

Airline alliances with a dominant presence at a particular airport also enjoy important marketing advantages. Their customer loyalty schemes make them more competitive in the local market since they are available for a large range of services from that airport. They are also in a position to gain travel agency loyalty through offering higher commissions or over-ride commission. Because of the range of services available they can tie in the large corporate clients who provide much of the higher class travel.

While most airline chairmen claim – they would, wouldn't they? – that the aim of the alliances they are entering into are to increase competition and to generate benefits for consumers, there can be little doubt that reducing or even eliminating competition is a factor in many alliances. The crucial question is whether the lessening of competition is so significant as to require alliances to be regulated by the competition authorities. This is discussed later.

4.6 Bypassing regulatory barriers

The preceding discussion has focused on the economic forces driving airlines towards closer co-operation. But the form which such co-operation has taken has resulted from the regulatory environment within which international air transport operates. In other industries and even in other service sectors, the economic pressures towards larger size, wider marketing spread and globalisation have resulted in acquisitions and mergers of companies across national boundaries. One has seen this in both the hotel industry, with global chains such as Stardust (Sheraton and others), Ladbroke, Inter-Continental or the French Accord group, and in the holiday and travel business.

In air transport, the nationality clause in bilateral air services agreements has limited and distorted the form of cross-border airline co-operation. In order for airlines to be designated by their governments to operate the traffic rights which their states enjoy under the air services agreements they must be 'substantially owned and effectively controlled' by nationals of that state. In the United States and many other countries this is interpreted to mean that foreign ownership should be no more than 25 per cent. Among a few states, including those of the European Union, a figure of close to 50 per cent is acceptable, that is, less than majority control. In fact, for airlines registered in a member state and operating purely within the EU, ownership is freely open to nationals or companies from any other EU state. But if an EU airline wishes to operate internationally to points outside the EU then the ownership rules in the air services agreement with the country it wishes to fly to become operative. Thus, EU airlines wishing to fly to points outside the European Union cannot be majority owned by non-nationals of their own country. (See Chapter 3, section 3.2 for fuller discussion.)

Apart from the nationality or ownership rules there are many other regulatory barriers to airline acquisitions and mergers. These arise primarily from attempts by governments to avoid anti-competitive behaviour or the abuse of dominant market position. Regulations exist in most developed countries aimed at ensuring that competition is not distorted. Such regulations may be enforced directly by governments and/or by special competition authorities such as the Bundeskartellamt in Germany or the Monopolies and Mergers Commission in the United Kingdom. In the

United States both the Department of Justice and the Department of Transport have a say in domestic airline mergers while the State Department may become involved in issues related to co-operative agreements between US airlines and foreign carriers. Clearly many governments or regulatory bodies make decisions in relation not only to domestic regulatory issues but also take decisions with an extra-territorial dimension. In the case of the European Commission its competition rules and mergers policies have clear extra-territorial scope (Soames, 2000). Moreover, many decisions of the Commission's Competition Directorate (DGIV) have related directly to co-operative agreements and alliances not only between airlines of EU member states but also on those between EU and non-EU airlines.

It is the nationality or ownership rules, together with various national and extra-territorial regulations that have forced the airline industry to move towards complex inter-airline alliances which take many forms from purely marketing agreements to more strategic partnerships. Only rarely do such alliances involve true cross-border acquisitions and mergers which would be natural in other industries.

In effect, there is a fundamental contradiction in the growth of alliances. The gradual liberalisation of international regulations made cross-border airline alliances both necessary and possible, yet the remaining vestiges of regulation, especially the ownership and nationality rules, constrained the form which such alliances would take. If, as has been suggested in Chapter 3 above, the nationality rules are relaxed during the early years of the 21st century, then there will be a new bout of alliance making, but based on airlines taking over effective control of carriers in other countries. The alliance groupings may then look quite different from those at the beginning of the millennium.

4.7 Cementing alliances

On 22 June 1999 two of the four global alliances then emerging were suddenly transformed. Air France announced a tie-up with Delta, Swissair's long-time partner, as the first pillar of a new global alliance. In the process Delta also destroyed the Atlantic Excellence alliance it had entered into with Swissair, Sabena and Austrian Airlines. On the same day, Swissair and Sabena, as a reaction to being abandoned by Delta, unveiled a new transatlantic code-share agreement with American Airlines. While Swissair said it would not at that stage be joining the Oneworld global alliance, led by British Airways and American, it was clearly a longer-term option.

The fact that Delta switched partners from Swissair to Air France is significant in two respects. First, it showed that longevity of an existing partnership may not in itself be enough to ensure its survival. Delta, together with Swissair and Singapore Airlines, had created the first global alliance in 1988. As mentioned earlier, Singapore Airlines withdrew in

1998 when it teamed up with Lufthansa. Ten years of working together was not enough to cement the alliance. Second, the fact that there were cross-shareholdings was also not enough to keep the alliance partners together. Swissair owned 4.6 per cent of Delta, who in turn held 4.5 per cent of Swissair shares. While these were relatively small shareholdings there are several other examples where substantial shareholdings were not enough in themselves to ensure the continuation of an alliance. At one time British Airways had a 24.9 per cent holding in USAir, SAS owned 19.9 per cent of Continental and Iberia had purchased 85 per cent of Aerolineas Argentinas. But all these partnerships broke up. The dowries paid were not enough to ensure that the marriages survived.

Swissair has had unfortunate experiences with alliance partners in which it has had a shareholding. Singapore Airlines, Delta and even Austrian, where it had a 10 per cent share, all abandoned their alliance with Swissair. The cross-shareholdings were not sufficient to cement these alliances. Despite, or perhaps because of, these setbacks, Swissair has insisted on building up its European Qualiflyer grouping through purchasing more substantial shareholdings in its partners. By early 2000 it had a 49.5 per cent share in Sabena; 70 per cent in Crossair; 49 per cent in the French airline Air Littoral and 49 per cent in AOM, another French carrier; 89 per cent in the Italian airline Air Europe, 20 per cent in South African Airways; 42 per cent in Portugalia; 10 per cent in the Polish airline LOT, which was expected to increase to 37.6 per cent. Swissair was also expected to finalise the purchase of 20 per cent of Air Portugal as well as a shareholding in Turkish Airlines (THY). But will such shareholdings, except where they exceed 50 per cent, be enough to ensure alliance cohesion?

In fact, share ownership may turn out to be a barrier to closer co-operation, as happened with KLM's 19 per cent voting stock in Northwest. The latter feared that the Dutch airline was seeking to gain control of the company and in a protracted lawsuit launched in 1995 Northwest sought to limit KLM's shareholding. The bitter two-year dispute ended in August 1997 when KLM agreed to sell its shares in four tranches and Northwest committed itself to a long-term alliance with KLM.

If neither long-term co-operation and working together nor share purchases are in themselves enough, then what is needed to cement a partnership into a real long-term alliance? There are three phases of alliance building (Figure 4.3). As one moves through them alliance partners' operations become more integrated and the alliance more durable. The first phase is oriented primarily towards generating extra revenue through network expansion and joint marketing (see section 4.3). There may be some cost-saving through joint sales offices or the sharing of CIP lounges but the focus is on revenue generation. While there may be an alliance brand shared by all partners, they each maintain their separate brand and identity. Agreements in Phase 1 are essentially commercial alliances, easily

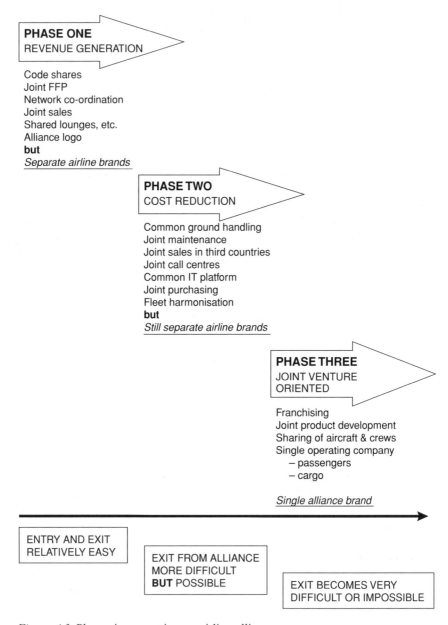

Figure 4.3 Phases in cementing an airline alliance.

entered into and easily abandoned. An example was the Delta–Swissair–Singapore Airlines alliance, which had really not progressed beyond the first phase. This is why abandoning the alliance was relatively easy. Phase 2 is also commercial but the focus is more on cost saving (see section 4.4), while continuing and reinforcing co-operation on the Phase 1 revenue aspects. The second phase will probably involve separate agreements in one or more specific areas where joint operations can reduce costs, as in ground handling or maintenance.

The greater the number of such agreements and the wider their scope, the more difficulty there may be in breaking away from the alliance. But it is still possible. Some airline partnerships jump into Phase 2 without implementing any of Phase 1. Such partnerships are opportunistic and generally focus on a single activity, such as joint ground handling or the Lufthansa and Swissair involvement in Shannon Aerospace, a jointly-owned maintenance company. They may not be part of a coherent alliance strategy.

Implementation of the first two phases does not necessarily cement an alliance. Break-up and separation is still possible, though increasingly difficult the longer the alliance has been in existence, especially if co-operation in most of the cost-cutting areas has been implemented.

The third phase in cementing an alliance is when partners begin to co-mingle their assets and use them jointly. This will involve joint product development and the creation of joint companies to manage different aspects of their operations. For instance, Swissair and Sabena took a step towards complete integration with the launch on 1 July 1999 of a single airline management company to run their flying operations. Other members of the Qualiflyer Group of airlines would be able to put their own services under this company later (Schorderet, 1999). The KLM-Alitalia alliance launched towards the end of 1998 aimed at creating two joint venture companies, one for passenger services and a separate one for cargo operations. At the end of July 1999 these two airlines signed an agreement which went further than any of the other global alliances in integrating the two companies' operations without being a full merger. A jointly appointed 'Network Organiser' would provide a unified management structure for the two joint operating ventures to which each airline would offer its existing fleet and staff and those of its close subsidiaries as service providers. In the first year, each airline would be able to keep Euro 450 million of its earnings. But revenues above that level would be shared on a 50:50 basis (*Aviation Strategy*, 1999).

During this third phase alliance partners will move from having separate brand identities to emphasising and even adopting a single alliance brand. They may even have a single set of consolidated company accounts. Untangling such an alliance or partnership clearly becomes very difficult The cement is beginning to set. The ultimate, of course, is a full merger once the nationality and ownership rules are relaxed.

To be able successfully to move from Phase 1 to Phase 3 and cement an alliance, airlines need to manage their partnership carefully. In particular they need to work very hard to ensure that:

- Alliance benefits to all partners are apparent and broadly in balance in terms of

    - marketing and revenue generation,
    - cost reduction and synergy,
    - reduced competition.

- Long-term vision and objectives are shared by all partners.
- Vision and objectives are communicated to all levels of staff and understood by them.
- Clear, neutral but strong alliance governance is in place either through a 'network organiser' or an executive committee. To be effective this requires

    - close working relationship and mutual trust between managers in each airline,
    - motivated staff,
    - mutual appreciation of cultural or organisational differences.

- High customer-oriented service standards are maintained by all partners.
- There is staff willingness to 'own' all customers and problems, even those generated by partners' clients.

It is clear that, despite the rhetoric, by the year 2000 many of the regional alliances and some of the global alliances had not moved much beyond the first phase. A case in point was the Oneworld global alliance which was still primarily revenue-oriented and focused on Phase 1 activities and, to a very limited degree on handling or other joint activities and then only between some of the partners. Such alliances were clearly vulnerable to the sudden exit of individual members, as happened when Delta abandoned its Atlantic Excellence partners in June 1999. This explains the pressure on Swissair and Sabena or KLM and Alitalia to cement their own alliances by moving quickly to set up joint companies to manage their flying operations. However, this too may be risky. Rushing too rapidly into the third phase without successfully implementing the first two phases and building up the other internal prerequisites listed above may lead to the collapse of an alliance from unresolved internal contradictions. This was the risk faced by the KLM-Alitalia alliance which aimed to move rapidly to Phase 3 before fully implementing the earlier phases. By February 2000, the KLM President, Leo van Wijk, was complaining that since Alitalia was scaling back its operations at Milan Malpensa airport contrary to earlier plans the alliance might have to be renegotiated! In fact, by May 2000 the alliance collapsed when KLM walked out citing difficulties at Malpensa, Milan's new airport, and the delay in privatising Alitalia as the key reasons. Clearly, the partners had jumped too quickly to Phase 3. There is a lesson here for other alliances.

In brief, it appears that the most effective way to cement an alliance is by moving successfully from a marketing alliance with emphasis on cost reduction (phases one and two in Figure 4.3) to the implementation of a real strategic alliance oriented towards a joint venture approach. This may prove more lasting than a minority shareholding.

4.8 Are alliances anti-competitive?

Alliances, whether route-specific, regional or global, have an inherent risk of becoming anti-competitive in one or both of two ways. First, if alliance groupings become very powerful at one or more hub airports through having a very dominant share of total departures and available seats, there is a danger that they may abuse that dominance to stifle new entrants and competition in their prime home market. This could be done by changing timings and increasing frequencies to make the new entrant's services less attractive. For instance, by scheduling departures for the same destinations ten to twenty minutes before those of the competitors. It can also be done through selective fare reductions. A clear example of what may happen was illustrated in the suit brought by the US Government against American Airlines in May 1999 on anti-trust grounds. The government claimed that the airline and its regional subsidiary AMR Eagle had in recent years unfairly driven three low-cost competitors, Sun Jet, Vanguard and Western Pacific, out of Dallas-Fort Worth airport through fare reductions and increased frequencies. The Justice Department argued that 'American's conduct was predatory because the costs of the flights it added exceeded the revenues they generated' (*International Herald Tribune*, 14 May 1999). The suit detailed the allegedly predatory practices in great detail. For instance, in the case of Vanguard, the suit stated that American reduced its average one-way fare from Dallas-Fort Worth to Kansas City in April 1995 from $108 to $80 when Vanguard began operating three daily non-stop flights. From May to July 1995 American also increased its daily flights on the route from eight to fourteen, by adding six more round trips, with the aim of driving Vanguard from the market. The fare cuts forced Vanguard to cut its frequencies to one a day and also drove Delta Airlines entirely out of this market by May 1995. American Airlines denied the charges in the government's suit and argued that its actions were those that any tough competitor would take in a highly competitive industry. American Airlines at the time operated two-thirds of the flight departures at Dallas-Fort Worth. At many of the world's major hubs, especially in Europe, the creation of alliances has significantly increased the base airline's dominance of slots. This was shown earlier in Table 4.4. In Amsterdam, KLM has been able to increase its share of scheduled departures from 42 per cent to 71 per cent as a result of its numerous alliances. In Copenhagen a similar picture emerged in 1998. SAS's share of scheduled flights rose from 53 per cent to 74 per cent when alliance partners were included. Thus, as in the United States, the risks of anti-competitive behaviour increase because alliances significantly increase hub dominance.

Slot dominance in itself creates a barrier to entry for new carriers or for those wishing to start competing on an existing route, even if those dominating the slots have no malign intentions. It is for this reason that, when at the end of 1987 British Airways added British Caledonian's operations at London-Gatwick to its own flights at that airport, the European Commission insisted that it surrender a large number of its slots to airlines wishing to launch new scheduled services. The same reasoning was behind the July 1999 recommendation of the UK's Director of Fair Trading that British Airways' purchase of its franchisee City Flyer based at London-Gatwick be approved, but only on condition that their joint share of all slots for the following five years be reduced from 46 per cent to 41 per cent.

The second inherent risk arising from the formation of alliances is the reduction or elimination of competition on specific routes. The risk appears greatest *on short-haul domestic or international routes* with flight times of less than two-and-a-half hours or so.

This is because indirect services on such routes via transfer airports invariably increase the journey time by one to two hours even if there are convenient and frequent connections and by much more if there are not. The vast majority of the denser international routes in Europe are of less than two-and-a-half hours. Therefore it becomes attractive to reduce competition by entering into alliances on such routes. The UK Civil Aviation Authority came to the same conclusion in a 1998 report:

> In some cases, these airline partnerships have lead to a reduction in competition at the route level, most notably perhaps on the main German/Scandinavia routes. In other cases, there has been a reduction at the country level, for example in the link between Austrian and Lauda Air.
>
> (CAA, 1998, p. 167)

The CAA did say, however, that in some cases alliances may strengthen a weaker carrier against their national airline as was the case with AirUK (later KLM UK) or Eurowings in Germany. Both became KLM's regional partners and thereby more effective competitors to BA and Lufthansa. On many international routes the old revenue sharing pools, which had never been permitted on routes to the USA and which were banned by the European Commission as anti-competitive, have been replaced by code-sharing alliances. But the effect on routes without a third airline to provide competition may be the same. Namely, that the alliance partners can push up or keep up fares by holding back on capacity growth through schedule co-ordination. This creates a shortage of seats and enables them to push up yields and load factors at the same time. Duopolistic routes can become effective monopolies.

On *long-haul routes* it may not be so easy to reduce competition by entering into an alliance with another carrier on the same routes. There are two reasons why this is so. First, because only a small proportion of the traffic on an individual long-haul route is local traffic between the two airports at either end. On the London–New York route in summer 1998 only 51 per cent of passengers were local and were not connecting onto or from other flights at either end of the route (estimate based on UK Civil Aviation Authority data). From other major European airports to the east of London such as Frankfurt or Zurich the proportion of local non-connecting passengers on transatlantic flights is even less. Lufthansa claimed that in 1998 only around 19 per cent of passengers on the code-shared flights with United between Frankfurt and Chicago were purely local, travelling just between these two cities (Table 4.5). The remaining 81 per cent were on connecting flights at one end of the route or the other or at both ends. Surprisingly 38 per cent were on connecting flights at both ends of the route (Kropp, 1999). For passengers who are not local and are not flying purely between the two points at either end of the route a large number of convenient and competitive options are available. In comparing direct and indirect flights to New York from four secondary European airports it can be seen that by transiting through the European hubs of one of the global alliances, passengers have journey times which are two to three hours longer but in most cases have a choice of higher frequencies and more departure times (Table 4.6). The longer journey times are less significant on long-haul routes since one is losing a day or a night travelling anyway. There is little difference in terms of total journey time or frequencies between the alternative connecting hubs. The fares are also broadly similar. Thus, it would be difficult to argue that competition for connecting passengers from Dusseldorf or Milan to New York is significantly reduced because of an alliance between Lufthansa and United on the section Frankfurt–New York. Passengers could fly equally quickly, or even faster, via London, Amsterdam or Zurich.

The second reason why alliances may not eliminate competition on long-haul routes is that even for local point-to-point traffic, especially leisure passengers, there may be reasonable routings via alternative hubs. Thus, the 19 per cent of local passengers on the Frankfurt–Chicago route in 1999, could have taken alternative routings via Amsterdam, Zurich or especially London, where frequencies were high (Table 4.7). But in all cases three-and-a-half hours would be added to the journey time. For time-sensitive passengers these would not be reasonable alternatives. For leisure

Table 4.5 Traffic distribution on code-shared Frankfurt–Chicago flights, 1998

	Average passengers per flight		Average distribution (%)
	United Airlines	Lufthansa	
Local point-to-point traffic	25	50	18.8
Feeding to/from Chicago	89	–	22.4
Feeding to/from Frankfurt	–	84	21.1
Feeding at both Chicago and Frankfurt	98	52	37.7
Total	212	186	100.0

Source: Kropp (1999).

Table 4.6 Comparison of interconnecting services from four European cities to New York-JFK via European hubs, summer 1998

Journey origin	Service aspect	Connecting European hub				Direct flight from origin
		Amsterdam-Schiphol (KLM)	Frankfurt (Lufthansa)	London-Heathrow (BA)	Zurich (Swissair)	
Dusseldorf	Journey time (hrs:mins)	10:00	11:45	10:40	11:30	8:20
	Frequency (flights per week)	14	27	21	13	7
Geneva	Journey time	11:00	11:00	10:25	10:30	8:45
	Frequency	14	28	25	30	7
Milan	Journey time	11:00	10:45	10:45	11:15	9:00
	Frequency	14	21	28	13	28
Oslo	Journey time	11:15	12:50	11:05	13:45	8:20
	Frequency	14	14	21	6	7

Note
Journey time includes connection time.

Source: AEA (1999) and author.

Table 4.7 Comparison of direct and indirect services on Frankfurt–Chicago and London–New York routes, summer 1998

Journey	Service aspect	Connecting European hub and airline				Direct flights from FRA or LON
		Amsterdam-Schiphol KLM	Zurich-Kloten Swissair	Frankfurt Lufthansa	London-Heathrow BA	
Frankfurt–Chicago	Business fare (US$)	6,514	6,514		6,514	6,514
	Journey time (hrs:mins)	12:25	12:25		12:30	9:00
	Frequency (flights per week)	7	7		21	28
London New York	Business fare (US$)	5,147	5,297	5,297		4,147
	Journey time (hrs:mins)	10:55	11:40	11:50		7:40
	Frequency (flights per week)	14	14	21		49

Source: AEA, OAG.

or other passengers, who are less time-sensitive, flying via these other hubs is an option, particularly if lower fares are offered. Some clearly take this option. A study has shown that while in 1998 62 per cent of leisure traffic between Frankfurt and Chicago went by indirect flights, only 2.6 per cent of business traffic did so (AEA, 1999). Clearly, there is real competition for this leisure market, but for the local time-sensitive business market the alliance between Lufthansa and United has reduced competition. Only American Airlines was left to compete with them on the Frankfurt–Chicago route. In the case of local traffic between London and New York, going via a European hub is even less attractive since it involves a three-and-a-half to four hours longer journey time (Table 4.7). Here too it is competition for the time-sensitive market segment which is reduced if the two biggest operators on the route, BA and American, become alliance partners though two other strong competitors, Virgin Atlantic and United, would remain.

While there may be possible anti-competitive elements in some alliances they nevertheless produce benefits for consumers. Unless this was the case alliance partners would not be able to claim increased traffic levels as a result of their alliance. If the prime driver of alliances is the need to obtain marketing benefits then it follows that such benefits will only arise if consumers, or at least some consumers, perceive a benefit from using the alliance's services. Those benefits may arise from higher frequencies, improved transfer times, the availability of more destinations with online connections with airlines in the same alliance, improved ground and in-flight service levels, more attractive loyalty schemes. In so far as alliances may lead to lower operating costs through the realisation of cost synergies described earlier, customers are likely to benefit from lower fares if cost savings are reflected in lower fares. They may also benefit more directly from lower discounted fares offered by the alliance on routes involving a transfer at a hub. Lower fares on such routes may arise from two factors. The alliance may discount fares to compensate passengers for the inconvenience of a transfer connection if there is an alternative direct flight between the two points being flown. Or if the alliance's connecting service is competing only with connecting flights offered by two airlines not in an alliance, the former's fares are in any case likely to be lower. This is because the non-allied carriers are each likely to insist on getting the highest pro-rate fare for their sector of the route, while the alliance partners see capturing the passenger as their joint priority. This has been confirmed by a 1998 study at the University of Illinois which examined data collected by the US Department of Transportation's passenger surveys to study fares paid by passengers travelling with alliance partners on a given journey and by those using two separate airlines for the same journey. The study concluded that those travelling on non-allied airlines paid on average 36 per cent more than alliance passengers (Brueckner and Whalen, 1998).

From the preceding analysis it would seem that the greatest risks to the maintenance of an open competitive environment as alliances develop further arise in two areas: either through alliance dominance at major hubs, especially those with slot constraints, or on short- to medium-haul routes where alliances may transform duopolies into monopolies while making it difficult for other airlines to enter those routes.

4.9 Controlling alliances

The United States and Europe have taken different approaches to tackling the perceived threats to open competition from mergers and alliances. In the United States in the mid-1980s, the peak period for airline acquisitions and mergers, it was the Department of Transportation which oversaw airline mergers. The Department believed in the concept of '*contestable markets*' and therefore waived through all the mergers referred to it. Subsequently the United States has relied more on anti-trust legislation and the Justice Department to deal with anti-competitive airline behaviour in domestic markets as in the American Airlines Dallas-Fort Worth case mentioned above. In the international sphere the United States' approach has been somewhat contradictory. The State Department believed that the opening up of competition truly arising from 'open skies' air services agreements outweighed the risks to competition inherent in code sharing and other alliance features. The United States, which had for four decades categorised inter-airline revenue-pooling agreements as anti-competitive, offered anti-trust immunity to cross-border airline alliances provided the countries concerned signed 'open skies' bilaterals with the US. Following the first such bilateral with the Netherlands in 1992, KLM and Northwest applied and received the first full anti-trust immunity. This enabled the two airlines to plan and promote joint services, products and pricing. Other alliances were also granted immunity following 'open skies' agreements, most notably the United-Lufthansa alliance in 1996. The major exception was the British Airways-American Airline alliance first announced in June 1996, which fell foul of the inability of their respective governments to negotiate a new bilateral during 1998 and 1999.

While the US Government felt that 'open skies' liberalisation was enough to ensure adequate competition, the European Commission took a more interventionist view. It believed that where mergers or alliances resulted in a significant reduction of competition the merged or partner airlines involved should give up airport slots and, in some cases, route licences to encourage and facilitate new operators to enter and compete directly with them. The first key decision related to the takeover by British Airways of all British Caledonian's operations at London-Gatwick at the end of 1987. The Competition Directorate of the European Commission imposed even more stringent conditions than the UK's Monopolies and Mergers Commission. BA had to surrender close to 100 weekly slots and give up all domestic route licences from Gatwick, plus several international licences to key markets including Paris and Brussels. It was also limited to operating no more than 25 per cent of the slots at Gatwick. All this to encourage competition. A similar approach was adopted three years later in 1990 when Air France in acquiring UTA also achieved control of Air Inter, France's largest domestic airline, where previously it was a 37 per cent minority shareholder. In order to approve the merger of these three airlines, the Commission required Air France to give up eight domestic and up to fifty international route licences and to make slots available at Paris-Charles de Gaulle airport for other French airlines to use for domestic routes. Air France also had to sell its 35 per cent shareholding in TAT, the third-largest domestic carrier, subsequently acquired by British Airways.

The pattern was set. In subsequent cases the Commission insisted on partner airlines giving up slots, either immediately or when asked to do so, and in some cases surrendering route licences. They did this in 1992 when Air France took a significant shareholding in Sabena (which it later gave up), and again in 1995 when Swissair bought 49.5 per cent of Sabena and in 1997 when Lufthansa and SAS entered into an alliance on the

Scandinavia–Germany routes. But the evidence to date suggests that in most of these cases little real competition has emerged to challenge the alliance partners. The Switzerland–Belgium routes and the six major routes between Germany and Scandinavia were still alliance monopolies early in 2000 while BA and its partners were operating on most of the international routes from Gatwick that they surrendered in 1988 while their share of scheduled slots was up to 66 per cent. Thus, the European Commission's policy of trying to stimulate competition through withdrawal of slots when alliances take place has apparently failed.

Yet the European Commission has persisted in this approach, most notably in key decisions on two of the global alliances. Early in July 1998, Karel van Miert, Europe's Competition Commissioner, in his long-awaited ruling, issued similar conditions for approval of both the British Airways-American Airlines (BA-AA) alliance, originally proposed in June 1996, and the Lufthansa-SAS-United Airlines alliance. In the case of BA-AA, the Commission's key competition concerns were the reinforcement of these airlines' dominant position on three hub-to-hub routes and the significant barriers to entry that would be created by the alliance. In order to approve this alliance, the airlines were required to make several concessions (Official Journal, 1998):

A reduction of 50 weekly frequencies in total by BA and American on the London–Dallas, London–Miami and London–Chicago routes that link BA's major hub to American's three primary hubs [Table 4.8]. These slots were to be released to competitors on these routes.

An additional 217 weekly slots were to be made available for rivals to use for North American services from Heathrow or Gatwick, but these could be transferred from other BA or AA routes not necessarily their own transatlantic flights.

All slots were to be released without compensation.

The Commission's target was to ensure that the alliance partners jointly had no more than 45 per cent of frequencies on any route. But the above conditions were much more demanding than those recommended by the UK's Office of Fair Trading, which had earlier suggested that less than 200 weekly slots should be surrendered. Its director had also stated that he saw no reason why such slots should not be sold.

The Commission imposed similar conditions for approving the Lufthansa-SAS-United alliance. Namely, a reduction of frequencies by Lufthansa and United on the hub-to-hub routes Frankfurt–Chicago and Frankfurt–Washington and the release of slots from any route for rivals to use on other transatlantic services. A total of ninety-three slots to be surrendered at Frankfurt and fifteen at Copenhagen.

Table 4.8 European Commission conditions for BA-AA alliance, July 1998

	Weekly transatlantic slots 1997		
	AA/BA	Competitors	New slots open to competitors
*Hub-to-hub routes**			
LHR–Chicago	66	13	24
LHR–Miami	28	14	10
LGW–Miami	14	14	0
LGW–Dallas	40	0	16
*Non-hub routes***			
LHR–Boston	66	24	57
LHR–Los Angeles	48	52	7
LHR–JFK/Newark	204	162	87
LHR–Philadelphia	26	0	32
LHR–Seattle	14	0	17
LGW–Charlotte	14	0	17
Total LHR	452	265	234
Total LGW	82	28	33
Total	520	279	267

Notes
* On hub-to-hub routes alliance frequencies must be reduced and surrendered to competitors.
** On non-hub routes new slots will be from other routes/services.

Source: *Official Journal* (1998).

There were further conditions attached by the Commission to approval of both alliances aimed at ensuring that competitors did take up the liberated slots. The alliance partners were required either to refrain from pooling their frequent flyer programmes or to allow other airlines to participate in them. Displays on CRS screens could not be overburdened on the first page by one flight having different airline codes and appearing several times. Competitors on the relevant routes had to be allowed to interline with alliance members at least for their fully flexible fares. More surprisingly, member states were asked to authorise any Community airline which wished to do so to operate services on the routes from the member states to the United States so as to ensure that competitors could enter these transatlantic markets (*Official Journal*, 1998). But this assumed that the United States would authorise such Fifth Freedom services.

Despite all these conditions, the Commission has proved ineffectual here too. Faced with giving up so many slots without any financial recompense and with continued uncertainty about whether the United States would approve their alliance and under what conditions, BA and American decided early in 1999 to downgrade the alliance to a looser and wider marketing arrangement under the Oneworld banner. As a consequence, by the end of 1999 they had not given up any Heathrow slots. Nor had Lufthansa and their partners, because they had appealed against the Commission's decision and new hearings were taking place.

In essence we have two approaches for dealing with the perceived or potential risks to open competition arising from the creation of global alliances. The United States' view is that if international alliances are operating within 'open skies' bilaterals then free market forces should guard against anti-competitive behaviour. The European Union's approach is essentially to require alliances which create hub or route dominance to give up runway slots to rivals. The latter strategy does not appear to have been very successful in generating greater competition on routes where it has been applied. But equally, the US approach may be suspect, because the Departments of Transportation and of Justice have adopted different criteria for assessing domestic alliances to those used for international markets. The Justice Department has baulked at assuming that open market access in itself is sufficient to ensure competitive markets domestically and has tried to hold up or question some more recent attempts by US airlines to set up domestic alliances. For instance, in November 1998 it tried to stop Northwest buying a controlling interest in Continental.

4.10 A response to economic forces or to uncertainty?

The alliance frenzy of the second half of the 1990s was undoubtedly a response to the escalating competition and structural changes resulting from the liberalisation of international air transport. At the same time it was very much a response to the economic characteristics of the airline industry. The marketing benefits of large size and scope combined with the cost synergies arising from joining existing networks and operations into larger units were pushing airlines inexorably closer together. Larger international airlines saw clearly the strong economic logic for setting up regional or global alliances. They were also a way of reducing competition on many common routes. However, for managers in many smaller airlines, alliances were a response to uncertainty and did provide comfort that the firm was taking action, though it was not necessarily the right action.

Economic and marketing pressures will continue to push airlines into setting up even more alliances in the early years of the twenty-first century. But airline alliances are transitional devices. They are a response to the particular regulatory environment of air transport which effectively hinders cross-border takeovers and mergers. Once the ownership and nationality restrictions are removed, the existing alliances and partnerships will be shaken up and may change dramatically. New groupings will emerge as a result of major share purchasers, takeovers and, ultimately, mergers.

At the start of the new millennium, the airline industry is going through a process of globalisation but not consolidation. Consolidation is the next phase. It will come about as existing alliances are transformed from being essentially commercial to being more truly strategic and as the ownership rules are relaxed or removed. Consolidation will see the emergence of six to eight very large transnational airlines, each created through the merger or takeover of several different airlines. Each will also have commercial agreements and alliances with numerous regional and niche airlines, though the number of such carriers will have declined. The consolidation phase will begin to emerge in the middle of the current decade, around 2005 or so.

In the even longer term, it is unlikely that all the large transnationals that initially merge will ultimately survive. As happened with the oil industry, in 1998–99 there will be a second period of consolidation when the transnational airlines will be reduced in number. This will happen because over time the management of some of these very large carriers will become slow-footed and sluggish. They will be unable to foresee the next period of consolidation and will be slow to act. Those without long-term secure executive management in place will be most vulnerable. Such airlines will seek the comfort of merging with their more successful competitors when the industry is going through a major cyclical downturn, which it does every eight to ten years.

In the meantime, there is little doubt that public and government disquiet about the threats to competition from ever larger and stronger international airline alliances will not go away. In fact, as the four more global alliances become stronger, more integrated and more strategic in the early years of the new century concern will increase. To deal with this growing concern two things need to be done. First, one must identify where the threats to competition really arise, particularly for passengers and other users of air services. They are not in the creation of long-haul alliance networks as such but appear to be linked more with growing hub dominance and the creation of alliance monopolies on short- or medium-haul routes. One must identify the form and nature of such threats to competition in order to identify the actions necessary to ensure continued competition or at least to avoid the abuse of dominance. Unless, of course, one decides that deregulated open skies are sufficient in themselves to ensure that dominance is not abused. This is unlikely. The second requirement is to establish a common approach internationally to dealing with anti-competitive behaviour. The current situation where airlines, especially European airlines or those in alliance with them, have to satisfy different competition rules and authorities in their own countries as well as those of the European Union and possibly for global alliances those of the United States, is clearly absurd. A global internationalised industry needs consistent rules to fly by. It is right that governments should act if and when an alliance is so dominant that it can act in a way that is detrimental to consumers and undermines free competition in particular markets. Airlines and alliances should not have to deal with several different and competing

national or international regulations on competition. It may be very difficult to harmonise the competition rules for air transport in different
countries. But in the context of the moves towards setting up a Transatlantic
Common Aviation Area, as discussed earlier (Chapter 3, section 3.4) it
should be possible to try and ensure the convergence of competition policy.
This would be an important first step.

5 Labour is the key

Labour costs represent the single largest threat to airline unit costs in the US.
(*Airline Analyser, August 1999 – Update*, Warburg Dillon Read)

If we do not want to make losses again, we have to do something about
our personnel costs. Otherwise I can calculate right now when we go bust,
at what ticket price.

(Jurgen Weber, CEO Lufthansa, *The Times*,
27 February 1997, London)

5.1 The importance of labour costs

In recent years, airline executives have increasingly focused their attention on the cost of labour, both because it has become the largest single
cost element and also because it is a major factor differentiating one
airline's unit costs from another's. In the early 1980s, following the second
oil crisis of 1978–79, the cost of fuel had risen to around 30 per cent or
more of total costs. For most airlines it surpassed labour as an input cost.
Those days are long gone. As the price of aviation fuel declined significantly in real terms during the 1980s, labour costs became increasingly
critical. Today, while fuel fluctuates between 10 and 15 per cent or so of
total costs for most airlines, labour, including social security fund or
pension contributions and other labour-related costs, accounts for between
15 per cent and 40 per cent. It is for this reason that controlling labour
costs is so crucial for airline managers. In the early years of the 21st
century it is the key to cost control because, unlike fuel and other inputs
whose prices are externally determined, airlines can and must influence
their labour costs.

There are significant regional variations in the impact of labour on total
airline costs. A review of 1998 labour costs as a percentage of total operating costs, before interest payments and taxes, shows that among large
North American airlines labour represented 27 per cent to 40 per cent of
total expenditures (Table 5.1). In fact, for most of these airlines labour
costs were at the higher end of the range, at 35–40 per cent. Among the

Table 5.1 Wages and associated costs of labour as a percentage of total operating cost, 1998

North American		European		East Asian/Pacific	
USAir	40.4				
Delta	38.5				
United	38.4				
American	37.7				
TWA	36.1				
Northwest	35.3				
		Air France	34.6		
		SAS	33.6		
Continental	30.6				
				Qantas	28.8
		Iberia	28.4	Cathay Pacific	28.4
		British Airways	27.8		
		KLM	27.5		
Air Canada	27.2				
		Alitalia	20.9		
		Lufthansa*	20.4		
				All Nippon	19.2
				Korean	17.6
				Thai	17.5
				SIA	17.4
				Malaysian	16.5
				JAL	15.3

Note
*For the Lufthansa Group the figure was 25.6 per cent in 1997.

Source: Air Transport Group, College of Aeronautics, Cranfield.

major European carriers the figure is somewhat lower, at between 20 per cent and 35 per cent. Labour is least significant as a cost among airlines in East Asia, where it frequently represents only 15 per cent and 20 per cent of total costs, except for Cathay Pacific, where labour costs are 28 per cent of total costs, as are those of Qantas.

The importance of labour costs in the overall cost structure of an airline is dependent on the interplay of two groups of factors, those relating to the relative cost of labour and those that determine the productivity of the labour which is used. In other words, labour costs depend on the unit cost of labour as an input and the amount of that labour that is required to produce a unit of output.

5.2 The cost of labour

Many factors determine the unit cost of labour and its impact on an airline's cost structure. Undoubtedly, by far the most significant variable affecting labour costs is the prevailing wage rates in an airline's home country and

Table 5.2 Average annual remuneration for pilots and cabin crew of selected major airlines, 1998

Region/airline	Average annual remuneration (US$)	
	Pilots/co-pilots	*Cabin attendants*
North America		
Continental	154,400	34,600
American	143,300	37,400
Northwest	142,600	30,700
United	140,500	33,300
USAir	138,600	36,400
Delta	121,900	35,100
TWA	94,500	27,600
Air Canada	83,200	20,500
Europe		
Alitalia	201,600	58,500
Iberia	190,900*	61,800
SAS	163,700	72,600
Lufthansa	155,100	51,900
British Airways	125,200	29,600
East Asia/Pacific		
JAL	229,900*	62,900
Cathay Pacific	215,800	39,400
All Nippon	167,400	32,600
SIA	120,700	36,200
Qantas	114,600	42,000
Thai Airways	83,800	13,200
Malaysia Airlines	50,800	19,200
Korean	35,500	n.a.

Note
* Includes flight engineers.

Source: *Digest of Statistics*, Series F-P, Fleet and Personnel 1998, ICAO, Montreal.

any associated social charges that have to be met by that airline. Significant variations exist in wage levels for similar categories of staff between different regions of the world and between airlines in the same region. Table 5.2 shows the average annual remuneration in 1997 for two discrete types of airline employees for most of those airlines whose labour costs were compared in Table 5.1. As one would expect, salary levels are most homogeneous among the larger United States airlines, because they have the same home base. With the exception of TWA, pilots at the US majors were being paid between $125,000 and $155,000, while cabin crew received between $27,000 and $37,000. For smaller US airlines not shown here remuneration would be lower, especially for low-fare carriers. Salary differentials were widest among East Asian airlines. Because of heavy dependence on expatriate crews, Cathay Pacific was paying its pilots $215,000 which was over 50 per cent more than many US airlines.

Following currency devaluations in 1997 Thai, Korean and Malaysia Airlines pilots were paid less than $85,000 per year while their flight attendants too were by far the lowest-paid. Among the sample of European airlines Alitalia's and Iberia's salaries were the highest, higher even than those of US airlines, while British Airways' were the lowest.

Differentials in pilot salaries are important because, while cockpit crews represent only a small part of any airline's total workforce they account for a disproportionate part of salary expenses. Among North American carriers cockpit staff are generally around 10–12 per cent of total employees, while among European airlines they are on average a smaller proportion, around 6–9 per cent. But because they are by far the best-paid airline employees, cockpit crews, for most airlines, represent 20–30 per cent of total labour costs. It is for this reason that controlling pilot salaries is so critical for airlines and why negotiating an agreement with pilots is a key part of any airline's labour relations. Pilots in most airlines are well organised and in strong unions. Unlike other airline employees, except cabin crews, they have no other group in a country's labour force with whom their salaries can be compared or equated. Pilots, like cabin crew, have no counterparts. They only assess their salary levels with those of pilots in other airlines, often in other countries. There is therefore a strong inherent tendency for pilot salaries to rise both in absolute and real terms. Countering this tendency is a major preoccupation for airline managements.

Some variation in pilot salaries may be due to differences in flight equipment, since pilot salaries vary with type of aircraft flown, or with the age and seniority of the pilots. Nevertheless the salaries and wages paid depend primarily on the market conditions for labour in an airline's home country and on the cost of living in that country. In a country with free wage bargaining it is the interplay of supply and demand for the categories of labour required by the airline(s), together with the strength of particular unions, which will broadly determine the level of wages that an airline has to pay for its various categories of staff. In other countries wage levels may be set by national agreements between governments or employers' associations and the trade unions. In some cases governments themselves virtually determine the salaries to be paid and impose them on employers and employees alike. In all cases the prevailing wage levels are related to the standard and cost of living in the country concerned. Airlines can negotiate with the unions representing their employees, but usually only within a fairly narrow band whose level is pre-determined by the prevailing wage levels in the country concerned. In countries where airline labour has been unionised and well organised there has inevitably been strong upward pressure on wage levels.

In some countries, the shortage of trained pilots or engineers has forced the home airlines to employ expatriate cockpit crews, engineers or even in some cases cabin staff. Where this is the case labour costs are pushed

Table 5.3 Level and impact of social charges on European airlines' labour costs, 1998

	Average annual social charges per employee (US$)	Increase in total salary cost (%)
KLM	20,300	+ 52
Air France	17,500	+ 38
Lufthansa	16,300	+ 29
Swissair (1997)	15,700*	+ 30
SAS	14,100	+ 27
Finnair	12,400	+ 32
Austrian	12,200	+ 24
Sabena	11,800	+ 31
Iberia	11,800	+ 31
Alitalia	11,200	+ 25
Olympic	7,900	+ 24
Air Portugal	7,700	+ 26
British Airways	6,400	+ 15
Cyprus Airways	6,400	+ 21
Aer Lingus	5,700	+ 16
Turkish	4,700	+ 24
Malev	3,600	+ 46
Czech Airlines	3,000	+ 39

Source: Compiled by author from various data sources.

up significantly not only because of the need to pay higher wages to attract foreign staff but also because of the need to cover additional costs such as housing, schooling and so on. This explains in part why labour costs as a proportion of total costs at Cathay Pacific are so high when compared with other East Asian carriers (Table 5.1). In addition to basic salaries and overtime payments, airlines in most countries may also be required to contribute to their employees' pension schemes, to the state's social security funds, and they may have to pay other employee-related charges such as payroll taxes. All these charges raise the cost of labour to levels that are well above the cost of salaries and wages alone. Moreover, such social charges may vary significantly between neighbouring countries. This is nowhere more evident than in Europe, where airlines not only pay, as we have seen, significantly different wages but must also meet widely varying social charges (Table 5.3). In 1998 social charges among European airlines were lowest in absolute terms among airlines of Eastern Europe, such as Malev and Czech Airlines, where the annual charges totalled less than $4,000 per employee. At the other end of the scale, Swissair, Air France and Lufthansa were each paying more than $15,000 per employee each year and KLM over $20,000. Such charges increased their unit labour costs, which were already among the highest in Europe, by almost a third. It is interesting to note that annual social charges were very low for British

Airways ($6,400) and Aer Lingus (£5,700), and added only around 15 per cent to labour costs. This reflects the low levels of such charges in the UK and Ireland and is one reason why so many low-cost, no-frills airlines have been launched there. Pension contributions, related benefits and payroll taxes are somewhat higher in the United States, adding around 25 per cent to payroll costs.

Apart from the absolute level of wages and social charges, two other factors affect the significance of labour costs in an airline's overall cost structure. The first of these is the relative importance of other input costs. If one or more of the other significant cost items are relatively low then this inevitably pushes up labour costs as a percentage of total costs. This occurs among United States airlines. In the United States, aviation fuel prices are below prevailing prices elsewhere while airport and en-route charges are much lower than, say, in Europe because aviation infrastructure in the US is financed differently (Cranfield, 1998). Some other costs are also relatively lower for US airlines. The fact that several non-labour costs are comparatively low partly explains why labour costs as a proportion of total costs among US airlines appear to be so high in Table 5.1. It cannot be because their wage rates are much higher, since it is evident from the comparative analysis in Table 5.2 that they are not.

The fluctuation in an airline's home currency is the second variable that impacts on the significance of labour costs. While the vast bulk of salaries and associated costs are paid in an airline's home currency for its home-based employees, many other costs are paid in foreign currencies. Fuel prices are always denominated and paid in US dollars, loans for aircraft purchases are in hard currencies and aircraft leases are normally paid for in US dollars. In addition, airport and en-route charges when flying abroad, as well as ground handling fees and many sales and distribution costs are paid in foreign currencies. Given this situation, if an airline's home currency is devalued, then its labour costs, the bulk of which are mainly in that currency, will become cheaper in relation to the airline's hard currency expenditures. Labour costs will become a lower proportion of total costs. This is what happened during 1998 in those countries such as Korea, Thailand and Malaysia, whose currencies were devalued as a result of the East Asian economic crisis which unfolded at the end of 1997. This partly explains why labour costs are so low (in Tables 5.1 and 5.2) for Korean Airlines, Thai Airways and Malaysia Airlines. Conversely, if the home currency is being revalued upwards the opposite effect can be observed. Labour costs will become a growing proportion of total costs as expenditures in foreign exchange become relatively cheaper.

5.3 Productivity of labour

As previously mentioned, the significance of labour costs to an airline depends not only on the wage rates paid but also on the productivity of

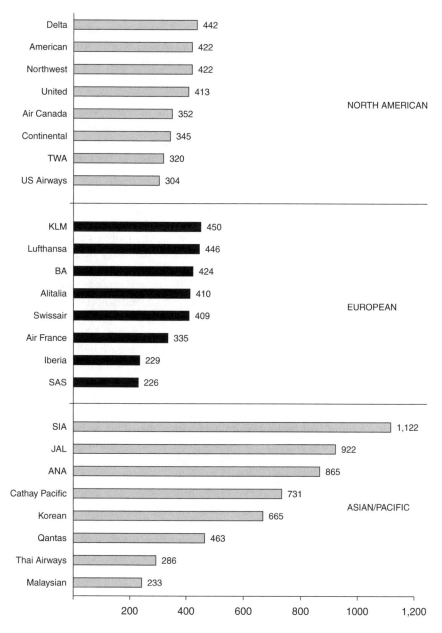

Figure 5.1 Available tonne-km ('000) per employee, 1998.

that labour. Traditionally, labour productivity has been measured in terms of output, that is, available tonne-kilometres, per employee. The productivity of our sample of major airlines from three regions of the world in 1998 is shown in Figure 5.1. Broadly speaking, North American and European airlines appear to be equally efficient in their use of labour as an input, though the two airlines with very low productivity in 1998 were both European: Iberia and SAS. When one examines the Asian/Pacific group of airlines there is a quantum jump in labour productivity. The five most efficient of these airlines achieved productivity levels one-and-a-half to three times as high as the better North American and European carriers, though there were also some very poor performers among Asian carriers.

Labour productivity depends partly on institutional factors such as working days in the week, length of annual holidays, basic hours worked per week, maximum duty periods for flying staff and so on, which vary significantly between countries, and partly on a number of operational factors, such as size of aircraft, average sector distance, frequencies per sector and level of involvement in freight. There are significant economies of size when operating larger aircraft since the labour inputs required such as pilots, flight dispatchers, ground handling staff and so on either do not increase with aircraft size or increase much less than in proportion to size. Sector distance impacts on productivity because such labour-intensive activities as passenger check-in, passenger and baggage handling, aircraft provisioning and aircraft cleaning take place less frequently. Size and sector distance frequently reinforce each other. That is to say that where airlines operate primarily long-haul sectors with very large aircraft then inevitably they can achieve high labour productivity. Cathay Pacific and Singapore Airlines are prime examples. Conversely, short domestic sectors operated with small aircraft inevitably lead to low labour productivity. This is why airlines such as SAS, Iberia and Thai Airways, or Malaysian, with extensive domestic or short-haul networks operated by relatively small aircraft, suffer low productivity. High frequencies can improve labour productivity in two ways. They produce economies of scale because ground and other support staff at all the outstations served do not increase in proportion to the frequencies offered. The same number of station and ground staff at the destination airport can normally handle one flight or, say, four flights per day. High frequencies also enable airlines to achieve higher utilisation from pilots and cabin crews, thus reducing the numbers required. Finally, airlines in which freight is a major part of their output, especially if they are flying a significant number of all-cargo aircraft, invariably appear to achieve high labour productivity because freighters do not require cabin crews or so much ground staff nor does cargo need so many sales and marketing staff. This is a factor which partly explains the very high labour productivity of SIA, Cathay Pacific and Korean in Asia and the relatively good productivity of KLM and Lufthansa in Europe.

These are airlines that generate nearly half of their international traffic from the carriage of cargo.

A further factor affecting labour productivity is the degree of outsourcing which an airline undertakes. If labour-intensive activities such as flight kitchens, heavy maintenance, aircraft cleaning or IT support are outsourced, then an airline's own staff numbers are invariably reduced and output per employee is enhanced. Conversely, if an airline contracts in catering and maintenance from other airlines, its own staff numbers will be swelled without any corresponding increase in traffic though there may be an increase in revenue generated. During the last decade, many airlines, especially in Europe, have begun to outsource key functions, as British Airways has done with its ground transport at Heathrow and Gatwick airports and its catering, which was sold to Swissair's Gate Gourmet in 1998. In 1999 Aer Lingus went so far as to sell off its entire maintenance division to FLS Engineering, who would henceforth undertake the airline's maintenance. Other airlines, such as Lufthansa have converted some of their divisions into separate subsidiary businesses to whom the core airline business sub-contracts functions such as engineering or ground handling. In the process they take many staff off the core airline's head-count, thereby artificially improving their labour productivity. While Lufthansa's three airline divisions, Lufthansa German Airlines, Lufthansa Cityline and Lufthansa Cargo, had around 34,500 employees at the end of 1998, a further 28,000 or so worked in several subsidiaries, such as Lufthansa Tecnik or LSG Lufthansa Services, grouped into six strategic business segments. These subsidiaries undertook airline maintenance, catering, ground handling and other functions for Lufthansa's own passenger and cargo divisions as well as for many airlines world-wide. In such situations it is difficult to establish how many of the subsidiaries' 28,000 employees are required for work on Lufthansa's core airline divisions and should be included when assessing Lufthansa's labour productivity.

Because of differences between airlines both in terms of their institutional environment and their operational characteristics, benchmarking of labour productivity must be treated with caution. Nevertheless, each airline's management operating within its own institutional and operational constraints is under constant pressure to try and improve the productivity of each group of employees. Since reducing operating costs is the ultimate objective, managers must juggle and balance salaries paid per employee with the number of employees required for each activity so as to produce the desired combination of service standards and unit costs.

While available tonne-kms (ATK) per employee is the traditional measure of labour productivity, in the highly competitive world of international air transport it is not the number of employees which is critical but the cost of such employees in relation to the output they generate. It matters less if an airline is apparently overstaffed if it pays relatively low salaries. If labour is a cheap resource there may be operational or service benefits in

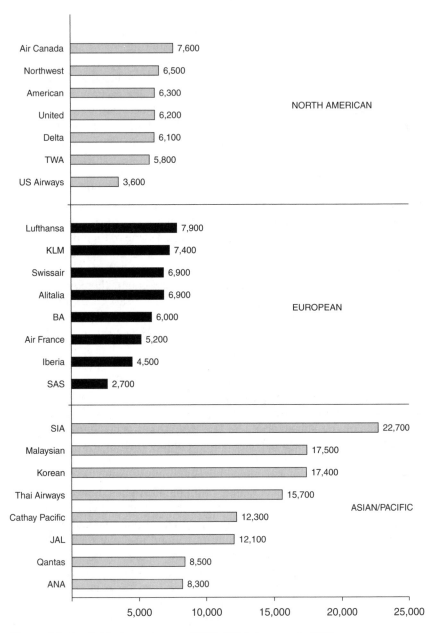

Figure 5.2 Available tonne-km per US$1,000 labour cost, 1998.

employing more staff than is strictly necessary. Conversely, if wage rates are very high, the need to improve labour productivity is even greater. Since comparative wage rates vary enormously it may be more indicative of efficiency in the use of labour to compare airlines in terms of output (that is, available tonne-kms) per $1,000 of labour cost (Figure 5.2), rather than ATKs per employee. Many of the Asian carriers now come into their own, because of their low salaries. Airlines such as Thai Airways or Malaysian that appear overstaffed in Figure 5.1 now achieve labour productivity figures more than twice as high as those of their European or North American competitors. Surprisingly, SAS, which, according to Table 5.2, has among the highest wages, fails to offset high unit labour costs by significantly improving its labour productivity and has the lowest productivity among the major airlines sampled.

5.4 Growing pressures to reduce the cost of labour

The traditional view, long held within the airline industry, was that management could do little about the unit cost of labour. It was argued that salaries and wage rates were largely externally determined by prevailing wage levels and the cost and standard of living in an airline's home country. Moreover, airline unions were generally very powerful, especially in North and South America and in Europe, since any small group of employees, such as flight despatchers, could ground an airline by withdrawing their labour. Management saw its role primarily as that of trying to keep a lid on the wage increases demanded in the annual pay negotiations. It was felt that management's influence on the level of wage costs in highly unionised airlines was marginal. This was especially true at state-owned airlines, where governments were loath to face up to unions or to have to deal with strikes that were publicly damaging. Moreover, because employees in many such state-owned airlines were treated more or less as civil servants, employees received annual wage increments automatically or their wages were frequently index-linked, that is, to say they rose in line with the consumer price index. Or they had both annual increments and indexation, as is still the case with Cyprus Airways. In many Asian and African countries where unions were not strong, the social culture and/or government pressures prevented airline managements from reducing airline wage rates and often forced them to increase them more than in line with the consumer price index. Because management's influence on the unit cost of labour could only be marginal, airline executives focused their attention on improving labour productivity through the introduction of larger aircraft, computerisation and so on, while holding back, as much as possible, any increases in staff numbers as output increased.

During the 1980s, management attitudes to labour began to change dramatically as a result of deregulation and the successive cyclical economic crises that affected the airline industry. Growing domestic and international competition which was accompanied by falling fares and yields, made it increasingly clear that trying to improve labour productivity in itself was not enough to contain labour costs. This was especially so as the latter became a growing proportion of total operating costs with the decline in the real price of fuel. Airlines were forced to try and reduce the unit cost of labour.

In the United States, domestic deregulation in 1978 was followed by the emergence of a large number of new start-up airlines, many of which offered significantly lower fares than the traditional carriers. The new start-ups appeared to have little trouble in getting employees willing to work at lower salaries and with more demanding terms and conditions. The pressures the new entrants created on established carriers were exacerbated by the economic crisis of the early 1980s, which pushed many airlines into the red (see Chapter 1). The established US airlines reacted to the twin challenge of the new entrants and the cyclical downturn by persuading their own employees to accept wage standstills or even cuts, or by introducing a two-tier wage structure whereby new employees were taken on at much lower salaries than established staff. American Airlines was among those who initiated a two-tier wage structure. Few of the early start-ups survived into the 1990s, the notable and very successful exception being Southwest (see Chapter 6, section 6.2). But the pressure to hold down labour costs was maintained. The crisis years of 1990–93, when the US majors lost several hundred million dollars each, led to a new period of belt-tightening on labour costs. During this second phase major concessions were also won from employees, but, in several cases, only in return for shares and share options. Throughout the period the traditional US carriers kept on looking over their shoulders at the growing success and continued profitability of low-cost carrier Southwest and wondering how they could get their unit costs anywhere near the former's. Reducing labour costs became a priority.

In Europe, the real focus on reducing unit labour costs came later than in the United States because the impact of liberalisation was not really felt until the late 1980s. Three parallel developments pushed European airlines to place greater emphasis on cutting labour costs. The first was growing competition as bilateral air service agreements between European states were liberalised and as the regulations affecting air transport within the European Union were gradually relaxed from 1987 onwards. Denser European routes previously the duopolistic preserve of the two national carriers from either end of the route, became increasingly open to competitive pressures. Second, the crisis of 1990–93 hit European carriers just as badly as their American counterparts, especially the state-owned airlines. Third, several European governments decided that their loss-making national airlines, which they owned, needed to be restructured and made profitable in order that they could be privatised. The restructuring involved staff cuts, early retirement, freezing or even reduction of salaries and improved labour productivity. Moreover, governments, with the approval of the European Commission, pumped hundreds of millions of dollars into their airlines to facilitate this restructuring process (see Chapter 8, Table 8.4). By the mid-1990s, competition had become more acute on long-haul routes, while in Europe the new-entrant, low-cost, no-frills airlines were beginning to make a major impact. For European airlines the pressures to reduce labour costs were reinforced.

In contrast to developments in North America and Europe, the airlines of East Asia had not been so adversely affected by the cyclical down-turns of 1980–82 and 1990–93. This was largely because they were based on economies whose growth continued to be rapid and well above the average. The airlines themselves were growing very rapidly and in most cases profitably. There was little pressure to reduce labour costs, which were, in any case, quite low, except among Japanese carriers. The latter suffered from the steady appreciation of the yen, which pushed up their average wages rates in dollar terms (Table 5.2). It was not till the economic crisis that surfaced in the tiger economies towards the end of 1997 and became acute in 1998, that most East Asian airlines began to seriously tackle the issue of labour costs and overstaffing as losses became heavy. Pressure to do so also came from the desire of many of their governments to privatise their airlines which in turn required financial and operational restructuring. Airlines facing the most serious difficulties, notably Philippine Airlines and the Garuda Indonesian, brought in foreign management teams to turn these companies around. Cutting labour costs became here too a major priority.

5.5 Labour as a cost differentiator – the European case

As airline markets became more open and competitive it was increasingly apparent that reducing unit costs on each route was critically important. This was so both because lower costs offered airlines greater pricing flexibility and because the greater the competition the greater was the downward pressure on average yields. Lower route costs were and are a prerequisite for route profitability. Numerous factors affect the level of airline costs, some of which are largely externally determined, such as the price of aviation fuel or the level of airport charges, while others, such as the size of aircraft used, depend on the nature of an airline's operations. The unit cost of labour and the efficiency with which that labour is used is but one of the factors affecting overall costs. However, on a route-by-route basis, and especially in international markets, labour can become a major cost differentiator.

International air services within the European Union amply illustrate this. Europe's major conventional airlines compete against each other on dense and medium-sized routes radiating from their own country to major European centres, both capital cities and large regional airports. Within the European Union around 250 cross-border routes are flown by two carriers and close to 100 are operated by more than two carriers (Commission, 1999). The latter include routes operated by low-cost, no-frills carriers. On the 350 or so intra-EU routes on which there is competition one finds that the airlines competing against each other fly very comparable aircraft. On some routes the aircraft types will be the same. On any particular route, the aircraft being flown in competition should achieve broadly similar utilisation, that is, flying or block hours per day. The financing costs of the aircraft will not be identical but will be close enough to ensure that the impact on each airline's total costs are only marginal. The cost of spare parts consumed will be similar, especially if the aircraft are identical. The price paid for fuel on the route by each airline will be comparable, while the level of airport and en-route navigation charges will be identical. All the above costs taken together represent around one-third of total operating costs for intra-European scheduled services. But many other more discrete costs will not vary significantly between airlines such as the cost of in-flight meals and catering, of ground equipment, of airport office space, of advertising space and so on. Expenditure on items such as these will vary according to the amount of office space used or of advertising commissioned. This is up to each airline to decide. But the unit costs will not be so far apart as to make any of these items a major cost differentiator. With so many costs being more or less comparable, the cost of labour can be the most critical item in explaining cost differences between airlines competing on the same routes, though clearly it is not the only factor.

From the earlier discussion it is apparent that labour costs for European airlines represent 20–35 per cent of total operating costs and for most it is over 25 per cent (Table 5.1). But these are total figures. For their intra-European services labour costs will be even more significant since these are essentially short-haul routes that are more labour-intensive. Apart from pilots and cabin crew, which, on intra-European services, account for 11–14 per cent of total operating costs, labour is heavily used for sales and ticketing, for check-in and handling at airports and it is also a major component of maintenance cost which itself is increased as a result of shorter sectors. For most intra-European sectors fully allocated labour costs for most airlines are likely to represent 30–40 per cent of total operating costs. Therefore, differences in the unit cost of labour, when compared to that of its direct competitors, can have a major impact on an airline's comparative route costs.

For reasons discussed earlier, the level of wage costs per employee differs widely between airlines in different European countries. They may also vary markedly between airlines in the same country. An indexation of average wage costs per employee of European airlines in 1998 shows that the highest wages when all staff were included were being paid by SAS (Table 5.4). Though Lufthansa and Swissair appear to pay more this

Table 5.4 Index of average annual wage costs per employee, European scheduled airlines, 1998

	Index of average wage cost*		Index of average wage cost*
Swissair	124	British Airways	75
Lufthansa	110	Icelandair	75
SAS	100	Aer Lingus	64
Air France	96	Olympic	63
Austrian	94	Air Portugal	59
KLM	90	Cyprus Airways	56
Alitalia	85	British Midland	55
Finnair	78	Turkish	37
Sabena	76	Malev	17
Iberia	76	Czech Airlines	17

Notes
* SAS = 100. Index based on salaries paid plus social security charges.

N.B. Lufthansa and Swissair indices exclude maintenance, traffic handling and catering staff.

is because certain categories such as maintenance, ground handling and catering staff are excluded. Below SAS, wage levels, including the cost of overtime and social charges, varied enormously. Eight of the twenty airlines sampled had wage levels that were less than two-thirds of those paid by SAS. Several were around half or less. The lowest wage costs were and still are among the airlines of Eastern Europe such as Malev in Hungary and Czechoslovak Airlines. Their wage costs per employee in 1998 were around 17 per cent of those of SAS.

In view of the fact that labour costs represent over 30 per cent of total operating costs on intra-European routes and that costs per employee varied so widely between the airlines competing in these markets, it was inevitable that strategies to reduce costs, as competition increased, should focus mainly, but not exclusively, on cutting labour costs. The same thinking has underlain the emphasis placed on reducing labour costs among North American and East Asian airlines.

5.6 Strategies for reducing labour costs

Experience in Europe in the 1990s amply illustrates the strategies airlines can adopt to cut labour costs. As the cyclical downturn of the early 1990s began to bite, European airline chairmen announced crisis measures to reduce costs. Among privatised or partly privatised airlines such as British Airways, Swissair or KLM, explicit cost reduction targets were set for the three or four years up to 1994 or 1995. These generally involved reducing total costs from between 10 per cent to 14 per cent, while continuing to increase traffic. For the state-owned airlines of Europe cost reduction became part of a more complex operational and financial restructuring required in order to obtain approval from the European Commission for the capital injections ('state aid') provided by their governments (see Table 1.1). The explicit aim of such state aid was to ensure that in the future these airlines could operate profitably without recourse to further state support which in any case would not be permitted by the Commission. Airlines aimed to achieve their cost reduction targets through various measures. These included cutting unprofitable routes, business re-engineering, financial restructuring to reduce debt payments and outsourcing. But reducing labour costs was in all cases the most significant part of any cost reduction programme. It was also the most difficult. It was high-profile, contentious and most likely to create adverse reaction from employees.

As pointed out earlier, not only are labour costs the most significant single cost input but there are also wide variations in average wage costs among European airlines. Thus, it was inevitable that cost reduction measures in the early to mid-1990s should focus on cutting labour costs. To achieve the latter several strategies were adopted. The first and most obvious has been to *cut staff numbers*. Most European airlines announced staff cuts early in 1991. Few actually achieved their targets apart from British Airways, which lost 6,400 staff that year: a reduction of 12 per cent. Further job cuts were announced by most airlines in 1992, though targets once again were only partially met. Indicative of the pressures to reduce staff numbers was Lufthansa's 'Programme 93' cost-cutting exercise, the main thrust of which was to cut 1,800 jobs in 1992 and a further 3,100 each year in both 1993 and 1994. Though such cuts were not fully achieved both Lufthansa and British Airways were employing 9 per cent less staff in 1994 compared to 1990, and this despite a significant growth in traffic. Most airlines introduced attractive but expensive schemes to facilitate voluntary redundancies. The most dramatic cuts in employee numbers were among some of the state-owned airlines undergoing restructuring as a prerequisite for privatisation. Between 1990 and the end of 1994 Iberia lost 18 per cent of its staff, Air Portugal 17 per cent and Olympic Airways 13 per cent. Some of the state aid was used to fund early retirement schemes and redundancies. A few airlines, such as Air France, however, failed to cut back on staff numbers while at Sabena employee numbers rose sharply in the early 1990s. Among smaller independent European airlines, such as British Midland or Crossair, staff numbers also rose. This was in response to their rapid growth as these airlines took advantage of deregulation to expand their routes and operations. With these exceptions, there was a strong downward trend in staff numbers. But, while reducing their permanent employee numbers, many airlines began to make greater use of part-time seasonal labour to meet peak traffic demands, especially during the European summer. For example, Lufthansa increased its part-time employees from about 4 per cent of total staff in the early 1990s to 17 per cent in 1998.

As traffic growth accelerated again after 1994 and the fortunes of the airlines improved, there was a tendency for staff numbers to drift upwards, in some cases quite markedly so. This was to be expected, since airline output grew rapidly in the second half of the 1990s. However, the new staff taken on, being much younger, were employed at lower salaries than the staff made redundant in the early years. But when airline financial results began to worsen in 1998–99 staff cuts again became the order of the day for several European airlines. Thus, in January 2000 British Airways' chief executive, then Robert Ayling, announced that around 6,500 jobs would be axed during the next three years. The following month KLM stated it would axe up to 3,000 jobs in an effort to return to profitability.

The second strategy adopted in parallel to reductions in staff numbers was to *renegotiate terms and conditions of employment*. Inevitably, those who continued in their posts were required to adopt more flexible and productive work practices to compensate for the fact that there were fewer of them. At the same time, existing wage and salary levels were frozen for a year or two or even renegotiated downwards. Thus in August 1992 Lufthansa negotiated a one-year wage freeze and a cut in bonuses with its unions, who also agreed to changes in working conditions and productivity improvements. In 1993 Air France introduced work rule changes for flight and cabin crew that saved almost US$150 million. Meanwhile, during the summer of 1993 Sabena negotiated wages cuts ranging from 2.5 per cent to 17 per cent. Swissair has claimed that, as a result of revised labour contracts, it was able to cut the cost of flight crew per block hour of flying from Swiss Francs 1,368 in 1995 to 1,057 in 1997, a drop of 23 per cent (Bruggisser, 1997).

Another way to get around existing labour agreements was for airlines to *set up low-cost subsidiaries*. These aimed to have lower wage scales and/or more flexible terms of employment. This is why Iberia set up Viva Air which, while initially operating charters, took over more and more of Iberia's scheduled services in leisure markets, though this policy was later changed. KLM too began using its subsidiary charter airline Transavia for leisure-oriented scheduled services. Lufthansa has done the same with its subsidiary charter airline Condor, which now flies scheduled services to some tourist destinations in addition to more traditional charter flights. Lufthansa also has a separate airline called Lufthansa CityLine operating regional jets with staff employed on different terms from those of the parent company.

An alternative approach but with a similar objective was for airlines to *buy into or to franchise smaller independent airlines*, with lower unit wage costs, to operate on their behalf, especially on thinner domestic and short-haul routes. The best example perhaps in Europe has been Swissair's use of Crossair to serve a network of thinner routes radiating from Zurich and Geneva as well as Basel, Crossair's original base. Crossair was an independent and successful operator of smaller regional jets and turbo-props in which Swissair initially bought a minority shareholding. But Crossair staff worked with more flexible terms and conditions and were paid less, in some cases much less, than comparable Swissair staff. Crossair was altogether more efficient and cost-conscious. Crossair unit costs are high because of the nature of its operations, but it is still able to operate at lower unit costs than could be achieved by Swissair's main-line services operating on thinner routes out of Switzerland. Swissair eventually took a majority shareholding but Crossair continued to operate as a more or less independent airline serving routes requiring aircraft of 100 seats or less on behalf of its parent. British Airways used Gatwick-based City Flyer Express in a very similar way, but as a franchisee. City Flyer in BA colours operated thinner domestic and regional routes out of Gatwick at lower unit costs than could be achieved by British Airways. Eventually in 1999 British Airways bought this airline outright to safe-guard these routes and also its numerous slots at Gatwick. Most of the larger European airlines have used smaller franchise partners in order to take advantage of the latter's lower labour costs, though there were also marketing advantages from such franchising agreements (see Chapter 4, section 4.4).

Effectively airlines were outsourcing the flying of loss-making routes to lower-cost carriers. Another prime example occurred in October 1996 when Sabena asked Virgin Express to operate its nine daily flights between Brussels and London-Heathrow on Sabena's behalf. Virgin Express has much younger and more poorly paid staff. Sabena claimed the routes became profitable and extended this outsourcing to other routes (see Chapter 6, section 6.3).

A further way to reduce labour costs was through *outsourcing or contracting out* activities previously done in-house by an airline's own staff. This not only helped an airline to reduce its own staff numbers but also enabled it to shop around among service providers to obtain the best deals from companies, possibly other airlines, with lower labour costs. In-flight catering, aircraft cleaning, passenger handling, aircraft maintenance, revenue accounting, informatics were among the activities that could be outsourced. For instance, in the early 1990s KLM outsourced its catering and Swissair its aircraft cleaning. As mentioned earlier, British Airways in 1997 outsourced all its ground transport services at London-Heathrow and Gatwick to Ryder and in 1998 sold its catering services at Heathrow to Swissair's SAirRelations for around US$105 million. Austrian Airlines closed its own heavy maintenance facility and now sends its aircraft to other airlines for such maintenance. It still does base maintenance up to C-check level but employs less than 700 engineers and technicians for a fleet of forty or so aircraft compared to 1,000 staff for a fleet half that size in the very early 1990s. (*Airline Business*, March 1999). Other medium- and small-sized airlines have followed this path.

In some cases airline managements used the threat to outsource an activity as a way of obtaining concessions from its own employees in that area. Thus, in May 1997 British Airways cargo staff voted for a two-year pay freeze and a loss of 400 out of 1,400 jobs so that the airline would not outsource their work.

Finally, airlines in high wage economies started to *move certain activities away from their home base* to countries where wages were much lower. Swissair was the first to do this by moving some of its accounting services to Mumbai in India. Others have followed. Austrian Airlines has also outsourced its revenue accounting to Mumbai. Much of British Airways' software development for its management information systems is now also done in India. Together with Lufthansa, Swissair has set up Shannon Aerospace to provide major aircraft overhaul and maintenance facilities while taking advantage of much lower labour costs in Ireland. Another way of achieving reductions has been to employ flight crews or cabin staff based in countries with lower wage rates. Swissair has done this by using Asian flight attendants. This trend to export or *relocate* airline jobs to lower-wage economies will accelerate.

In trying to reduce labour costs, airline managements will use all or some combination of the above strategies. Sabena provides a clear example. In 1996, Swissair having bought a 49 per cent share, appointed Paul Reutlinger, one of its own senior executives, as the new President of Sabena. His plan to turn round the airline, announced in June 1996, involved a reduction in labour costs of US$64 million. This could be achieved in one of three ways: a 12 per cent cut in salaries, 1,270 job losses, or revised and tougher work schedules. This was the choice offered to the employees and their unions. A compromise was eventually agreed combining elements of all three proposals. Salaries were cut by 2 per cent, 730 employees retired or left and there was some tightening up of work practices. As mentioned earlier Sabena also obtained union approval to outsource some of its flying to low-cost operators Virgin Express and City Bird.

During the early to mid-1990s European airlines made strenuous efforts to reduce all costs, but especially labour costs. But this was not enough. As international competition intensified in the later 1990s and as average yields per passenger-km or freight-km continued to decline, European airlines were put under great pressure once again to cut costs. A new round of major cost reductions was announced in 1997 and 1998 (Table 5.5). These mirrored similar announcements made in 1991 and 1992. The targets set were very demanding in terms of the expected cuts in unit costs. The cost of labour per ATK among European Union airlines had gone down in real terms by about one-third between 1989 and 1994 (Alamdari and Morrell, 1997). But once again since labour was a major

Table 5.5 European airlines' cost reduction programmes (as at July 1998)

Airline	Cost/efficiency target	Period
Air France	Unit cost cut 15 per cent	By 2001
Alitalia	US$340 million savings Unit labour costs cut 10 per cent	By 2001
Austrian Airlines	Unit cost cut 17 per cent	By 1999
British Airways	US$1.7 billion savings	By 2000
KLM	Operating cost cut 10 per cent	1997–2000
Lufthansa	Unit cost cut 20 per cent	1996–2000
Swissair	Unit cost cut 24 per cent	1996–2000

cost differentiator a major part of the proposed cost reductions was expected to come from lower labour costs.

All the labour cost reduction strategies once more came into play. Even at Lufthansa, which began to make substantial profits in 1995 and 1996, there was tremendous pressure to reduce costs. In late 1996 the company launched a programme to reduce costs by DM1.5 billion and demanded concessions from the employees. According to Jurgen Weber, the chief executive, the choice was clear. 'If we do not want to make losses again, we have to do something about our personnel costs. Otherwise I can calculate right now when we go bust, at what ticket price' (*The Times*, 27 February 1997). The Lufthansa unions agreed to more or less a standstill on wages for two years in return for a small, one-off payment and some profit-sharing bonuses.

It is relatively easy to squeeze concessions out of airline employees in periods when the airline industry is clearly in deep crisis and airlines are losing money hand over fist. This was the situation in the early 1990s. But when airlines are profitable and things are going well employees rightly want to share in the profits generated. It is difficult to persuade them that a new crisis is impending as a result of intensified competition and that to avoid future losses and an airline's possible collapse it is essential for them to make sacrifices now. To overcome this problem European airlines were forced increasingly to offer performance or profit-related bonuses and/or shares in exchange for concessions on pay or conditions of work.

A recent example of the latter was Air France's deal late in 1998 with its pilots, the highest-paid in Europe. The airline needed to reduce labour costs, push up labour productivity and ensure industrial peace. Yet in 1997 it had produced a substantial profit of around US$320 million, the first in seven years. Against this background of apparent success, the management could only achieve the necessary wage reductions and significant productivity improvements through offering equity handouts. The pilots agreed to a three-year wage freeze to 2001 with the possibility of extending it for a further three or four years without adjustments for inflation. This would save the airline around US$42 million a year. They also accepted changes in work practices to increase productivity and to bring them into line with practices at airlines such as British Airways or KLM. Finally, a scope agreement allows Air France to outsource services requiring aircraft of less than 100 seats to other operators. In exchange, pilots received share options. When the airline was partially privatised in 1999, the pilots found themselves owning around 7 per cent of the equity. Moreover, together with other employees, they elect seven of the eighteen members of Air France's board.

5.7 Sharing the spoils: employee stock option plans

The strategies adopted by European carriers to reduce costs and especially labour costs very largely mirrored those adopted by United States airlines. For example, Delta, having come close to collapse in the period 1991 to 1994 with net losses of around $1.7 billion, launched a very ambitious cost reduction programme in April 1994. Its 'Leadership 7.5' project aimed at an operating cost reduction of $1.6 billion, so as to cut costs per available seat-mile by 20 per cent from 9.3 cents to 7.5 cents within three years. This was to be achieved through a cut in staff numbers, more outsourcing and the elimination of unprofitable routes. The targeted reduction was not achieved although unit costs did go down to around 8.3–8.4 cents. Two years later, in April 1996, Delta made a new deal with its pilots producing further cost savings, but also allowing Delta to set up a low-cost subsidiary Delta Express employing pilots at lower salaries. Meanwhile, in 1993 Northwest had secured a three-year package of wage concessions from its own employees which effectively meant freezing pay at the 1992 levels. The wage concessions were worth almost US$900 million in cost savings.

In one very important respect the United States airlines were innovators. They pioneered the concept of offering equity to employees in return for concessions on pay and work conditions. Eastern Airlines and other carriers had some initial success with the idea in the mid-1980s but early enthusiasm did not last. Later, faced with the huge losses suffered in the early 1990s, managements saw employee stock option plans, ESOPs as they were called, as a way of achieving major reductions in labour costs. In July 1994 United Airlines took the boldest leap of all by offering 53 per cent of the company's shares to its two largest unions and three out of twelve seats on the board in exchange for a four-year agreement involving pay cuts, which averaged around 15 per cent, and work-to-rule concessions. In the process, United created the largest employee-owned company in the United States. Significantly, its 20,000 flight attendants did not join the buyout.

It was estimated that United employees had effectively bought their airline for around $5 billion, which was the value of the wage concessions obtained. Unions also agreed to the setting up of the low-cost United Shuttle whose purpose was to compete with low-fare Southwest. Other airlines, Delta, Northwest and TransWorld among them, also offered shares and stock options in return for concessions on pay. All the major US airlines now have employee shareholders and employee representation on their boards, though only in the case of United are employees the majority owners.

As the profits of United States airlines soared after 1995, the honeymoon with labour began to falter. On the labour side employees wanted a greater share of the record profits than could be obtained from their dividends on stocks, especially as not all of them held stock. Yet all employees had made sacrifices to help their airlines through the crisis years of the early 1990s. On the management side, there was great pressure to prevent cost escalation as the earlier three- and four-year agreements began to unwind and salaries and wage rates reverted to the higher pre-concession levels. The potential for conflict was there. It came to a head most dramatically at Northwest in 1998. After the 1993 agreement with the unions came to an end in 1996 salary levels went back to the 1992 levels, which were higher, but for the employees these were no longer enough. Negotiations for new agreements dragged on until the unions lost patience. The mechanics went on strike in the spring of 1998 and the pilots in September, causing the cancellation of all flights for an eighteen-day period. The 1998 strikes cost Northwest well over US$1 billion in lost revenues and increased costs. But during the first half of 1999 the airline set about closing new agreements with each of its six major unions. The other majors also had union agreements coming up for renegotiation at the beginning of the new millennium.

Delta provides a good example. In September 1999 it entered into a tentative agreement with its pilots for flying the Boeing 777 which would make them the best paid in the United States. The deal included a proposal to convert the existing profit-sharing scheme into a 6 per cent pay rise. Delta had to conclude an overall deal with its pilots by May 2000. It was likely to prove costly as the pilots were expecting significant pay increases given Delta's high profits in the previous years. At the start of the new millennium American, United, America West and the other carriers were facing or were about to face similar problems with their pilots. Many airlines, including American, Continental, Northwest and US Airways, also still had to reach agreement with their cabin attendants. Significant wage increases for the pilots or flight attendants would inevitably cascade down through the airline to other labour groups. There is strong union and employee pressure for higher wages. How well and in what way they deal with this pressure may well be a defining moment for most US airlines. As investment bank Warburg Dillon Read claimed at the end of

1999, 'Labour costs do represent the single largest threat to airline unit costs in the United States' (*Airline Analyser*, August 1999 update).

Employee share schemes or ESOPs in the United States have been used by airline managements with two objectives in mind. The first is to improve labour–management relations as well as employee motivation and good-will by giving employees a stake in the airline and in its well-being. This has been done through payment of profit-related bonuses and, in the case of government-owned airlines, by offering employees free or cheap shares when such airlines are privatised. Often employees enjoy both bonuses and preferential access to shares. This has happened both with Singapore Airlines and British Airways. In 1984 British Airways was one of the first to offer staff annual bonuses whose level is linked directly to the annual profits generated. Such annual profit-related bonuses can also be taken in the form of cash or shares. When it was privatised in 1987 BA encouraged staff to purchase shares by offering them some free shares as well as some shares at less than the initial price of the public offering.

The second objective has been to use offers of shares or stocks to employees or their unions in order to obtain very specific concessions on wages or work conditions. This was the purpose of United's ESOP deal with its two major unions in 1994 and of Air France's agreement with its pilots in 1998. In both cases a further aim was to improve labour relations but this was a secondary objective. Reducing labour costs was the primary aim of such agreements.

The results have been mixed. Employee share ownership in some cases does appear to lead to improved motivation and better relations between staff and management. This was certainly the case at British Airways after its privatisation in 1987. But it is not a guarantee of improved labour–management relations, as the very acrimonious strike by BA's cabin crews in 1997 showed. Nevertheless, involving labour in share ownership is beneficial overall and should improve industrial relations in the longer term. In the United States ESOP deals have not lived up to expectations in terms of a long-term and lasting improvement in labour–management relations. Where, as in the case of United, some unions did not participate in the ESOP there was additional friction. However, the ESOPs did appear to reduce work stoppages for a number of years during the mid-1990s.

However, the strikes at Northwest in 1998 and the more recent difficulties experienced by US airlines in trying to hold back wage demands suggests that giving employees or their unions shares or stock options is no longer attractive enough to achieve wage concessions over the longer term. They do not provide labour with a sufficient share of the spoils. The US experience suggests that ESOPs or similar schemes buy off real wage concessions only once and then for a short time only.

5.8 The labour challenge

During the first decade of the new millennium, the spread of 'open skies' agreements and the loosening of regulatory constraints in all markets, especially when the ownership rules are relaxed or totally abandoned, together with greater alliance activity, will lead to intensified competition. A consequence of that competition will be a continued downward pressure on airline yields arising from fare wars and overcapacity. When ownership rules are relaxed there will be further structural instability as new cross-border mergers and share purchases take place, destabilising existing alliances.

Against such a background of intensified competition and market instability, all airlines will be under great pressure to keep down or even reduce their operating costs. Because labour is the largest single input cost and because average staff costs can vary significantly between airlines, controlling labour costs will inevitably be a key part of any cost minimisation strategy. But this will be made more difficult by the fact that the mergers and much strengthened alliances which are foreseen for the early years of the new millennium will bring together airlines with different levels of wages and varying work practices. Employees within alliance partner airlines and their unions will seek to ensure that the wages paid within all alliance partners match those paid by the airline with the highest wages and that the least onerous work practices are also adopted. Duane Woerth, President of the US Air Line Pilots Association, has made it very clear that his union's goal is to harmonise wages and compensations across global alliances: 'It is clear that pilot groups are willing to stand up and support other pilots such as with Northwest and KLM. We won't allow one partner to be picked on and you will see more of that' (*Airline Business*, September 1999, p. 37). An example was the formation in September 1999 of a joint organisation, the Wings cabin crew union, linking together the UNC union in the Netherlands with three Italian cabin crew unions. Cross-border trade union activity and solidarity will intensify. Preventing an upward wage drift arising from union pressure to close pay differences between alliance partners will be one key challenge for airline executives.

Perhaps the greatest challenge to be faced will be how to reconcile the growing contradiction between controlling labour costs while enhancing service quality. Intensified competition from other alliances and from low-cost carriers means that airlines will need to be more customer-focused, requiring motivated and contented staff. On the one hand airline executives will be asking their employees to work harder, to be much more flexible in the way they work and to face up to the disruptions and uncertainty created by mergers and new alliances, while at the same time accepting minimal increases or even a freeze in their salaries and more performance-related pay. Yet on the other hand, they will expect those same employees in contact with customers to be open, friendly, helpful and very conscious of each customer's individual needs. Both in cost and marketing terms, labour is the key. Successful airlines will be those that can overcome these contradictions. They will be those airlines that can effectively implement strategies to reduce labour costs while maintaining and enhancing employee support and goodwill. Not an easy task!

6 The low-cost revolution

> We went to look at Southwest. It was like the road to Damascus. This was
> the way to make Ryanair work.
>
> (Michael O'Leary, Chief Executive, Ryanair)

6.1 A new phenomenon in Europe

In the spring of 1999 a survey of 19,000 British leisure passengers produced
some astonishing results. A much higher proportion of passengers would
definitely recommend low-cost 'no-frills' carriers such as Go or easyJet
to their friends than would recommend British Airways, British Midland
or many other European scheduled airlines. The discrepancy in rankings
was particularly marked on short-haul routes. For UK domestic flights, 63
per cent of easyJet's passengers would definitely recommend this airline
while among British Airways passengers the figure dropped to only 41
per cent. For flights to France, easyJet again received a firm recommendation from 63 per cent of its passengers while the figure for Air France
was below 25 per cent. While in relation to individual factors such as leg
room, comfort, catering, cleanliness or cabin crew all the 'no-frills' airlines
were generally considered among the worst, in terms of value for money
they were rated among the best. Clearly many passengers don't mind
roughing it on short flights if the price is low enough. Moreover, they
believe their friends would welcome this too. Interestingly, the 'no-frills'
scheduled carriers were also much more highly recommended than
European charter airlines which, like them, offer low fares but *with* frills
(*Holiday Which*, 1999).

The 1999 survey highlighted the revolution which was taking place in
European scheduled air transport as the new millennium approached. While
low-cost, no-frills services in Europe had been launched by Ryanair in
1991 it was only in the period after 1995 that they spread to European
markets other than those across the Irish Sea. The fact that within four
years they were being rated so highly in passenger surveys emphasised
their success in introducing a radical rethinking in how to operate scheduled services. Their success could also be measured in terms of traffic

growth. In 1994 less than three million passengers were flying on low-cost European carriers, most of them on Ryanair. By 1999, this figure had risen to around 17.5 million. The low-cost carriers during this period experienced very much higher growth rates on intra-European services than did the traditional European scheduled airlines. Another measure of the former's early successes after 1995 can be seen in the decision by British Airways to set up its own low-cost subsidiary named 'Go', which launched several routes in May 1998 from London's Stansted airport. It was the first of the European majors to do so. KLM was next, launching Buzz, its own low-cost subsidiary also based in Stansted in January 2000. Other majors are bound to follow.

In essence, the successful innovation which these carriers introduced into Europe was the provision of easily accessible scheduled short-haul services at very low unrestricted fares close to those of charter airlines but with 'no frills', that is, without many of the traditional product features of either scheduled or charter services.

Outside Europe and the United States the low-cost phenomenon has been slow to catch on. This is largely because the domestic and short-haul international markets have been too tightly regulated. In the early 1990s an airline named Compass launched domestic low-cost low-fare services in Australia, but it collapsed after a year or two. Several years later and after further domestic liberalisation, Virgin, a British company, announced it was to launch a low-cost Australian airline modelled on Brussels-based Virgin Express. The new airline was due to be launched during 2000. On trunk routes such as Sydney–Melbourne its announced aim was to offer fares at half the level of the existing discounted ticket prices. Meanwhile in Japan attempts to operate true low-cost based on the Southwest model have been thwarted by the aviation laws which required prior government approval of all domestic fares. It was not till 1 February 2000 that this requirement was replaced by a system of merely filing fares, allowing domestic airlines to set their own fares for the first time.

The low-cost, no-frills phenomenon in Europe coincided with the period of alliance frenzy entered into by Europe's conventional scheduled carriers (see Chapter 4). It seemed to suggest that there are two possible ways of making money in the airline industry. The first is through a network approach based on hub and spoke operations. It is exemplified by the development of alliances aimed at linking hubs. The second way is through a low-cost approach for which there are two distinct models. The traditional low-cost model has been that of the charter or non-scheduled airlines which have been such a success in Europe (Doganis, 1991). But the second model introduced into Europe in the late 1990s is that of the point-to-point, low-cost, no-frills scheduled airline. But will the new low-cost model survive in Europe in the coming decade and, if it does, how significant will it be not only in terms of market share but also in terms of its impact on the traditional scheduled and charter operators?

While relatively new to Europe, the low-cost formula is not new to the United States. Since the early 1970s many new US airlines have adopted a low-cost, no-frills strategy. Few of the earlier new entrants survived, with the notable exception of Southwest Airlines. The peak of low-cost new entry was between 1993 and 1995 when ten or so low-cost carriers launched operations, though only a small handful, including Valujet (renamed Air Tran) and Western Pacific, were still flying in 1999. In Europe, executives of new start-up airlines looked at Southwest's financial success over many years of operation and tried, in many cases, to use Southwest as their model. Michael O'Leary, Chief Executive of Ryanair, was very explicit on this. He stated that after several years of losses, while operating Ryanair as a full service airline, 'We went to look at Southwest. It was like the road to Damascus. This was the way to make Ryanair work' (*Financial Times*, 8 December 1998).

6.2 The Southwest model

Southwest Airlines is unique among United States airlines. It is the only one to have been consistently profitable for the last thirty years. Yet Southwest had an inauspicious start. Set up in 1967 to operate within Texas, it could not start flying till four years later because of court battles brought by its local competitors who argued that there was not enough demand to support a new entrant. Shortly after Southwest's operations began, Braniff and Texas International set off a price war in order to drive Southwest out of the Texas market. In response, at one point Southwest dropped its fare on Dallas–Houston to \$13. It survived. The other two carriers later collapsed.

Basing itself at Love Field, only 10 km from downtown Dallas (whereas the main airport at Dallas Fort Worth International was 35 km out), Southwest concentrated on a strategy of operating short sectors offering low and unrestricted fares, high point-to-point frequencies and excellent on-time departures. It did away with the traditional scheduled frills such as meals, pre-assigned seats and connecting flights, but developed a brand image of 'flying is fun' and trained its staff to ensure that it was. This marketing strategy worked. It diverted passengers from other carriers but much of its business was newly generated. It attracted leisure and business passengers to fly rather than drive the relatively short distances between most of the cities it served. The Southwest Chairman and CEO Herb Kelleher summed up this strategy by saying 'We are not competing with other airlines, we're competing with ground transportation' (Freiberg and Freiberg, 1996).

When it entered any new market, Southwest's low fares invariably stimulated demand faster than it could add capacity, so load factors were high. If competitors responded by dropping their own fares the total market was further stimulated and all carriers were able to maintain higher passenger load factors. Invariably when Southwest, or for that matter other low-cost carriers, entered particular routes, traffic growth rates were well above average. Airports, especially smaller secondary airports, were therefore keen to attract such airlines and were willing to cut their own charges to do so.

When US domestic deregulation came in 1978 Southwest was well placed to expand beyond Texas. But it did so cautiously, avoiding the calamitous over-expansion of many of the new start-up carriers of the 1980s. It took twelve years to grow its fleet to fifty aircraft. New capacity was used to add frequencies to existing routes and only a small handful of new routes were added each year. During those twelve years it focused its route development on its traditional Southwestern and West Coast markets. It was only in the 1990s that it ventured beyond the sun belt, adding Chicago in 1990, to establish a Mid West base, and Baltimore in 1993. In 1993 it took over Morris Air, based at Salt Lake City, though it did have some problems integrating it. It expanded into Florida in 1996.

Traditionally Southwest has picked routes where no one else was operating or where it could gain a dominant market share by offering high frequencies and low fares. By July 1993, Southwest was the dominant airline in ninety-three of its top 100 markets (CAA, 1999). It avoided head-on competition with the major airlines by using secondary airports or older terminals. A more recent example was the launch of services from New York in March 1999 using MacArthur Airport in Islip on Long Island about 70 km from downtown Manhattan. Yet when Southwest has had to face up to the majors head on it has usually been successful. This happened in California after United Airlines had launched its 'shuttle' services in late 1994. At first Southwest lost market share. But, forced to offer low competitive fares the United shuttle was unable to cover its costs and subsequently withdrew or scaled down its services on many Californian routes. As a result Southwest is now the dominant carrier on the busy intra-state markets within California.

From a relatively small Texan intra-state carrier Southwest had grown by 1999 into the fifth-largest United States airline in terms of domestic passengers or sixth largest in terms of domestic passenger-kms. This steady growth over nearly thirty years was accompanied by continued profitability in every year of operations. This is a remarkable achievement since this period spans two major cyclical downturns in the early 1980s and the early 1990s. The worst crisis was the one between 1990 and 1994 (see Chapter 1). During this period all the larger United States airlines recorded substantial losses for several years. The worst performers were Continental, Trans World Airlines and USAir, which posted losses for each of six years or more. Yet throughout this period Southwest continued to be profitable. Even in 1992, the worst year, when the other nine largest airlines collectively lost $3.2 billion, Southwest was able to generate a profit of $104 million. Yet Southwest's share of the US domestic passenger market was only around 8 per cent.

Southwest's financial success is due to its ability to operate at costs which are consistently below its revenues. Its unit revenues are not much below those of other competing airlines operating on the same or similar routes. The big difference is in unit cost. Southwest's great achievement has been to operate at cost levels which are 25–40 per cent below those of its major competitors.

It is Southwest's unique service and product features which have enabled it both to generate relatively high average yields and to operate with below average costs. Undoubtedly, Southwest's key product feature is its low, unrestricted fares. When Southwest enters new markets it prices not just to compete with other airlines but also against ground transport since its aim is to divert traffic from the latter. This means pricing 60 per cent or more below prevailing air fares in these markets. For instance, when the company opened a Cleveland–Chicago route the lowest unrestricted one way fare on other carriers was $310. Southwest's was $59 one way. After Southwest launched its Florida intra-state services in 1996 it offered some advanced purchase fares as low as $29–32. Such fares inevitably diverted substantial numbers of passengers from the roads. But the yields achieved, if measured in terms of revenue per passenger-km, are relatively high because the fares are all point-to-point. There is no interlining to dilute revenue by spreading it over two or more airlines or sectors, though some of its passengers do fly two sectors on the same aircraft. Also, Southwest's average sector lengths are short, so the fares, while low in absolute terms, may be relatively high when expressed on a kilometre basis. Southwest's fares are low, simple and unrestricted, that is, there are generally no complex conditions attached to them. This makes them particularly attractive. Any discounting through special more restricted fares is limited.

Low fares are combined with high frequencies and excellent punctuality. In fact, in recent years, the airline has tended to top the Department of Transportation surveys of on-time performance, baggage handling and customer satisfaction (Nuutinen, 1998).

Southwest tries, wherever possible, to use smaller, less congested airports to serve major cities. These include Love Field in Dallas, where it has exclusive rights, Midway in Chicago, Detroit City airport, Providence for Boston instead of congested Logan International, Islip on Long Island for New York. By using these airports average flight times can be reduced by 15–20 minutes as a result of short ground taxi times, fewer delays at the aircraft gates and less congestion and circling in the air when on approach. Punctuality is also easier to maintain. The fact that Islip serves New York but is outside the congested airways in the La Guardia-Kennedy-Newark triangle is a major advantage.

The combination of all these product features has enabled Southwest to attract not only leisure traffic but also substantial volumes of business passengers for whom high frequency and punctuality are especially important. They choose Southwest despite the fact that other service elements

Table 6.1 Comparison of Boeing 737-300 operating costs, United States carriers 1998

Airline	1 Costs* per seat mile (US cents)	2 Cost index **	3 Average sector (miles)	4 Daily utilis- ation (hours)	5 Seats per aircraft
Delta	5.54	100	708	9.80	126
United	5.20	94	668	10.32	128
US Airways	5.04	91	698	10.00	126
Continental	4.28	77	1007	10.55	129
America West	3.91	71	701	11.85	131
Southwest	3.10	56	461	11.31	137

Notes
* Direct operating costs only, i.e. fuel and labour cost of flying, all maintenance costs, aircraft depreciation and rentals.
** Delta = 100.

Source: Compiled by author using *Airline Monitor* (1999).

are poor if not Spartan. There is only high-density single-class seating. Passengers may be offered fast snacks, usually of cheese and crackers or peanuts, with soft drinks or cheap alcoholic beverages. But there are definitely no meals or expensive alcoholic drinks. Equally, there is no seat assignment prior to boarding. This in turn speeds up boarding and facilitates twenty-minute turnrounds.

In order to be able to offer low fares and still achieve profitability one must operate at very low costs. Southwest clearly does this. Historically, it has had unit costs well below those of its major competitors. The best way to assess this is to compare like with like by examining the costs incurred by Southwest's competitors when operating the same short-haul aircraft. Southwest has an all Boeing 737 fleet and the mainstay has been the 737-300 aircraft, of which Southwest had over 190 in 1998. It is evident from Table 6.1 that Southwest's direct operating costs per seat-mile for this aircraft in 1998 was 20 per cent to 40 per cent below that of other major airlines, though America West's costs were also well below the average (Table 6.1, column 2). Southwest's cost advantage is actually even greater when one allows for its very short sectors (column 3), which average 461 miles. The other airlines operating this aircraft have average sectors of close to 700 miles or over. Sector distance is a major cost determinant. Direct operating costs normally decline sharply as sector distances increase from short to medium. Because of this one would actually expect Southwest's unit operating costs to be higher than those of its competitors, given its much shorter sectors. The fact that it is actually 20 per cent to 40 per cent lower is a major achievement.

How does Southwest manage this? The direct operating costs referred to in Table 6.1 cover three major expenses – flying costs, maintenance and aircraft depreciation or rentals. Flying costs are composed of two main elements, crew costs and fuel. Clearly Southwest will be paying roughly the same prices for fuel as other carriers. But its crew costs like those of America West are substantially lower than those of the major airlines because they have largely non-union labour, which is highly motivated and more productive, even though wage rates may be similar. Southwest has also benefited from a ten-year agreement signed with its pilots in 1994. In return for share options, the pilots accepted a wage freeze for five years followed by annual increases of 3 per cent (Nuutinen, 1998). In maintenance, Southwest achieves economies by having a single aircraft type in its fleet, the Boeing 737. Though it does have four variants, the bulk are Boeing 737-300. Compared to airlines that have very mixed fleets there can be substantial savings especially in maintenance overheads. A single type fleet also helps in increasing pilot productivity. Because Southwest has a young fleet, its unit depreciation costs are higher than other carriers. On the other hand it appears to get better deals on leased-in aircraft and pays substantially less per block hour for lease rentals than other carriers. Its hourly depreciation and rental costs are reduced by the fact that on average it flies its aircraft one to one and a half hours longer per day than most carriers, thus spreading fixed annual costs over more hours (Table 6.1, column 4). Southwest achieves this very high daily utilisation through scheduling fifteen- or twenty-minute turn-rounds at most of the airports it serves. This is possible because of the use of uncongested secondary airports, minimal catering, no pre-assigned seating and highly motivated staff.

The aircraft hourly costs need to be converted into costs per seat-mile. Here again Southwest gains some advantage by packing more seats into its aircraft (Table 6.1, column 5) which increases the seat-kilometres generated per block hour. In fact Southwest, partly because of lower seat pitch and partly because of reduced galley space, is able to offer nine or ten seats more than most majors flying the same aircraft. This further reduces the cost per seat.

Southwest also achieves economies in many areas of indirect operating costs because of the nature of the product it offers. The use of secondary airports whenever possible usually means that airport charges and related costs for gates and so on are lower. This is especially so where such airports want to attract new scheduled services and are very keen for Southwest to come in because they know that rapid traffic growth will follow. Productivity of ground staff is also increased by using less congested airports and by ensuring high frequency of departures at each airport. Southwest aims to have at least twenty departures per day from any airport it serves to minimise gate and staff costs.

There are savings in distribution costs too. Traditionally Southwest has done its own ticketing and has not made its seats available on Sabre,

Galileo or other global CRS systems, thus saving $3 or more per booking. It was also the first to introduce direct online booking. As a result and in contrast to the US major airlines, around half of Southwest's sales are direct, which is a very high proportion. On these sales it saves agents' commissions which are 7–10 per cent or so of the ticket price. In January 1995 it was the first major airline to introduce ticketless travel systemwide, further reducing costs. In-flight catering is not a major cost item representing 2–3 per cent of most US airlines' costs. Nevertheless, by providing minimal catering Southwest reduces the cost of this to less than 0.5 per cent of its total costs. Limited catering and single-class cabins also mean fewer cabin crew. Southwest flies its Boeing 737 with three stewards or hostesses, whereas most airlines fly this aircraft with five or six cabin crew. All of these factors reinforce the direct operating cost advantages enjoyed by Southwest and discussed earlier.

Finally, the other key factor in Southwest's success is that it has a flexible and highly motivated staff. The management goes out of its way to treat its employees well, to give them a vested interest in and a share of the success of the company and to create a 'fun' atmosphere in which to work. This is possible because Southwest has developed a work ethic and culture in which individuality, taking initiative and ownership of problems is encouraged. Having a charismatic leader in Herb Kelleher, founder, chairman and chief executive, undoubtedly helps. Under his guidance, in 1973 Southwest was the first airline to offer profit-sharing to its employees. Each year a percentage of the profits before taxes are divided among employees based on their wages. This money can also be used to buy shares in the company. In 1998, the company paid out $91 million to its staff from its 1997 profits. This was equivalent to a bonus of about 11 per cent of annual salaries.

Over 10 per cent of the shares are owned by employees. Early in 1997 *Fortune* magazine declared Southwest to be 'the best company to work for in America'. Since staff are highly motivated and work rules, where appropriate, are flexible, labour productivity is high and this further helps to reduce costs. Motivated staff create a customer-friendly environment.

The key features of the Southwest model for low-cost, no-frills scheduled air services are summarised in Table 6.2. Over the last two decades several airlines and new start-ups have tried to follow a low-cost approach either without frills, such as People Express, or with frills, such as Muse Air and Florida Express. Few survived more than four or five years. The larger airlines have also created subsidiaries to operate low-cost services but initially only with limited success. Continental Lite was one of the first unsuccessful attempts. More recently low-cost, no-frills carriers have been more successful in establishing themselves. An example is Sun Country, which has taken on Northwest Airlines in its home base of Minneapolis-St. Paul. While the United shuttle in California withdrew from several routes it has survived. Recently Southwest has been facing

Table 6.2 The Southwest airlines' low-cost, no-frills model

Product features	
Fares	Low Simple, unrestricted Point-to-point No interlining
Distribution	Travel agents *and* direct sales Ticketless
In-flight	Single-class, high-density No seat assignment No meals Snacks and light beverages only
Frequency	High
Punctuality	Very good
Operating features	
Aircraft	Single type (Boeing 737), four variants High utilisation (over 11 hours/day)
Sectors	Short to average below 800 km (500 miles)
Airports	Secondary or uncongested 15–20 minute turnrounds
Growth	Target 10 per cent per annum Maximum 15 per cent
Staff	Competitive wages Profit-sharing since 1973 High productivity

a more serious challenge in several markets from Delta Express, set up in 1996 by Delta Airlines, and especially from MetroJet, launched by US Airways in 1998 to compete head-on in numerous East Coast markets.

Delta launched Delta Express in 1996 specifically to counter Southwest's growing market share in the Florida market, which it considered to be its own backyard. The low-cost airlines were forcing Delta to retreat from traditional markets and focus on higher-yield markets. The result was a steady loss of market share in Florida, one of Delta's biggest markets. Delta Express represented a change of strategy. The aim was to fight the low-cost carriers head on. Initially this strategy appeared to be succeeding. Delta's share of the Florida market rose from 22 per cent in 1996 to 28 per cent in 1999 (Corbin, 1999). But the problem faced by companies linked to larger parents is how to prevent their costs creeping up because of this linkage, as happened with Delta Express during 1998 (*Airline Business*, February 1999). They may also face limits to their expansion because of union opposition. For instance, MetroJet's fleet size could not go beyond fifty-four aircraft because of an agreement between its parent US Airways and the Air Line Pilots Association. There are in addition independent airlines such as Frontier and AirTran Airways (the reincarnated Valujet) that have successfully adopted the Southwest model and are vigorous challengers.

Faced with these potential threats, Southwest hit back in 1997 by launching some longer-haul services of over 1,000 miles, thus abandoning its long-held short haul strategy. This was a risky move because the longer the sectors the more difficult it becomes to ensure low-costs compared to other operators. It is too early to say whether the Southwest product features will enable it to attract sufficient traffic to do well in such markets, even if its cost advantage is less marked.

By early 2000 there were a dozen or so low-cost carriers operating in the United States in addition to Southwest Airlines. The youngest was New York-Kennedy based jetBlue launched in February 2000. With the exception of Southwest, most of these airlines had done very badly in 1996 and 1997 when their conventional competitors were chalking up huge profits. By 1999, however, most were posting profits or substantially reduced losses. Traffic growth and revenues were sharply up as passengers, including business passengers, switched from the majors who were pushing up fares sharply to compensate for falling yields and rising fuel prices. In Canada, WestJet Airlines, a young but successful low-cost operator, was poised early in 2000 to benefit from the takeover by Air Canada of Canadian Airlines, since the merged airline would have to steer clear of abusing its dominant position on domestic routes. In brief, the low-cost, no-frills model has clearly become a permanent feature of North American aviation. What about Europe?

6.3 The Europeans

Low-cost airlines are a much more recent and revolutionary phenomenon in Europe. The first low-cost, no-frills European airline to have any impact was the independent Irish airline Ryanair. When launched in 1985 it targeted the Irish ethnic market between Ireland and the United Kingdom by offering a more or less traditional type of service with a two-class cabin but at significantly lower fares. It stimulated a rapid growth of passenger traffic across the Irish Sea, much of it diverted from the sea ferries. On the London–Dublin route, where traffic had been stagnant for three years, passenger numbers more or less doubled in the next three years in response to the low fares introduced by Ryanair and to the lower fares forced on Aer Lingus and British Airways. But Ryanair was not profitable. Its unit costs, though lower than those of Aer Lingus, were not low enough to sustain its low fares strategy. By 1991 its accumulated losses amounted to close on (Sterling) £18 million and the airline was facing serious cash flow problems. It had also gone through five chief executives.

After a visit to Southwest Airlines in Texas in 1991 yet another new management decided to reinforce the low-fare strategy but to abandon all frills in order to reduce costs. It also moved its London base from Luton to Stansted airport, which was new and offered high-speed access to Central London. The new strategy slowly turned the company round and it recorded a small pre-tax profit in 1992. Subsequently traffic and profits grew steadily and in summer 1997 Ryanair was successfully floated on the Dublin and New York stock exchanges. In the financial year 1997–98 alone its profits rose by 51 per cent to US$53 million. Ryanair's sparkling financial performance was an encouragement to other European entrepreneurs to assess the low-cost, no-frills model as a way of entering European aviation markets.

In January 1993 international air services within the European Union were largely deregulated as a result of the so-called third package (see Chapter 2, section 2.4). It soon became apparent that most of the denser intra-European routes continued to be operated as high-fare duopolies by the traditional flag carriers. Even where third or fourth carriers had entered such markets as on London–Paris or London–Athens the downward pressure on fares had been limited. In the mid-1990s the existence of many such markets and an awareness that the Ryanair experience clearly highlighted how low fares greatly stimulated demand pushed several new entrants to follow the Southwest model. In October 1995 and June 1996 easyJet and Debonair respectively launched intra-European low-fare services from London's fourth airport at Luton. They were followed a year later by Virgin Express at Brussels, an airline fashioned out of an earlier company, Eurobelgian Airlines. Interestingly, it was only after these low-cost international airlines were launched that Ryanair, early in 1997, expanded out of its UK–Ireland niche and launched four routes to continental Europe from Dublin and Stansted. It added seven new European routes in 1998 and another eight in 1999. Meanwhile, in May 1998, after toying with the possibility of buying into easyJet, British Airways set up its own low-cost subsidiary, Go, operating from London's third airport, Stansted. It was followed by KLM whose own low-cost subsidiary, Buzz, started flying from Stansted in January 2000. Meanwhile the launch of Go had significantly increased competition among low-cost carriers. The first casualty was Debonair. At the end of September 1999, three years after its own launch and two years after a successful flotation which raised £28.2 million (US$46.5 million), Debonair stopped flying and went into receivership. More of this later.

It is noticeable that, apart from Virgin Express in Brussels, most of the low-cost development has been in the United Kingdom. New start-up airlines were attracted by the huge London market, the light-handed regulatory environment and the entrepreneurial culture. UK costs were also lower, especially labour costs, because of substantially lower social charges than elsewhere in Europe. However, by 1999 Air One in Italy, Color Air in Norway and Air Europa in Spain were spreading low-cost travel to other markets in Europe. Others were bound to follow. In some cases they might be hybrids, like Air Europa or the Greek airline Cronos, that is, to say, charter airlines moving into regular scheduled year-round services and offering very low fares.

To place the European, scheduled, low-cost carriers in perspective one should remember that, even by the end of 1999, their combined aircraft numbers amounted to less than half of Southwest's Boeing 737 fleet. It has been estimated that whereas in 1999 close to 15 per cent of US domestic passengers flew with low-cost carriers, less than 3 per cent of international and domestic passengers within the European Union used scheduled low-cost carriers primarily to tourist destinations. However, more than a third of Intra-European international passengers travel on low-cost, low-fare charters or non-scheduled services. This highlights that some major differences exist between the US and the European markets. The first is that the charter or non-scheduled airline industry, which also provides for very low fares, is much more significant in Europe than in the United States. The second difference is that, while virtually all low-cost airlines' traffic in the United States is domestic, in Europe it is mostly international. This cross-border element may impose certain additional constraints. Finally, on some European short-haul routes such as Paris–Brussels, low-cost airlines may face serious competition from high-speed rail services.

Following closely the Southwest model, all the European low-cost carriers offer very low fares compared to those previously prevailing. In the case of easyJet its policy is to set its highest fare at less than half its competitors' full economy fare and its lowest fare at around 20 per cent of the economy fare. In Europe the full economy fare on most routes is the Eurobudget fare. The impact of the low-cost new entrants on fares can be gauged from the London–Barcelona route in mid-March 1998 (Table 6.3). It is evident that Air Europa's, easyJet's and Debonair's lowest fares were around half or less of the cheapest fares offered by British Airways. Iberia's fares were close to those of British Airways. While Air Europa actually had the lowest fare at £80 return, it was restricted in that it both involved advance purchase and it had to be a return fare. Debonair's lowest fares were also only available as return fares. In contrast, easyJet's fares were also very low but could be bought as single, one-way fares, as could some of Debonair's. easyJet's lowest fare for a round trip £98 was close to 20 per cent of British Airways Eurobudget fare, while its highest fare, £198, was just 40 per cent of the latter. But all easyJet fares were available as one-way fares at half the price. The major innovation

Table 6.3 Impact of low-cost carriers on London–Barcelona return fares, March 1998 (Sterling)

BA fare type	British Airways	Low-cost airlines		
		Air Europa	*Debonair*	*easyJet*
Also available one way				
Club	£554			
Eurobudget	£498	£220	£138–258	£98–198
Return fares only				
Excursion	£392			
Pex	£233–311	£146		
SuperPex	£190–269	£120		
Apex		£80	£83–128	

Note
Air Europa fares higher in Summer 1998. Air Europa withdrew its services later in 1998 and Debonair collapsed in September 1999.

Source: Compiled by author using CAA (1998) data.

in airline pricing introduced by the low-cost operators was not only the very low level of fares but the availability of such fares on a one-way single basis and with no or only minimal restrictions. Previously, all the lowest fares offered by the conventional scheduled airlines were beset by restrictions such as the need to stay a Saturday night or to purchase in advance.

British Airways' initial response to the challenge of low-cost new entrants was not to try and fully match their lowest fares. In time, however, it changed its tactics. Not only did its own low fares move much further down but it also set up Go, its own low-cost carrier. As a result, by summer 2000, BA was offering a £169 return fare London to Barcelona, which required a Saturday night stay. This was close to Go's return fare of £130 and easyJet's fares which ranged from £100 to £120 return depending on time of departure. (Fares as quoted in April 2000 for mid-week June departure with return on Sunday. They exclude taxes.)

In many other markets too, the established flag carriers have been forced to introduce some very low fares though with restrictions and limited availability. Thus, in summer 1999 Virgin Express's single fares on Brussels–Milan ranged from US$68–132, Alitalia's prices ranged from US$76 to US$474 and Sabena's from US$96 to $474 (Godfrey, 1999). But the lowest fares offered by Alitalia and Sabena, though close to those of Virgin Express, generally had more restrictive conditions and the number of seats available at these fares were very limited. On the UK–Ireland market, Aer Lingus at first tried matching Ryanair's lowest fares, but ended up losing money. Aer Lingus's current strategy is to price its tickets about Sterling £10 to £15 higher than Ryanair's comparable fares, believing that passengers are prepared to pay this differential for the much better in-flight service and, in the case of London routes, for flying into or out of Heathrow.

As in the United States, the new entrants' low fares have stimulated demand and generated higher traffic growth than in other markets. It is the low-cost carriers that have captured much of this growth. The London–Barcelona market had seen only limited growth in passenger numbers during the three years 1994 to 1996. Late in 1995 Air Europa started serving Gatwick–Barcelona and in summer 1996 easyJet and Debonair launched services from Luton. The effect was dramatic. In 1996 total London–Barcelona traffic grew 25 per cent, well above growth rates in other UK–Europe markets. But all of this growth of about 150,000 extra passengers was carried on low-cost carriers serving Luton and Gatwick. There was no growth at Heathrow. In 1997 total traffic grew by a further 27 per cent, again most of it carried by the low-cost carriers. But during that year British Airways, by lowering its own fares and launching new services from Gatwick as Air Europa pulled out, had also shown good growth. In 1998 growth slowed down to 14 per cent but was still well above the average for European scheduled routes from London. In fact traffic on London–Barcelona almost doubled in three years from half a million passengers in 1995 to almost a million in 1998. The low-cost airlines' share of the total London–Barcelona market in 1998 reached around 25 per cent.

The same impact was felt in other markets too, even on domestic ones such as on the London–Glasgow route. Here the entry of Ryanair (Stansted–Prestwick) and easyJet (Luton–Glasgow) with low unrestricted fares pushed traffic up by 21 per cent in the first twelve months while UK domestic traffic as a whole grew only 10 per cent in that period (CAA, 1998). Ryanair's impact on routes to Dublin from UK regional airports was even more dramatic. Annual traffic on Birmingham–Dublin had dropped from nearly 200,000 passengers in 1990 to below 150,000 in 1993. Ryanair entered the market in 1994 and within three years traffic was close to 600,000 per annum. Similarly, Manchester–Dublin traffic shot up from 230,000 to just over 600,000 in three years. Clearly, as in the United States, the low-cost carriers are largely generating new traffic rather than robbing existing carriers of their passengers. However, it is noticeable that after three or so years of very rapid growth as low fares generate new demand, growth rates tend to fall sharply. This happened in 1998 on both the Manchester–Dublin and Birmingham–Dublin routes.

Despite their relatively poor in-flight services and the use of less accessible secondary airports, the low-cost carriers are attracting business as well as leisure passengers. On the London–Glasgow sector in 1996, 44 per cent of easyJet's passengers were travelling on business, while 28 per cent of Ryanair's traffic was for business. Though lower than the average for all London–Glasgow carriers, which is 55 per cent, easyJet's and Ryanair's figures show significant penetration into the business market.

On London–Barcelona, 10 per cent of easyJet and Debonair passengers are UK business travellers compared to 19 per cent for all carriers in this market (CAA, 1998).

In terms of the in-flight product there is some diversity among European carriers. Ryanair, easyJet and Go do not offer any complimentary drinks or catering or in-flight entertainment. But snacks, sandwiches and drinks are available for purchase at fair prices. They have a single-class high-density cabin. Debonair had business class as well as economy on most of its routes and offered some catering and free in-flight entertainment. Virgin is in a unique position because on five of its busiest routes out of Brussels, those to Heathrow, Gatwick, Stansted, Barcelona and Rome, it code shares its flights with Sabena which has withdrawn from these routes. Sabena buys about half the seats on these flights on a firm block seat basis and at a fixed price and requires a two-class cabin and in-flight catering. In theory, Virgin Express does not provide free catering or drinks for its own passengers on these or its other flights. The Sabena link means Virgin Express also provides pre-boarding seat assignment for business class passengers but not for others. Go offers its passengers pre-assigned seats, as did Debonair. Only easyJet and Ryanair have totally free seating.

In some respects the European carriers have gone even further in simplifying their products and reducing costs than Southwest Airlines in the United States. Like the latter, Go and easyJet are completely ticketless. Bookings and payments are made by phone or on the Internet. Customers only need to show their booking reference and/or passport at the check-in desk to receive their boarding pass. But, unlike Southwest, these two airlines have cut out travel agents completely. Passengers can only book directly with the airlines. Ryanair has continued to use travel agents, as did Debonair. Until 1997 around 70 per cent of Ryanair sales were through agents though this figure has been dropping. Virgin is again in an anomalous position because its code-shared flights with Sabena necessitate the use of both agents and tickets. Around 60–65 per cent of its sales are through agents. Where airlines do not use travel agents to generate sales, they have to spend proportionately more on advertising, as do Go and easyJet. But the additional expenditure on advertising is a lot less than the money saved from not having to pay agents' commission of 9–10 per cent.

The link-up with Sabena also makes Virgin Express different from its counterparts in another respect. Both Virgin and Sabena encourage passengers to interline to or from other Sabena services at the Brussels hub, especially Sabena's long-haul services. This means extra handling and other costs and creates potential for delays. Virgin also encourages online transfers between its own services at Brussels. In 1999 around 45 per cent of Virgin Express's traffic connected at Brussels. The other carriers, however, offer no interlining with other carriers and avoid transfers between their own flights. Their focus is very much on point-to-point single sector traffic.

All low-cost carriers have focused on a single aircraft type. In most cases this is one of the Boeing 737 series, though Debonair used the British Aerospace 146. Early in 1999 Debonair leased two Boeing 737-300s for the London–Barcelona route, thereby introducing a second type into its fleet. In all cases the seating density is higher than that of traditional scheduled airlines. This has been achieved by reducing the seat pitch, that is, the distance between the seats, and, for most of the airlines, by doing away with business class. Seat pitch is generally 29 or 30 inches, though Ryanair's seat pitch in its Boeing 737-200s is 32 inches. Here too Debonair, which did not survive, bucked the trend among low-cost airlines by offering 33-inch seat pitch and also a separate business class.

All carriers try to combine low fares with the high frequencies which are attractive for the business market. Thus, even on their thinner routes they aim to develop rapidly to three services daily. This helps to reduce their airport and related costs at the other end of the route. Higher frequencies and short turnrounds, ideally the target is thirty minutes or less, mean that daily aircraft utilisation can be pushed well above the levels achieved by their conventional scheduled competitors.

In order to achieve quick turnrounds and also to benefit from lower airport charges, all the carriers with one exception have based themselves at secondary and less congested airports and fly, as far as possible, to similar airports at the other end of their routes. Debonair and easyJet set themselves up in 1995 at Luton where they were given extremely favourable deals on airport charges and rentals. Ryanair got very good deals at Dublin airport and at Stansted when it moved its flights from Luton. The exception is Virgin Express, based at Brussels main airport Zaventem, which was relatively uncongested but not low-cost. Because they generate so much new scheduled traffic the low-cost airlines are very attractive to smaller airports and as a result can demand extremely low landing and other fees. The smaller and more unknown the airport the greater the concessions that can be extracted from its management. Both easyJet and Ryanair are masters at this. Since 1997 Ryanair has persuaded IATA to redesignate the unknown airports of Beauvais, Charleroi, Hahn, Torp and Nykoking respectively under the Paris, Brussels, Frankfurt, Oslo and Stockholm city codes, despite the fact that they were some distance from these cities. Ryanair was then able to obtain major concessions from these airports. But it also has to provide bus services to the city centres for its passengers. By using secondary airports, Ryanair has followed closely the Southwest approach. On the other hand, easyJet, while based at Luton, has tended to fly to established large or regional airports such as Amsterdam, Nice, Palma, Zurich, Geneva or Athens. Go has done the same from Stansted. However, easyJet does negotiate very advantageous deals with airport and handling authorities.

In terms of motivating employees and giving them a sense of involvement in the business as well as a share in its success, the Europeans have
generally not followed the Southwest approach too closely. Ryanair offered
2.1 per cent of its shares to employees when it was floated in 1997.
Ryanair, easyJet and others offer their employees productivity-based pay
incentives. In fact, for certain categories of staff, most of their pay is
productivity-related. Employees in easyJet's reservations call centre receive
no basic pay only a commission of 80 pence (about US$1.30) per flight
booking made. In Ryanair during the fiscal year 1996–97 productivity-
based pay incentives accounted for approximately two-thirds of an average
flight attendant's total pay package and about one-third of a typical pilot's
salary (Ryanair, 1997). The focus on performance-related incentives
undoubtedly increases labour productivity and reduces costs. But it is not
clear that this in itself is sufficient in creating an in-house company culture
of working together as a family in an enjoyable and egalitarian environment where all employees are valued and are encouraged to be innovative
and to be themselves and where all have a share in the company's success
and profits.

To summarise: the new low-cost European airlines are, with some variations, very similar to Southwest in terms of their key product features.
They offer high-frequency, scheduled, point-to-point short-haul services.
In order to offer very low simple fares they operate at very low-costs. To
ensure low-costs, they operate a single aircraft type with high-density
seating and aim at high daily utilisation by reducing turnrounds to thirty
minutes or less. They use secondary and less congested airports to reduce
airport related costs and to facilitate short turnrounds and high punctuality. Generally there is no free in-flight catering or entertainment and no
pre-assigned seating, though some Virgin Express flights are an exception. easyJet and Go have gone a step further than Southwest and have
completely cut out the travel agents. They only sell direct to their
customers.

Given these product features, can European low-cost operators achieve
a sustainable cost advantage compared to their conventional competitors
and how great is any such cost advantage?

6.4 A sustainable cost advantage

The paucity of statistical data makes it quite difficult to appreciate how
significant is the cost advantage enjoyed by the European low-cost, no-
frills carriers. While detailed aggregated cost data is available for Europe's
conventional scheduled airlines, such data covers all their services
including those on long-haul routes. It is virtually impossible to isolate
their true costs for short-haul intra-European routes similar to those served
by low-cost carriers. One can overcome this difficulty by focusing any
comparison on those conventional scheduled airlines that only operate

short-haul services. In the UK in 1998 two such airlines, British Midland and KLM UK, were comparable in many ways to, say, easyJet in the nature of their operations.

Like easyJet both these carriers operated smaller twin jets with on average less than 150 seats, though KLM UK also flew fourteen turbo-prop ATRs and Fokker 50s (Table 6.4). They both operated primarily short-haul domestic and intra-European scheduled services, though almost one-quarter of British Midland's flights were on charter services. In fact, their average sector distances are significantly shorter. While easyJet's average sector in 1998 was 764 km, British Midland's was 529 km and KLM UK's 472 km. However, there was enormous disparity in unit costs when measured in terms of total operating costs per seat-km. easyJet's unit cost was 58 per cent lower than British Midland's and close to 50 per cent below that of KLM UK. One would expect the costs of these two conventional airlines to be higher because their average sector distances were appreciably shorter than those of easyJet. However, the difference in unit costs is much too high to be due to this factor alone. Moreover, at that time KLM UK and British Midland were both much larger than easyJet. The latter was relatively small, with a total fleet of only nine aircraft and total output one-third of that of British Midland (Table 6.4). So both KLM UK and British Midland should have benefited

Table 6.4 UK conventional and low-cost scheduled airlines compared, 1998

1998*	British Midland conventional	KLM UK conventional	easyJet low-cost
Total seat-kms available (million)	5,485	3,642	1,800
Average sector length (km)	529	472	764
Average aircraft size (seats)	122	91	148
Passenger load factor (%)	67.1	58.7	69.2
Fleet composition	4 Airbus 321 7 Boeing 737–300 5 Boeing 737-400 12 Boeing 737-500 6 Fokker 100 3 Fokker 70	5 ATR-72 10 Bae-146 17 Fokker 100 9 Fokker 50	9 Boeing 737-300
Cost per seat-km	9.86 pence	8.60 pence	4.19 pence
Cost index: BM = 100	100	87	42

Note
* Data is for financial year ending 31 December 1998 for British Midland; 31 March 1999 for KLM UK and 30 September 1998 for easyJet.

Source: Compiled by author using airline reports and CAA data.

from some economies of scale to partially offset their shorter sectors. British Midland's costs would have also been depressed because 25 per cent of its output was on charter flights. Interestingly, Go's unit costs in its first year 1998–99 were around 4.00 pence per seat-km, but according to Barbara Cassani, the CEO, they were due to fall 13 per cent in the year 1999–2000 (Cassani, 1999). This would bring them down to around 3.50 pence per seat-km or well below easyJet's level in 1998. On the other hand, Debonair's costs per seat-km in the financial year 1997–98 were around 4.29 pence, which, though much lower than conventional carriers, was still higher than that of easyJet (Debonair, 1998). It was a contributory factor in its subsequent demise.

In order to establish how low-cost carriers such as easyJet or Go can achieve unit costs which may be as much as 60 per cent or so below those of more conventional scheduled airlines a more disaggregate cost comparison is needed. British Midland provides the most comparable benchmark. It is a relatively small conventional scheduled European short-haul carrier whose network and operations are most similar to those of Europe's low-cost carriers. It provides a relatively close match in terms of type and size of aircraft used as well as types of routes and sector distances operated. It has proved possible to compare easyJet's costs in the year to September 1998 with those of British Midland in the year to December 1998.

Low-cost airlines start with two initial cost advantages arising from the very nature of their operations, namely, *higher seating density* and *higher daily aircraft utilisation.* By doing away with business class, by reducing or removing galleys and by reducing the seat pitch, that is, the distance between seats, low-cost carriers can significantly increase the number of seats available for sale in their aircraft. Low-cost carriers may use 28- or 29-inch seat pitch compared to the 31–33 inches used by conventional airlines. On its Boeing 737-300 aircraft, easyJet packs in 148 seats. British Midland has 132 seats in the same aircraft. But its six-abreast seating is converted to five abreast to cater for business class. A seat is lost for every row of business-class seating. Though at peak times up to seven-teen rows can be converted in this way, a more average configuration would be for eight business-class rows. This reduces British Midland's average seat capacity on its Boeing 737-300 aircraft from 132 to 124 compared to easyJet's 148. If all their operating costs were similar, the fact that easyJet has twenty-four more seats in the aircraft would result in its cost per seat-km being 16 per cent lower than British Midland's when operating identical aircraft. This cost advantage, arising from higher seating density, is similar to that enjoyed by the other low-cost model, that of the charter airlines.

The use of secondary airports where possible, the reduced cleaning time required because there is no free catering, more rapid embarkation as a result of free seating and the absence of freight to load or off-load enables low-cost carriers to schedule for and achieve faster turnround of their aircraft. This in turn helps them to push up the daily utilisation achieved by their aircraft. Thus, in 1998 while easyJet flew its Boeing 737-300 aircraft on average for 10.7 block hours per day, British Midland managed only 8.4 hours for the same aircraft and British Airways even less, only 7.1 hours. In brief, easyJet was getting 27 per cent more flying out of its aircraft than British Midland. Or, in other words, each easyJet aircraft flew each day at least two one-hour sectors more than its conventional airline counterparts. All those costs which are fixed annual costs and are largely unaffected by the amount of flying done are spread over more flights and therefore the cost per seat-km is reduced. Depreciation, insurance, maintenance overheads and general administration costs clearly fall into this category. But some other costs too maybe reduced. For instance, cabin and flight crew costs may be lower per seat-km since staff achieve higher productivity because shorter turnrounds mean they do more flying per duty period.

At a disaggregate level, the lower unit costs of easyJet as opposed to those of the conventional scheduled airline are due in part to easyJet's higher seating density and better aircraft utilisation. This should be borne in mind in the comparison of the detailed cost data which follows comparing British Midland and easyJet costs in 1997–98 (Table 6.5).

Direct operating costs are all those costs which are dependent on the type of aircraft being flown. An examination of these costs in the top half of Table 6.5 suggests that the low-cost airlines enjoy marked cost advantages in four areas.

easyJet's unit costs of flight and cabin crew are over 50 per cent lower. As in other cost areas this is partly because of the higher seating density and the higher aircraft utilisation achieved. But in addition low-cost carriers use fewer cabin crew because there are no meals or snacks to serve. While easyJet will normally have three cabin crew on a Boeing 737-300, British Midland will have four or five. Basic salaries may also be lower for both pilots and cabin staff on low-cost carriers, especially when there is a high proportion of new and young staff. The low-cost carriers will also save expenses by not night-stopping away from base. Yet the conventional carriers such as British Airways, British Midland or Sabena invariably night-stop their last evening flight out of their base at most destinations. This is in order to get an early morning departure from the destination to attract business traffic.

As one might expect, there is a more significant saving in airport charges, that is, aircraft landing fees and passenger-related charges (Table 6.5, line 3). easyJet's airport charges per seat-km are about half those of British Midland. This is because it has negotiated very low rates as a new start-up carrier at its Luton base and as well as at its foreign destinations, which are generally major airports. Ryanair, by focusing all its network on small secondary airports, makes even greater savings in this area. According to

Table 6.5 Cost comparison: low-cost easyJet and conventional short-haul airline British Midland, 1998

Cost category	easyJet (pence per seat-km)	British Midland (pence per seat-km)	(%)
Direct operating costs			
1 Cabin/flight crew salaries and expenses	0.43	0.92	9.4
2 Fuel	0.35	0.55	5.6
3 Airport charges	0.55	1.20	12.1
4 En-route	0.39	0.41	4.1
5 Maintenance	0.58	0.75	7.6
6 Depreciation	0.02	0.26	2.6
7 Aircraft rentals	0.80	1.23	12.4
8 Insurance	–	0.02	0.2
Total direct	3.14	5.34	54.2
Indirect operating costs			
9 Station costs	0.01	1.36	13.8
10 Handling	0.31	0.40	4.1
11 Passenger services	0.04	0.63	6.4
12 Sales/reservations	0.18	0.47	4.7
13 Commission	0.01	0.78	7.9
14 Advertising/promotion	0.27	0.31	3.1
15 General and administration	0.17	0.44	4.4
16 Other	0.06	0.14	1.4
Total indirect	1.05	4.52	45.8
Total operating costs	4.19	9.86	100.0

Note
British Midland data for year ending 31 December 1998 and easyJet year ending 30 September 1998.

Source: Compiled by author using CAA data.

a Civil Aviation Authority analysis, Ryanair's airport charges per passenger are only one-third those of British Midland (CAA, 1998). Because on short-haul sectors in Europe airport charges can represent 10–13 per cent of an airline's total operating costs, then reducing such charges by half or more can cut overall costs by 6–7 per cent or so. However, is this cost differential sustainable in the longer run? The large discounts on airport charges offered to European low-cost carriers as start-ups opening new routes in the period 1995–99 may begin to unwind if the initial agreements were short-term (two to four years) and come up for renewal. Where secondary airports, especially those with minimal scheduled services, have been used it should be possible to renew airport charges agreements on very favourable terms. Ryanair is well placed in this respect. Where major airports are being served by low-cost carriers, the latter may be unable to obtain quite as favourable terms in the future. Thus, the sustainable cost saving in the longer term may be less than the 6–7 per cent enjoyed initially.

Another direct operating cost which appears to offer some cost saving is maintenance cost, where again the saving seems to be around 25 per cent (Table 6.5, line 5). It is likely that this is due to two factors. First, the decision of low-cost carriers to get the lowest possible costs by outsourcing most of their maintenance requirements and in some cases even their line maintenance. They have no top-heavy maintenance administration nor costly hangars and maintenance facilities of their own. Second, they keep their facilities and spare parts costs to a minimum by operating a single aircraft type. Compare easyJet's all Boeing 737-300 fleet with British Midland's fleet in 1998 which comprised thirty-seven aircraft of seven different types, though three of the types were variants of the Boeing 737 family with much commonality.

Surprisingly, easyJet's aircraft ownership costs, that is, depreciation plus lease rentals, are around 45 per cent lower than those of British Midland (Table 6.5, lines 6 and 7). easyJet's depreciation costs are negligible since all aircraft were leased. But British Midland has very much higher aircraft lease or rental costs per seat-km than easyJet. Since rentals are fixed annual costs, most of the difference is due to easyJet's higher aircraft utilisation and higher seating density.

From an examination of Table 6.5 it is clear that there are three areas of direct costs in which low-cost operators are unlikely to enjoy any marked advantages, namely, in fuel costs, en-route charges and insurance. Airlines pay very similar prices for aviation fuel. Though larger airlines may be able to negotiate marginally lower rates because of the larger volumes uplifted the price differences are small. But there are marked variations in fuel prices between airports. So the higher fuel cost per seat-km paid by British Midland is likely to be a function of the airports it serves and the lower seating density on its aircraft. En-route charges for using air navigation facilities are non-negotiable. All airlines on a route flying the same aircraft will pay similar charges. As with fuel the only cost advantage arises from low-cost carriers' higher seating density. The same is broadly true in relation to the unit costs of insurance, though these are further reduced by higher aircraft utilisation. Overall, easyJet's direct operating costs are about 60 per cent those of British Midland. In practice, low-cost carriers achieve their most dramatic and sustainable savings in most categories of *indirect operating costs* (bottom half of Table 6.5). These are mainly handling and marketing related costs which are independent of the type of aircraft used.

A huge saving can be achieved in so-called station costs, that is, the costs associated with providing ground staff, check-in staff, equipment, business lounges, office space and related facilities at each of the airports served by an airline. While conventional airlines maintain significant numbers of staff and equipment and may rent considerable space for business lounges and offices, especially at their base airport(s), low-cost carriers do away with much of this expenditure by outsourcing most of their passenger and aircraft handling and maintaining only very minimal numbers of their own staff. Where they need to rent space they negotiate very low rentals or at small secondary airports they may pay no rent at all. As Southwest does in the United States, they argue that their entry onto a route generates so much new traffic that smaller airports have much to gain by offering them free or very cheap space. And, of course, they do not need business lounges at all. For conventional short-haul operators such as British Midland, station costs represent around 11–15 per cent of total operating costs (Table 6.5, line 9) while easyJet has negligible costs in this area. On the other hand, the latter's handling costs, that is, the fees paid to other agencies for providing check-in services and passenger and aircraft handling are not much lower than the unit handling costs of British Midland which also outsources handling at some airports (Table 6.5, line 10). The small difference in unit handling costs between the two airlines is largely the effect of easyJet's somewhat longer sector distances and higher seating density.

Another area of major cost savings for low-cost carriers is that of passenger services which include the cost of meals, drinks and other services furnished to passengers as part of the fare as well as meals or accommodation for transit or delayed passengers. Since airlines such as easyJet or Go do not offer any free meals or drinks on board, but only a trolley from which passengers can buy drinks or light snacks, their passenger service costs are negligible and are in any case partly or fully covered by the revenue generated. Also, since they offer only point-to-point services they do not have to cater for transfer or transit passengers or their baggage. Virgin Express is an exception in that it does generate traffic connecting via its Brussels hub. For conventional short-haul airlines, passenger service costs represent 6–7 per cent of total operating costs. Low-cost operators can escape most of these costs (Table 6.5, line 11).

This is also true with cost of sales especially commissions paid to agents. Go and easyJet only sell direct and do not use travel agents at all (Table 6.5, line 13). They thereby save virtually all the commission payments paid by conventional airlines which average around 8 per cent of operating costs. Those low-cost carriers, such as Ryanair, that continue to sell through agents do not make comparable savings. But like the other low-cost carriers they do save on other sales and reservation costs by not setting up their own sales offices using expensive locations in the towns they serve and by not placing their seats through the global computer reservation systems, such as Sabre or Galileo, which charge a fixed fee of US$3 or more per booking made. Low-cost carriers have simplified the whole process of reservation and ticketing and, as a result, make substantial economies. If they offer ticketless travel, as Go and easyJet do, then they save money on printing tickets and on collecting and checking them. Since low-cost carriers only sell point-to-point on their own services and do not issue for, or receive tickets from, other airlines for interline transfers, passenger revenue accounting is greatly simplified and can be almost totally computerised. On a normal scheduled airline each ticket may be manually handled up to 13–15 times as it goes from issuing office to check-in and on to various stages of revenue accounting. A low-cost carrier may be completely ticketless with all revenue accounting done on computers or even if it uses tickets fewer people are required to process them. Thus, in 1999 while low-cost Virgin Express had five staff in revenue accounting, the conventional airline Virgin Atlantic had 115. Yet both airlines carried roughly the same number of passengers (Godfrey, 1999).

Moreover, low-cost carriers, easyJet in particular, have generally been among the first airlines to develop and actively encourage Internet sales, thereby further reducing sales costs. easyJet introduced Internet sales in the autumn of 1998. A year later they were over 30 per cent of total sales and had hit over 50 per cent during some promotional campaigns. easyJet also keeps its reservation costs low by paying its reservation staff purely on a commission basis. As previously mentioned, it pays them 80 UK pence (US$1.30) per booking made. As a result of all these savings, easyJet's sales and reservation costs are less than half those of British Midland (Table 6.5, line 12).

To offset the absence of travel agents as a selling tool, low-cost carriers tend to be more dependent on advertising. easyJet, Go, Ryanair and Virgin Express tend to advertise heavily especially in the press. However, when easyJet advertising expenditure is converted into a cost per seat-km it is slightly lower than that of British Midland. This may well be because as a smaller airline with a more restricted geographical spread, easyJet can more easily focus and target its advertising spend. It has also become very successful in generating a great deal of free advertising including two prime time UK television series made about the airline in 1998 and 1999. Nevertheless, with growing competition among low-cost carriers themselves, high advertising spend is likely to continue, though they will enjoy some economies of scale in advertising spend as their networks expand. However, low-cost carriers are unlikely to enjoy a cost advantage in this area.

Finally, by their very nature low-cost carriers are likely to have a smaller, tighter central administration partly because they outsource many activities and partly because as new start-ups they do not carry any of the administrative accretions that old established conventional airlines are burdened with. For instance they do not have large numbers of planning and other staff dealing with IATA issues or bilateral air services negotiations. Their small size and flexible staff also mean that in many areas one person will be undertaking two or three functions which in a conventional airline may

Table 6.6 Cost advantages of low-cost carriers on short-haul routes

Carrier type	Cost reduction (%)	Cost per seat
Conventional scheduled carrier		100
Low-cost carrier		
Operating advantages:		
Higher seating density	−16	84
Higher aircraft utilisation	−3	81
Lower flight and cabin crew salaries/expenses	−3	78
Use cheaper secondary airports	−6	72
Outsourcing maintenance/single aircraft type	−2	70
Product/service features:		
Minimal station costs and outsourced handling	−10	60
No free in-flight catering	−6	54
Marketing differences:		
No agents' commissions*	−8	46
Reduced sales/reservation costs	−3	43
Other advantages: Smaller administration costs	−2	41

Note
* Assumes 100 per cent direct sales and none through agents.

require two or three separate people or even departments. Low-cost carriers would expect to achieve administrative costs per seat-km which are half or less than those of their conventional competitors. In the search for lower costs, low-cost airlines can operate more or less as virtual airlines outsourcing most of the non-core functions to the cheapest suppliers. For instance, in the case of Go, only flight and cabin crew, flight operations and the UK call centre are provided in-house. All other functions are outsourced. These include passenger check-in and ramp handling, all maintenance, the European call centre, the reservations system and the Internet website (Cassani, 1999).

Following a detailed assessment of the data on which the cost comparison of British Midland and easyJet was based as well as a review of other similar studies, it is possible to identify where low-cost carriers can continue to enjoy sustainable cost advantages. The results are shown in cascade form in Table 6.6. This aims to show how and where low-cost carriers' costs per seat can be reduced on a sustainable basis when compared to those of a conventional airline operating on the same or similar routes.

It is clear from the cascade analysis that the low-cost airlines should be able to maintain cost levels per seat available which are around 40–45 per cent of those of conventional airlines operating on the same or parallel routes. The UK Civil Aviation Authority, using a different and less detailed approach, came to a figure of 48 per cent per passenger (CAA, 1998). Our cost analysis has been made on a per seat basis. It assumes that achieved passenger load factors on such routes are broadly similar for conventional and low-cost carriers. In 1998 British Midland and easyJet did achieve very similar passenger load factors, though the latter's was 2.1 per cent higher. If low-cost carriers do manage to achieve markedly higher passenger load factors than conventional competitors, then the cost advantage per seat identified in Table 6.6 would be further magnified when converted into a cost per passenger.

Two reservations arise in relation to what is sustainable. First, can low-cost carriers continue to enjoy much lower airport charges or will the special rates they achieved as start-ups gradually unwind until they end up paying the same rates as the conventional carriers? The assumption made in Table 6.6 is that this will not happen if they use a small regional or secondary airport at least at one end of the route, or have entered into long-term agreements on airport charges. Ryanair is well placed in this respect. However, this cost advantage will be eroded over time if low-cost carriers operate into airports such as Amsterdam, Geneva or Rome. When runway capacity at such airports is largely used up the airport managers will have no interest in selling it cheaply.

Second, as low-cost carriers get larger and more established, with fleets of 40–50 jet aircraft, will wage rates begin to rise while labour productivity declines and will they too become top heavy with high central and administrative costs? Will their suppliers and contractors, to whom they outsource functions such as aircraft maintenance, try to push up their own prices once they see the low-cost carriers are more profitable and larger? Clearly there will be strong upward pressures on costs once they are no longer considered as start-ups. But the experience of Southwest in the United States and that of Ryanair since 1991 suggests that costs can be controlled. Significantly lower costs are sustainable. Low-cost airlines must ensure that they maintain their 50 per cent or so cost advantage or they may not survive.

6.5 Revenue advantages

It is the very low unit costs that enable the low-cost airlines to offer such very low fares (see Table 6.3). These fares attract passengers from other conventional airlines and from surface modes, but above all they generate entirely new business encouraging people to undertake trips they had not made before or to make certain trips more often. The ability to book very cheap one-way fares, a facility not available on conventional airlines, makes travel with low-cost carriers especially attractive.

However, to break even at the very low fares initially marketed low-cost carriers would need to achieve very high load factors year round.

This is virtually impossible when offering relatively high daily frequencies on a scheduled basis. Daily and seasonal variations in demand mean that passenger load factors fluctuate. Low-cost carriers, like other scheduled carriers need to practise yield management to try and maximise the revenue generated per flight.

Low-cost airlines can apply revenue management more easily and simply than the conventional carriers because, with rare exceptions, such as Virgin Express, they only sell point-to-point single sector tickets. As a result they do not face yield assessment problems arising from multi-sector tickets and from tickets sold in a wide range of different currencies and different values. Instead of having twelve to twenty-four different booking classes low-cost carriers can manage with four to six to reflect the separate fares they may offer on any individual route. This makes effective yield management easier and cheaper to implement. This is especially so if only one ticket price is available at any one time for each flight. This is easyJet's practice, and further simplifies yield and revenue management. The marketing strategy is to start selling the cheapest advertised fares when bookings for flights open and then to progressively move to higher fares as departure dates approach or as sales at the lower fares pass certain pre-planned levels. During peak periods relatively few seats on a flight may be available at the lowest published fare. The overall aim is to maximise the revenue per flight. In this process effective yield management ensures that average yield per passenger on most flights is well above the level of the lowest fare. easyJet's fare changes and yield management in response to booking patterns for its services in November 1999 on the London–Zurich route are shown in Table 6.7. Out of the fares shown, only one was available for each flight at any one time, changed week by week as the departure date approached or in response to rising sales (i.e. demand). This was particularly true for the fare on the last flight on Sunday from Zurich, which went up week by week. Other fares for less popular flight times remained low and constant for much of the time and only rose a week or two before departure.

The benefits of a relatively straightforward yield management system in ensuring good yields is reinforced by the absence of yield dilution from multi-sector tickets and interline passengers. For instance, on a sector such as London (Luton) to Amsterdam easyJet collects the full published fare at which each ticket has been sold. But KLM on this sector will be carrying a significant proportion of passengers transferring to other KLM flights at Schiphol or even to another airline. Because of the way multi-sector tickets are pro-rated for each sector flown, KLM may receive much less per transfer passenger on the London–Amsterdam sector than it collects from a local point-to-point passenger. Such revenue dilution can significantly reduce the average yield per passenger on many short-haul sectors, serving major hubs. Low-cost airlines do not face such revenue dilution. Nor, as

Table 6.7 EasyJet's yield management: London–Zurich case, October to
November 1999

Flight departure time	Date of fare quotation on Internet				
	2 Oct (£)	9 Oct (£)	16 Oct (£)	23 Oct (£)	30 Oct (£)
To Zurich Friday 5 Nov 1999					
Dep. 08.30	19	19	19	29	34
Dep. 13.15	19	29	34	39	49
Dep. 18.20	29	29	29	34	49
From Zurich Sunday 7 Nov 1999					
Dep. 06.55	19	19	19	19	34
Dep. 11.50	19	19	29	34	49
Dep. 16.15	39	44	49	59	59

Notes
One-way fares quoted on easyJet website changed week by week as departure date
approached.
Fares did not include taxes which were about £15 for a round trip.

previously mentioned, do they lose revenue through commissions to agents
if they sell all or most of their seats direct to passengers without using
any agents.

The major revenue advantage enjoyed by low-cost airlines is that where
they sell direct to the public without using agents, passengers must pay
by credit card when they make the booking. They cannot make a reservation without paying. This means that airlines, such as Go or easyJet
who sell only direct, generate all their cash revenue before flights are
made. This contrasts with their conventional competitors who selling
through various agencies world-wide may not receive all the payments
for individual flights until several months after the departure date. This
difference facilitates the low-cost airlines' cash flow and cash management and may enable them to generate interest income from their cash
deposits. This is an advantage also enjoyed by charter airlines.

A further advantage is that bookings once made and paid for cannot be
changed, except in some cases on payment of a surcharge, and tickets
normally cannot be refunded. This means that there are very few 'no
shows' on departure. When they occur, the airline still collects the revenue
from the ticket since an unused reservation cannot be changed or re-used
subsequently.

In brief, the cost advantages enjoyed by low-cost carriers are reinforced
by more limited advantages on the revenue side. This is especially true
for those airlines selling their entire inventory directly by telephone or the

Internet. These benefits are somewhat diluted for those airlines, Ryanair or Virgin Express among them, that continue to use travel agents as well.

6.6 A passing phase or a model for the future?

In September 1999 KLM announced that its UK subsidiary KLM UK would launch a low-cost airline early in 2000 with eight BAe 146 jet aircraft flying from London's Stansted airport initially to seven European destinations. Only nine days later Debonair, a low-cost airline identical in many respects to the one being set up by KLM, collapsed. Debonair operated a fleet of BAe 146 four-engined aircraft to seven European destinations from London-Luton, an airport less than an hour's drive from Stansted. Was the close juxtaposition of a new entry and a sudden failure indicative of a fundamental malaise and uncertainty within the low-cost sector or did it signal a weeding out of weaker operators in order for the strong to survive? Do the low-cost, no-frills airlines represent just a passing phase for European aviation or are they a model for the future?

The collapse of Debonair three years after its launch in the summer of 1996 was not surprising. Faced with growing competition from other low-cost carriers it had added more and more frills ending up as a 'low-cost, high-frills' operation. Yet its initial prospects had looked very bright. Its flotation and share offering in July 1997, which raised £28.2 million, was three times oversubscribed. But the airline was already haemorrhaging badly. Three factors lead to Debonair's collapse. First, the BAe 146 aircraft it was using did not produce low enough seat-mile costs compared to the Boeing 737 aircraft used by other low-cost operators. Second, its attempt to differentiate its product from that of its competitors inevitably pushed up its operating costs even further. It progressively abandoned the key features of the simple low-cost model, as exemplified by Southwest (see Table 6.2). It offered what it claimed was the most generous seat pitch in the European scheduled market, 33 inches as opposed to 29–32 inches, thereby reducing the seats on offer but increasing the cost per seat. There were complimentary refreshments on board and a choice of economy or business cabins. All passengers received seat allocations and sales were mainly through travel agents. Shortly before its collapse, Debonair joined IATA in order to allow its passengers to interline with Lufthansa and Swissair at Munich and Zurich. Four days after it stopped flying Debonair had been due to launch a new upgraded business-class product which included a chauffeur-driven car for the day at the destination airport. This is hardly 'no frills' and certainly not low cost. All these product features pushed up Debonair's costs and confused its brand image as a low-cost operator. Finally, while its costs were rising, growing competition for the low-fare markets especially after the entry of Go and the expansion of Ryanair into Europe pushed down its fares and yields. Debonair was trapped in a downward spiral of growing losses. Attempts in 1998–99 to halt the downward drift by wet leasing aircraft to Lufthansa and Swissair were only partially successful. Debonair lost £32.3 million in its first two years of operation and, despite the capital injection from its flotation, it had accumulated debts of £36 million by the time it stopped flying.

Given the growing market share of low-cost airlines, the entry of KLM into this market segment was expected. It was after all following British Airways. But the manner in which it launched Buzz, as its entry into low-cost operations, was surprising. To use KLM UK which, as has been noted earlier, is a high-cost operator (see Table 6.4) as the nucleus of the new airline and for Buzz to fly KLM UK's costly BAe 146 four-engined aircraft, similar to those operated by Debonair, suggested desperation on the part of KLM. The latter was trying to tackle two different problems at the same time. First, how to reduce KLM UK's mounting losses and declining market share. Second, how to counter the growing success of the low-cost operators. One can only assume that the use of BAe 146 was an interim measure until they could be replaced by aircraft with lower unit costs. However, it would have been easier to ensure minimal operating costs for a new low-cost carrier by starting afresh from the bottom up, as happened with Go, rather than migrating Buzz out of a costly KLM UK operation. Moreover, KLM UK continued to operate as a separate brand offering feeder services from Stansted and UK regional airports to Amsterdam. This would initially confuse KLM UK's and Buzz's brand images at Stansted.

By the end of 1999 conflicting signals were emerging. On the one hand Debonair, a much smaller UK airline AB Airlines and the Norwegian low-cost carrier, Color Air, had all stopped flying in the second half of the year, while Go had announced a loss of £19.6 million in its first 17 months of trading. On the other hand, Ryanair was continuing to show rapid growth and steadily rising profits – from Irish £25.4 million in 1997 to £37.7 million in 1998 and £45.3 million in 1999 – while in September 1999 easyJet posted its first profit of Sterling £9.1 million before tax for its third year of operation. The uncertainty reflected in these mixed signals was justified. At the start of the new millennium, low-cost carriers in Europe, as in the United States, face a number of difficulties which must be successfully overcome if they are to survive in the longer term.

The first real problem is that there is growing competition both among the low-cost carriers themselves and from the conventional airlines fighting back to retain their market shares on key routes. Following the launch of Buzz in January 2000 there are now three low-cost carriers based at Stansted serving the London market and another not far away at Luton airport. By early 2000, there were ten or so routes out of London, such as Frankfurt, Venice, Madrid, Barcelona, Lyons and Geneva, where two low-cost operators plus two or more conventional carriers were operating. Price competition was bound to become increasingly intense. One will see frequent seat sale periods when fares drop to ridiculously low and uneconomic levels. For instance, during its October 1999 seat sale Ryanair was offering 160,000 free seats from London to eight European destinations on selected mid-week and Saturday flights for a two-month period from mid-October to mid-December 1999. Plus another 850,000 seats at £24.99 return. The only condition was that passengers had to pay the airport taxes, which were around £15 for a round trip. These absurdly low fares are indicative of the level of price competition in many short-haul markets as a result of the entry of low-cost carriers. Price wars have tended to be especially acute when there is seasonal overcapacity in the market or when new entrants enter particular markets. Inevitably, as they receive more aircraft, low-cost carriers will find themselves competing head-on with other low-cost operators on more and more routes. The Ryanair 'seat sale' mentioned above coincided with falling demand after the summer peaks and with increased winter frequencies by both Ryanair and Go from Stansted as well as easyJet out of Luton. The conventional carriers will also selectively cut fares especially at periods of low demand. The competition between low-cost carriers is intense even when airlines are not operating on the same routes. This is because at the very low fare end of the market leisure passengers are frequently indifferent as to the destination. Their prime objective is to go away cheaply for two or three days. Low price, for many, becomes more important than destination.

Competitive pressures will worsen if more European conventional airlines, other than BA and KLM, launch low-cost carriers. The US experience is telling. After deregulation in 1978, the US majors reacted to competition from new entrant, low-cost airlines by cutting fares and increasing frequencies. They lost some of these battles but even when they won they did so at great cost to their own bottom line. After a decade or more they finally concluded that in the long run they would continue to lose market share in key markets if operating with their existing cost base. To fight back they had to set up their own low-cost subsidiaries. United Airlines set up Shuttle in California, Delta launched Delta Express in Florida and US Airways has set up MetroJet in Baltimore. If other European majors follow BA and KLM along this path competition and the downward pressure on fares will be exacerbated.

A second problem faced by low-cost carriers linked to that of intense price competition is the very real risk of overcapacity arising from too rapid growth. Ryanair has been geared to growing at about 20 per cent each year and at the end of 1999 had 25 Boeing 737-800 aircraft on order to add to its fleet of twenty-one Boeing 737-200s. easyJet was operating eighteen aircraft with thirty on order with early deliveries during 2000 while Go was planning to double its fleet of eight aircraft in the same year. All this before the entry of Buzz early in 2000. All these airlines were planning to grow very rapidly at rates of 20 per cent per annum or more. Yet the success of Southwest in the United States, while other low-cost carriers failed, was due in part to its strategy of steady but low growth.

In the early years it was targeting annual growth of no more than 10 per cent and it is only more recently that growth of 15 per cent per annum has become more frequent. It took Southwest twelve years to reach a fleet size of 50 aircraft. It may well be that the European low-cost carriers by growing too rapidly are endangering their own survival. Too rapid growth creates strong pressure to reduce fares to fill up so much additional capacity. It may also involve launching many new routes that are marginal or require time to build up or where they may face intense competition from other low-cost airlines. Rapid growth places an airline's management and organisation under strain and controlling costs becomes more difficult.

Controlling costs is the third problem area. Not only are costs going to be under pressure from too rapid growth but more generally from the fact that low-cost airlines will no longer be in the start-up phase when they can negotiate the best deals with airports and suppliers of outsourced services. For instance, many key contracts between low-cost operators and airports will need to be renegotiated in the period 2000 to 2002. Will the former get as good deals second time round as they did when they were genuinely new entrants? It may become more difficult to do so when there are several of them. As they become more established there may also be greater pressure from unions and employees to push up salaries and consequently wage costs. One way of reducing such pressure is to introduce greater employee participation in the airline's profits as both Southwest and Ryanair have done.

In Europe, the low-cost market has been dominated hitherto by UK- or Ireland-based airlines. Nevertheless, new low-cost airlines are sure to emerge elsewhere in Europe as Virgin Express has done in Brussels. But such non-UK-based carriers will in most cases face a major problem which has also been faced by Virgin Express. This is that in many European countries, especially in Central and Northern Europe, staff costs are significantly higher than in the UK or Ireland, partly because basic airline wages are higher but more especially because social security payments and taxes are much greater. Thus, while in Belgium employers must pay social and insurance costs which may be equivalent to 31 per cent of an employee's salary increasing staff costs by one-third, in the UK and Ireland such charges are around 15 per cent (Chapter 5, Table 5.3). Corporate taxation is also substantially lower in the UK and more especially in Ireland compared to the major European countries. It is for this reason that Virgin Express in 1999 set up a separate Irish subsidiary while meeting much opposition from its Belgian unions and the Belgian Government. Since staff costs may represent 25–30 per cent of a low-cost operator's total costs, then being based in the UK or Ireland offers a distinct cost advantage. But while European low-cost new entrant airlines will be looking to move towards the UK or Ireland, the Irish and British low-cost airlines will look to expand on the mainland of Europe. To ensure their longer-term growth and survival they must look to developing operations from bases in other European countries. easyJet has already set up a Geneva based operation after taking over a small Swiss airline, TEA, in 1998, and is planning another base in Amsterdam. Go has also been evaluating the establishment of a base in mainland Europe. The Irish and British low-cost airlines will need to develop and expand such bases in major European markets without allowing their operating costs to escalate, because of higher wage rates, social costs and so on. This will be yet another difficult challenge to be overcome.

The final problem that will increasingly be faced by Europe's low-cost scheduled airlines is whether they can compete effectively in the largest low-fare short-haul markets, those currently served by the charter airlines. The latter carry over one-third of international passengers between the European Union member states. Most of their routes are two to two and a half hours in length and generate some of the densest leisure passenger flows in Europe. These markets represent a major challenge for the new low-cost airlines. Traditionally, charter airline seats were sold by tour/travel companies as part of a holiday package which included accommodation. But increasingly during the 1990s European charter airlines or the tour operators sold off spare capacity on charter flights on a seat-only basis without accommodation. Fares for such seat-only sales in particular markets are generally 30 per cent to 40 per cent below the lowest scheduled fares offered by competing conventional airlines. In this respect seat-only fares on charter flights in Europe are comparable to fares offered by low-cost scheduled airlines. The latter by the end of 1999 had themselves launched services on many European routes where charter airlines were dominant. From London these included routes to Palma, Ibiza, Alicante and Malaga in Spain, Rimini, Ancona and Venice in Italy and Faro in Portugal. More such services into markets traditionally the preserve of the European charter carriers were being planned as the new millennium dawned. Were the two low-cost models set to fight it out? If so, who would survive?

Certainly low-cost carriers and charter airlines enjoy certain common operational and economic features. Both sell seats at very low fares. In contrast to conventional scheduled airlines both collect their revenues up front before flights take off. Both reduce their unit costs through high density seating and through achieving very high daily utilisation of their aircraft. However, the charter airlines have certain additional advantages which gives them a powerful and sustainable competitive advantage vis-à-vis the new low-cost scheduled carriers. These advantages, when both are operating on the same route, are summarised on Table 6.8.

In brief, the charter airlines can produce even lower seat-km costs than those of low-cost scheduled airlines through using larger and more economical aircraft and flying them for longer hours each day by operating during the night. Since they sell most of their capacity directly to a few holiday tour operators and not to the public, they also have minimal selling and advertising expenditure for the bulk of their capacity. This is particularly

Table 6.8 Charter airlines' cost advantages compared to low-cost scheduled carriers

Advantage	Details
Use larger more economical aircraft	• 180 to 350 seats compared to 130–160 seats.
Higher daily aircraft utilisation	• Fly through the night.
Capacity offered closely matches demand (despite higher seasonality)	• High daily frequencies not important.
	• No need to offer flights in low season.
Higher passenger load factors (85–90 per cent, not 65–75 per cent)	• Flights pre-sold to holiday tour operators.
	• Poor flights cancelled or consolidated.
Very low sales or advertising spend	• Most capacity sold to a few large tour operators.
	• Vertical integration with largest tour operators.
BUT – some frills and more expensive in-flight service	

so when they are vertically integrated, that is, to say the airline and its major customer are part of the same parent company. For example, Britannia, the largest UK charter airline, and Thompson Holidays are both part of Thompson Travel. Low seat-km costs are converted into even lower costs per passenger because of the very high passenger load factors achieved by charter airlines. On an annual basis these normally range between 85 per cent and 93 per cent, whereas low-cost carriers will be aiming for 70 per cent to 75 per cent. Clearly, by getting more passengers on board, the costs per passenger will go down. Though charter airlines face greater seasonality in the demand for their services they face up to this by very closely matching the capacity or flights they offer to the demand. They only plan to fly at times of the day or week required by their main customers, the holiday tour operators, who charter most of their flights and seats. They don't need to maintain high frequencies through the day every day to be competitive nor to fly at all in periods of low demand. All flights are only flown because they have been pre-chartered by one or more tour operators who are responsible for selling the seats. When sales are poor, operators will often combine flights by cancelling some flights. This further ensures high load factors.

Some European charter companies have tried to fight back against the threat of very low fares on scheduled services by launching their own such services. Monarch, the UK's third-largest charter airline, has been operating scheduled services from London's Luton airport, which is also easyJet's base, to several holiday destinations in Spain. These are points for which there is substantial demand for seat-only sales from British owners of villas and apartments. However, when easyJet launched a Luton–Palma service in 1999 it forced Monarch off this route. It is unlikely that charter airlines can compete effectively head on with the low-cost carriers for this market segment by offering their own scheduled services. This is in part because their sales and distribution systems are not as extensive. In Germany, charter airlines faced with the threat of cheaper competition from lower-cost UK charter companies and in order also to ensure long-term access to runway slots at congested airports, have converted their regular charter flights into so-called 'scheduled' flights. While one can buy seats only on these flights the bulk of the seats are still sold in blocks to holiday tour operators. But scheduled flights cannot easily be cancelled or consolidated when bookings are poor as happens with charter flights. So one consequence of the German charter airlines' strategy is that their passenger load factors have dropped to around 80 per cent compared to over 90 per cent for the UK companies that remain traditional charter operators.

Because their own unit costs are likely to be higher and also because the charter airlines cater primarily for the needs of holiday tour operators, it seems unlikely that the low-cost airlines in their pure form can make major inroads into the markets currently served by the charter airlines. However, they can compete with the latter for certain smaller market segments such as independent travellers that do need very low fares but do not require hotel accommodation or other holiday package add-ons that need to be arranged in advance. Such segments include leisure passengers who have their own homes or want to make their own arrangements at the holiday destination, 'back-packers' and students. These have hitherto benefited from seat-only sales by charter airlines. The low-cost carriers offer them much greater flexibility in terms of departure days and times as well as the option to buy one-way tickets. These market segments, depending on the routes concerned, may represent 10 per cent to 25 per cent of the passengers currently carried by charter airlines. It is here that competition between the two types of low-cost operator will be most acute, for the charter airlines will not willingly give up these markets. They will find ways of fighting back. The bulk of the charter business, however, will not be threatened by the low-cost new entrants. It would seem wise for the low-cost airlines to focus on competing against conventional scheduled airlines and on developing entirely newly generated or repeat business rather than to target their charter counterparts.

All the above difficulties and problems will ensure considerable turbulence in the short-haul low-cost sector of the European aviation market during the early years of the new millennium. Experience in the United States during the 1980s suggests that few of the early start-up low-cost carriers will survive. Three of the early European low-cost carriers collapsed in 1999. In the coming years one is bound to see the emergence of new airlines entering the low-cost, no-frills market, some of these will be subsidiaries of existing conventional carriers. But in the longer term Europe is unlikely to have more than two or possibly three low-cost carriers of any size.

To ensure their long-term survival low-cost airlines must do two things. First they must maintain a sustainable competitive advantage over their conventional competitors. In essence this means they must focus on the essentials of the low-cost product in order to ensure that their costs per passenger-km are 50–60 per cent below those of conventional airlines while offering a product which, despite the absence of frills, is very highly rated by passengers in terms of value for money. The essential features they must stick to are short-haul routes with single aircraft type offering high-density seating and operating, where possible, from secondary airports. Frequencies should be relatively high and punctuality and regularity among the best. Sales should be 100 per cent direct by telephone or, ideally, via the Internet and ticketless. On-board catering should be minimal and of good quality but not free. Many of the functions of the airline should be outsourced to minimise their cost. Airlines that lose a clear focus and diverge from these essential features of the low-cost product are likely to lose their way as Debonair did in 1998–99.

The second requirement for long-term survival is for low-cost carriers to ensure that on most of their routes they become the number one or number two carrier in terms of market share. This dominance, combined with their low fares, gives them a very powerful defensive position should new competitors attempt to enter, while also ensuring a strong cash flow base on which to mount further expansion. Southwest's survival and success is due in no small measure to its growth strategy, which has focused on becoming dominant in most of its markets. As mentioned earlier in 1993 it was the largest carrier in ninety-three of its top 100 markets (CAA, 1998). This is also an explicit objective of Ryanair's growth. Michael O'Leary, Ryanair's Chief Executive, has claimed that in 1999 Ryanair displaced Alitalia as the largest carrier on London–Turin in its first month of operation, it displaced British Airways on London–Genoa after three months, while its traffic on London–Carcassonne quickly surpassed Air France traffic levels on the competing London–Toulouse route (O'Leary, 1999). Ryanair had already replaced Aer Lingus as the largest carrier on many of the UK to Ireland routes some years earlier. Becoming a dominant carrier is more difficult to achieve if low-cost airlines enter major dense routes which already boast three or four operators or where two or more low-cost carriers are operating on the same or parallel routes. Nevertheless, becoming the largest or second-largest carrier on most of their routes must be a prime objective for low-cost carriers wishing to ensure their longer-term survival.

At the beginning of the year 2000, there were four significant low-cost carriers operating in Europe – Ryanair, easyJet, Go and Virgin Express – as well as some smaller ones elsewhere in Europe. KLM's Buzz was the new boy on the block. Additional short-haul low-cost airlines were sure to emerge. Of the larger group Ryanair, easyJet and Go were most clearly focused on the essential features of the low-cost model as described above. Virgin Express, as was evident from the earlier analysis (in section 6.3) appeared to have a confused market strategy and no clear focus. After a small profit in 1998 it made a loss of US$5.4 million in 1999 and began dropping routes in May 2000. Ryanair, up to that time, was the most successful in achieving a dominant position in many of the markets it served, partly because it has been in existence nearly ten years longer than the others and partly because of its early focus on UK–Ireland routes where it has only faced limited and weak competition. The cost advantages enjoyed by these three airlines from having a UK or Irish base means that they will be among the long-term survivors. However, their dependence on the UK market and increasing competition between them, as their networks overlap more and more, makes it very unlikely that all three will survive!

7   E-commerce@airlines.co

A new electronic marketplace has emerged with different rules.
(David Guillebaud, Vice-President, Arthur D. Little)

7.1 Increasing focus on the customer

Soon, a businessman or his secretary in New York, using only a single
airline or travel agency website, should be able to book a return flight to
London, reserve a car on arrival, as well as three nights at his favourite
hotel, a ticket to the Royal Opera House and two nights at an out-of-town
hotel for the weekend. On arriving at the airport, the airline's electronic
ticket machine will print out his boarding pass and details of his itinerary
and other reservations including his room number at both hotels. As he
is a frequent flier member, the airline website already knows he wants
rooms on non-smoking floors. It will also print his opera ticket. This will
automatically be for a seat in the grand circle which he is known to prefer.
All he has to do is swipe his frequent flier or credit card through the automatic ticketing machine (ATM). At London's Heathrow airport his car is
waiting on confirmation of his identity at another automatic machine. If
during his stay in London he has to change his itinerary he can do this
effortlessly by calling into the airline's website on his palmtop computer.
On his return to New York, details of his trip and all expenses are fed
automatically to his company's travel manager who ensures budget control
and that travel policies are being adhered to. A leisure traveller may have
different requirements. For instance, he will want to find the cheapest fare.
But the travel service should be just as seamless and readily accessible.

All this is possible because of developments in information technology
and the Internet. The enabling technology has largely been mastered. That
is now the easier part. But electronic commerce (e-commerce) is not just
about reservations, or automatic ticketing or monitoring expenses and travel
policy. It is about changing the whole relationship between suppliers, in this
case the airlines, and their customers – but also the relationship between
the airlines themselves and their own suppliers of goods and services. The

whole process of 'doing business' is being transformed. Some of the changes will be far-reaching and they may not all be beneficial for the airlines. Airline managements must understand the fundamental nature of the changes that are already taking place in their customer relations so as to avoid potential pitfalls and maximise the benefits that e-commerce can bring. This is the challenge.

Business priorities within the airline industry have changed. The economic downturn of the early to mid-1990s focused airline managements' priorities on reducing costs and financial restructuring. After 1994, as the industry climbed out of recession and found itself in an increasingly deregulated environment, the priorities switched to alliance building. As the new millennium approached the strategic focus changed once more. The customer became king. Airline executives saw their key business priorities being increasingly focused on customer-related activities. A 1999 survey by IBM of senior executives and board members of 119 of the world's leading airlines found that improving customer service and customer loyalty were considered to be the two most critical strategies in meeting their airlines' financial goals (IBM, 1999).

The rapid development of information technology during the 1990s has provided airlines with several new tools with which to woo customers and to improve customer service in many areas of airline operations. In the area of marketing and distribution two in particular will play an increasingly important role. These are sales and distribution through the Internet and electronic ticketing. Together they represent the key elements of the application of electronic commerce to air transport. They will undoubtedly transform dramatically the way that airline services and products are marketed and distributed. The process is well under way but the full impact of e-commerce has still to be felt by airlines or their customers. In particular they need to appreciate that the new electronic marketplace will have different rules.

FedEx, the integrated cargo carrier, was the pioneer. Having developed a very efficient and fully computerised system for tracking individual parcels anywhere on its network it took the next logical step. In 1994, through its website, it allowed its customers to book and pay for its services without restriction via the Internet. The United States scheduled airlines introduced electronic ticketing a year or two later but were slower to implement Internet sales. The lead in this respect was taken by specialist online-only travel agencies such as Expedia and Travelocity, though the conventional airlines subsequently followed suit. The most enthusiastic proponents of e-commerce have been the low-cost carriers who saw it as one of the tools by which they would reduce costs.

While electronic ticketing spread rapidly in North America and less rapidly in Europe in the later 1990s, sales through the Internet lagged far behind. For instance, by 1999 around 40 per cent of Continental Airlines' domestic sales in the United States involved electronic ticketing. But its ticket sales through its website, while rising rapidly, were still very small in value terms. In fact it was estimated that in 1999 close to 4 per cent of total US airline tickets were booked on the Internet, almost double the previous year's figure. The penetration of Internet sales in global markets outside the United States at that time was less than 1 per cent. But the potential for the growth of e-commerce was and is enormous.

A 1999 survey of the state of IT among the world's leading airlines found that 43 per cent of them expected that within five years, that is, by the end of 2003, they would be selling over half of all their tickets online through the Internet (Ebbinghaus, 1999). Yet at the time of the survey in 1999 none was selling more than 10 per cent of tickets online and for most the actual figure was much lower. While Delta, Northwest and US Airways took around 7 per cent of their bookings on the Internet in 1999, for British Airways and most European airlines it was less than 1 per cent (*Aviation Strategy*, 2000). Yet growth in Internet sales can be extremely rapid, as the low-cost carriers have shown. easyJet, in the UK, introduced Internet ticketing at the end of 1997. Within a few months around 10 per cent of its sales were through the Internet and by the end of 1999 Internet sales were averaging close to 40 per cent. There is little doubt that very rapid growth in e-commerce sales will be achieved. All the forecasts are optimistic, but vary widely, since the phenomenon is so new. In the United States, forecasters predicted that 32 per cent of all US business travel will migrate online by 2003 and 10 per cent of leisure travel (*Herald Tribune*, 15 October 1999).

If one focuses on airline sales alone the potential is enormous. United Airlines, one of the first and most successful of the major international airlines to sell online, expects to be selling about 20 per cent of its tickets through the Internet by 2003. If one were to assume a similar penetration of Internet sales for both passengers and cargo among all the airlines of the four major alliance groupings (see Chapter 4, section 4.1), then revenues generated would be around US$34 billion in 2003. Perhaps not all the alliance members will be in a position to achieve such high Internet sales by 2003. However, any shortfall will be more than offset by Internet sales by several non-alliance airlines who will be achieving high Internet sales by 2003 or earlier. Among these will be several low-cost carriers in North America and Europe including Southwest, Ryanair and easyJet. Already by 1999 the US low-cost carriers were achieving a high proportion of their sales through the Internet. For AirTran it was 17 per cent and for Southwest 15 per cent (*Aviation Strategy*, 2000). Thus, the US$34 billion total is a realisable figure. The 20 per cent penetration assumption is in any case low. The 1999 survey by SITA mentioned earlier showed that of the 150 top airlines 43 per cent expected to be selling over half of all tickets online by 2003 (Ebbinghaus, 1999). This from airline tickets and cargo sales alone. If one were to add sales of hotel accommodation, car hire or other services packaged together with air travel, the total sales revenue generated from the airlines' e-commerce would be very much higher.

7.2 Drivers for change

Developments in information technology including the Internet, together with the wider availability and ownership of cheaper personal computers, have been driving the penetration of electronic commerce in many service sectors and industries of which air transport is only one. New and cheaper technology has been the facilitator. But an additional factor has undoubtedly been changing attitudes towards information technology, especially among younger consumers. Increasingly, they find it as natural and easy to purchase goods and services electronically as through conventional outlets. A cultural and fundamental change is taking place in the way consumers in developed economies perceive the processes of shopping for goods and services. Within air transport, in addition to these general trends, there have been some very specific factors pushing airlines to move towards greater use of e-commerce and away from their traditional distribution systems.

The first driver for change has been the need to *cut distribution costs*. Ticketing, sales and promotion costs, taken together, have in recent years represented around 17 per cent to 18 per cent of the total operating costs of international airlines. These are the airlines' costs of distribution. Historically they have been the largest single functional cost element. According to a 1996 IATA study, commissions paid to agents and other airlines, net of commissions received, accounted for almost 42.8 per cent of these distribution costs, equivalent to 7.5 per cent of *total* operating costs. Reservations and ticketing represented a further 31.0 per cent of distribution costs and payments to computer reservation systems an additional 7.1 per cent (Table 7.1) Today's figures are still broadly comparable. Falling yields in recent years have made cost reduction a vital priority for all airlines. Initially the emphasis was on reducing labour costs but once progress had been made in this area, the focus switched to reducing costs in particular functional areas.

Because distribution costs represent such a large share of total costs it became critically important to attack these costs and especially the commissions paid to agents. Two strategies were adopted. The first was to reduce the level of commissions paid. In the United States commission payments had peaked at 10.2 per cent of total operating costs in 1993. The airlines fought back step by step. Early in 1995 Delta introduced commission caps on domestic tickets of $25 one way or $50 return and was quickly followed by the six largest US airlines. The quick matching induced the American Society of Travel Agents to file an anti-trust suit. Though a $86 million settlement was finally made in the travel agents' favour, the capping stayed in place. In mid-1997 United went further and lowered base commissions

Table 7.1 Breakdown of airline distribution costs, 1996

Costs	As % of total operating costs	As % of distribution costs
Net commissions	7.5	42.8
Reservations and ticketing	5.4	31.0
Advertising and promotion	2.2	12.5
Computer reservation system fees	1.2	7.1
Credit card commissions	0.7	4.0
Frequent flyer programmes	0.4	2.1
Other	0.1	0.5
Total distribution costs	17.5	100.0
Other operating costs	82.5	
Total operating costs	100.0	

Source: IATA (1996).

on domestic and international ticket sales from 10 per cent to 8 per cent. Delta and American and others adopted the same policy. Two years later in October 1999 United Airlines announced that it would cut commissions from 8 per cent to 5 per cent and cap them at $50 for a domestic round trip and $100 for international tickets. Not only did all the majors follow suit but so did many of the smaller United States airlines. Many travel agents responded by introducing flat fees to customers of around $10 per ticket issued.

The same pattern of trying to reduce commission rates was repeated in Europe but the lead here was provided by national flag carriers' cutting commissions within their own home markets where they were strong enough to overcome adverse reaction from travel agents. Thus, in 1997 Lufthansa cut domestic commissions in Germany from 7.5 per cent to 5 per cent and was followed down by Deutsche BA. Commissions on international ticket sales, which in Europe were 9 per cent, were reduced by several airlines in the late 1990s including SAS which cut the commission on intra-Scandinavian flights from 9 per cent to 5 per cent and then 4 per cent. At the end of 1997 British Airways cut its standard 9 per cent commission to 7 per cent and 7.5 per cent respectively for domestic and international tickets but introduced an incentive-based 3 per cent additional commission for high-performing agents. This was subsequently ruled to be anti-competitive by the European Commission. Attempts by airlines to reduce agents' commissions by 1 per cent, 2 per cent or 3 per cent were important in controlling costs but their overall impact on total costs was and is only marginal.

More dramatic cost reductions could be achieved by maximising the opportunities offered by e-commerce. This was the second strategy. By selling direct to customers, whether passengers or freight forwarders, airlines could cut out commissions altogether for that part of their inventory that was sold in this way. Avoiding commission payments could reduce total distribution costs by up to 43 per cent (Table 7.2). If, while selling online, ticketing is provided through automatic ticketing machines then ticketing costs can also be reduced. Or one can go all the way and provide ticketless travel as the low-cost airlines have done. The Air Transport Association, the body which represents US airlines, has estimated the cost to an airline of processing a ticket sold by an agent to be $8 compared to $1 if sold through the airline's website. Websites are also cheaper than telephone call centres since the number and cost of reservation staff can be significantly reduced or even eliminated altogether. Further cost savings arise if by using an internal reservations system, online callers can by-pass the global CRSs to whom the airlines would normally pay $3.00 or more per sector booked. Conversely, credit card commission costs will increase since all sales will be based on payment by credit card. Advertising costs may also need to increase over all if an airline is not using agents to publicise and promote. On balance nearly two thirds or more of distribution costs could be avoided by Internet sales on an airline's own website (Table 7.2). Since distribution costs represent 16–20 per cent of total costs, cutting them by two thirds would reduce total costs for international airlines by 10–12 per cent if all sales were through the web.

America West, a medium-sized US domestic airline, claimed in 1999 that direct distribution costs could be reduced from $23 to $6 per ticket

Table 7.2 Distribution costs via Internet sales compared to current sales outlets

Costs	Current costs of distribution* (%)	Estimated cost changes if all sales through own website (%)	
Net commissions	42.8	All costs saved	−42.8
Reservations and ticketing	31.0	Much lower	−20.0
Advertising and promotion	12.5	Higher	+5.0
Computer reservation system (GDS) fees	7.1	All costs saved	−7.1**
Credit card commissions	4.0	Higher	+2.0
Frequent flyer programmes	2.1	Unchanged	2.1
Other	0.5	Unchanged	0.5
Cost saving			−62.9**
Total distribution cost	100.0		37.1

Notes
* Current costs cover all distribution outlets including travel agents, airlines' own sales offices and call centres (source: IATA, 1996).
** If existing GDS reservation system is not by-passed, then cost saving is less, at around 56 per cent.

by online sales (*Airline Business*, July 1999). Airlines appreciate that if they could transfer up to half of agents' sales, currently averaging 70–80 per cent of total sales, as well as some part of their own existing direct sales, through the telephone or their own high street sales offices, to the Internet, then they could make significant reductions in their distribution costs. This provides airlines with a very strong incentive to speed up their use of e-commerce.

The second major driver for change is the strong trend towards *disintermediation*, which aims to bypass travel and freight agents, or other intermediaries, so as to link the airlines directly to their customers. The purpose is not just to reduce costs by cutting out or reducing commission payments and other distribution costs as described above. The trend towards disintermediation also arises from changes in the tripartite relationships between customers, agents and service providers which have been affected in part by developments in information technology. In the first place, it is becoming apparent that agents' ability to determine customers' choice of airlines is becoming less and less. Increasingly, it is the passengers who decide which airline to fly with. In the case of business travellers, numerous surveys show that choice of airline is influenced above all by the convenience of an airline's schedules and timings, though other factors such as in-flight comfort, safety and reputation for punctuality are also important. The travel agents can help in identifying the airline which best meets the potential travellers' requirements, but the business traveller will often have done this for himself on the basis of previous experience or through accessing information, previously available only to agents, through a PC or laptop or a company intranet. The traveller's choice will also be influenced by airline branding, when it is successful, and by loyalty schemes such as frequent flyer awards which aim to tie frequent business travellers to particular airlines. Of course in many cases a further limiting factor on choice of airline may be company travel policies or special pricing deals made directly by corporates with individual airlines. With so many factors other than the agents' recommendation influencing the choice of airline it clearly makes little sense to pay commission to agents on the grounds that they can be or have been instrumental in the choice of airline for a particular journey. In the case of leisure travel the decline of agents' influence is not yet so marked. But here too growing knowledge and awareness of the options, airline branding and frequent flyer programmes are eroding the role of agents. As access to and familiarity with the Internet spreads then this process of disintermediation will accelerate. It will affect not only travel agents and tour operators but also other intermediaries such as providers of global distribution systems (previously called computer reservation systems).

While the ability of travel agents to influence customers' choice of airline is declining, effective use of the Internet provides airlines with *increased marketing power*. The need to take advantage of the unique opportunities offered by the Internet is the third driver pushing airlines into e-commerce. The Internet enables them to market their services world-wide, cheaply and effectively to anyone who has access to an online computer. Without having to deal with and through hundreds, if not thousands, of travel agents. Travel information on their website can be clear, correct, precise and uncluttered. Changes to services, schedules, prices or other information can be made available to customers or potential customers anywhere in the world instantaneously. At the same time, the ability of airlines to develop more robust relationships with customers is increasing because of the developments in information technology. When customers book direct with an airline, by telephone, via the Internet or through its own sales offices, it is the airline which captures key details regarding the customer for its database and not the intermediary. The latter might be a travel or tour operating agent or an independent computer reservation system. The airline can then use that database both to provide services more closely attuned to customer needs and to market pro-actively directly to clients. For large corporate or business customers an airline, through effective use of IT, can provide many of the services previously offered by agents such as monitoring company travel policies and expenses.

In fact, effective use of the Internet to interact directly with customers can help airlines create new markets, particularly those based on last-minute impulse buying. A good example of pro-active marketing based on exploiting close relationships with particular market segments is provided by American Airlines. In 1999 its 'NetsAAver Fares' programme provided special last-minute fares marketed to members of its AAdvantage club through the members' own home page. Customers were informed by e-mail every Wednesday of special low fares for the following weekend. Tickets had to be purchased on Thursday with travel starting on the Friday. One million customers were participating in the scheme. In this way American Airlines were able to sell capacity that would other-wise be wasted. At the same time these low fares reinforced the loyalty of their regular customers who felt that their loyalty was being rewarded through these exclusive fare deals. This example shows how e-mails targeted specifically to a frequent flyer database and based on known travel needs and patterns can not only enhance customer loyalty but can also reduce pricing transparency. Whereas special fares marketed to travel agents via the GDS are known and available to everyone and can quickly be matched, special offers to targeted customers are more difficult for competitors to respond to.

It should be borne in mind that the Internet can be much more effec-tive as a direct marketing tool than the telephone because customers can view things on their screens that they cannot 'see' on the phone. They can be shown photographs or even films of locations, hotels or airports. They can also view the interior layout of different aircraft cabins and choose their seat in relation to the exits, toilets, or any other factor which is important for them. At the same time, since there is no physical product to deliver other than a ticket which can be printed and delivered electronically, air travel is particularly suitable for e-commerce.

The fourth major driver pushing airlines to make greater use of e-commerce is the fact that it makes *airline pricing more dynamic, interactive and market-focused,* as in the American Airlines example mentioned above. It is clearly much easier to respond quickly to changing market conditions such as fare cuts by a competitor or a shortfall in late bookings which leave departing flights with many unsold seats. Fare increases or reductions, whether triggered by a yield controller or automatically by a computer programme, can be fed to the market instantaneously. Such fare changes can be marketed either directly through the airline's own website or indirectly through online-only ticket agencies such as Travelocity or Expedia or regular travel agents or consolidators. More important, e-commerce enables prospective customers to access new fares and to make reservations quickly and at short notice directly with the airline concerned, ideally without the need to go via an intermediary. There is a growing trend among many airlines, especially in the United States, to sell their cheapest discount tickets only via the Internet. This makes them more quickly available and cuts out the cost of agents' commissions on what are in any case deep discounted fares.

In addition to the four major drivers discussed above, there are a number of other factors which reinforce the benefits which arise from greater use of e-commerce within the airline industry. On the revenue side, there is considerable scope for airlines to sell other products and services on their websites, not only obvious ones such as hotel rooms, car hire, travel insurance or even tickets on other airlines, but also less obvious products such as books, wines, theatre tickets and so on. Because some airline brands are very strong cross-selling of this kind would be relatively easy. If done well it would enhance the attractiveness of an airline's website and help build up customer loyalty, while generating additional revenue and profits.

On the cost side, greater use of e-commerce can bring two further advantages. All Internet buyers pay by credit card, though large customers may have credit facilities. This significantly improves airlines' cash flow since payments are received within two or three days whereas when sales are made via agents revenues generated will normally take one to two months to reach the airline. But they may take much longer. Since air travel is highly seasonal with very marked peak periods, receiving cash up front helps reduce working capital and may well generate additional bank interest. Greater Internet use, especially for business-to-business dealings, also reduces costs in other areas. For instance, online monitoring and ordering of supplies such as aircraft spare parts, stationery, in-flight catering or products for in-flight sales can save labour costs, reduce stock holding and improve efficiency. Costs can also be reduced by switching from traditional telecommunication links to web technologies. It is for this reason

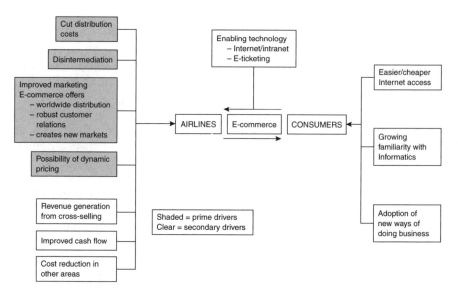

Figure 7.1 Forces driving rapid growth of e-commerce in air transport.

that British Airways in November 1999 signed a contract with SITA to set up a modern intranet Protocol platform, linking its 60,000 computers world-wide. The Internet also makes it easier to outsource activities formerly done in-house to external suppliers or to relocate labour-intensive functions such as revenue accounting to areas with lower wage costs. In other words economies are also achievable in the supplier-to-supplier relationships.

The interplay of all the forces and trends pushing the rapid adoption of e-commerce in air transport are shown in Figure 7.1.

7.3 Problems and dangers

Internet shopping is increasingly accepted and used by consumers. This trend will accelerate. But with regard to air travel there are still some barriers which need to be overcome to ensure that the potential for e-commerce is fully realised. Access to the Internet is clearly still an issue. Not all potential airline passengers have access to and can use a computer. Computer ownership per head is lower in Europe than in North America and even lower elsewhere. This is partly because computers appear to be much more expensive in Europe. Even those Europeans who do have use of a computer at work or at home may be inhibited by the much higher Internet access costs in Europe than in the United States. Wider computer ownership and easier Internet access is clearly an essential prerequisite if the global airline alliances are to achieve 20 per cent of sales online by the end of 2003, as suggested earlier. Another barrier to overcome is the fear of credit card fraud when buying online. Numerous surveys have shown this to be the single most important inhibitor of Internet sales. As more and more people actually do buy online without suffering fraud, which in any case is very minimal, public perceptions are changing. Nevertheless there is a lingering fear. A more active advertising and public relations campaign to show why such fears should be unfounded is necessary. In the United States companies selling via the Internet go to great lengths to protect their customers and to reassure them that they are doing so.

Fear of fraud is one of the reasons why the ratio of 'lookers' to 'bookers' on travel websites is very high, certainly much higher than with telephone call centres. But there may be numerous other reasons for this, too. Lookers may find it difficult to navigate through the particular travel or airline site they have called into. Many sites are still not customer friendly and may be hard to read or slow to navigate. They may demand a great deal of information from online customers before giving them real access or force them to view proprietary pages before reading booking sites. Many modems are too slow, creating connection problems and making trawls through travel websites laborious for the 'lookers'. Also, many airline websites only provide information of their own services and prices and not those of competing airlines, thus forcing customers to look elsewhere if they want to weigh up the alternatives. Of twelve major European airline websites surveyed in 1999 only one, Lufthansa's, offered booking on other airlines. But even for Lufthansa the lookers to bookers ratio was a poor 162:1 in 1998 but expected to fall to 115:1 in 1999. In contrast, the conversion rate at its telephone call centres was 30:1 in 1998 (Salomon Smith Barney, 1999). Uncertainty or lack of familiarity with buying on the Internet may also be an inhibiting factor. Converting more 'lookers' into 'bookers' is going to be a major challenge for airlines and online travel agencies.

A potentially more serious and longer-term problem for airlines is that the balance of market power has shifted in favour of the consumer. The electronic marketplace offers consumers both fast, borderless and efficient access to information on airline services, timings and prices and the ability to make rapid and effortless reservations and payments. In economic terms greater knowledge means greater market power. Despite much deregulation and liberalisation in international air transport there were in the late 1990s still many imperfections in the major international markets. One of these was inadequate knowledge, among consumers, of alternative routings and pricings available to them. Their knowledge was hazy. E-commerce is removing the haze and making the marketplace more competitive. Falling yields across the board and loss of business and first-class traffic in long-haul routes was blamed by British Airways and other carriers, such as KLM, for a serious erosion of their profits in 1998–99. It was assumed that this was due primarily to overcapacity in key markets, especially the North Atlantic. It is likely that these deteriorating traffic and yield trends were aggravated by greater knowledge in the market-place. This enabled both leisure and business travellers to be much more selective in their choice of airline, especially when trying to reduce their travel costs.

A feature of the new electronic distribution is the speed with which knowledge of new fares or fare changes can be circulated in the market-place. The technology makes this almost instantaneous. This means that lower fares or special offers can be closely monitored by competitors or their computers and rapidly matched. In many cases this might be done by the computerised yield management systems more or less automati-cally. In turn this may generate a counter response from the original price leader. As a result, in very competitive markets, prices may change several times during the day. Such computerised revenue management systems further reinforce the market power of consumers and the downward pres-sure on fares and yields.

One major consequence of increased consumer power arising from the further extension of electronic commerce will be the commoditisation of the airline product. This means that attempts, which hitherto were partly successful, to differentiate and brand an airline's product in order to charge a premium or ensure customer loyalty will become increasingly difficult. Product features will become more or less standard. In fact the develop-ment of global alliances makes this more likely. As alliance members are forced to produce a standard seamless service it becomes very difficult for the maverick innovative airline to produce on its own a unique product that leap-frogs ahead. The airline product will become a commodity – a seat from A to B – with more or less standard product features irrespec-tive of the airline providing the service. It will be readily available for sale in the open market at prices that are widely known. Commoditisation creates the very serious risk that the airline marketplace will become increasingly auction-based, thereby undermining attempts to maintain or improve yields and manage revenues. The dangers are enormous.

Up to now, online ticket auctions have been used by airlines primarily to sell excess capacity, so-called distressed inventory, to a wider market or to very specific market segments. The latter might be the airline's own frequent flyers, as with American Airlines' 'NetsAAver' fares discussed earlier, or particular corporate clients. Some airlines such as Cathay Pacific have managed their auctions through their own websites while others have used specialist online agencies. For instance, in November 1999, British Midland offered 30,000 tickets to thirty European destinations for auction through the Internet auction site QXL. The best known for airline tickets is perhaps the US-based Priceline.com, in which Delta Airlines is a share-holder. Callers request a seat on specified routes and dates and bid the fare they are prepared to pay. Priceline then tries to find the requested seat at that price by interacting with potential suppliers. If it can match the bid fare the customer must accept and pay for it. If the best fare available is higher than the bid price, the customer has the option of accepting or rejecting it. Price is the determining factor in that consumer's choice. The name of the airline or other product features are unimportant. This is commoditisation.

The real question is whether such auctions will be limited to selling only distressed inventory and special offers or whether commoditisation is inexorably leading airlines in very competitive markets or routes to rely more and more on auction-based pricing for selling most of their capacity. It requires only one airline in a market to start auctioning its seats, which it can now do so easily through the Internet, and others are bound to follow. If that happens existing computerised revenue management and inventory control systems and procedures will be unable to cope effectively with the more dynamic and highly segmented marketplace being created. New revenue management controls will need to be introduced based not on historical precedent and statistical forecasting, as current systems are, but on an understanding of consumer behaviour and the price elasticity of different market segments. There is a very real threat that if auctions spread it will become increasingly difficult in such very competitive markets to stem the downward drift of fares.

That auctions will become more common is an inevitable consequence of commoditisation. However, it is less certain how far and deep they will spread. There is also some uncertainty about the next logical step which is the development of a travel futures market. Already by late 1998 one company was reported to be trying to set up a travel commodities futures exchange (Guillebaud, 1999). The concept is simple enough. Through the exchange, blocks of, say, 50, 100 or more airline seats for specific routes could be bought for delivery in the future. Prices would move up or down in response to changing patterns of supply and demand in relation to specific delivery dates. Buyers and sellers could speculate on market developments and also hedge their risks as in any other commodity exchange. Airlines might not only be sellers but also buyers when market conditions changed. Trading would also take place in blocks of hotel beds or in car hire capacity. The development of a travel futures exchange would reinforce the commoditisation of air travel.

Another problem which e-commerce creates as a result of the disintermediation which it makes possible is the worsening relationship between airlines and travel agents. Not only are airlines putting agents under pressure by reducing commission rates on ticket sales but they are actively taking business away by developing both their Internet sales and their telephone call centres. With regard to business or corporate travel, which is the most profitable market for airlines, growing competition between airlines has forced them to go even further. Most airlines now make direct deals on fares with large or even medium-sized corporations as a way of ensuring their business. This is more effective than relying on increased incentives to travel agents, such as high override commissions, to tie in large corporate customers. Very large international companies, such as General Electric or major global banks, will cut deals with different airlines to provide tickets for particular geographical regions or markets. Travel agents may still be used for ticketing, though electronic ticketing means that even this may no longer be necessary. The role of business travel agents has changed from reservations and ticketing to provision of travel advice and related services such as hotel or car hire bookings, monitoring travel expenditure, enforcing company travel policies, finding and offering the lowest fare alternatives and so on. Smaller business travel agents do not have the technology or expertise to supply all these services and are being forced to consolidate or go out of business. Instead of relying on commissions from the airlines, which in any case are being cut and capped, business travel agents are increasingly charging corporate clients a management fee. This will normally be based on the actual cost of services offered by the agent plus a small profit margin. The fee may also be related to the travel cost savings obtained by the agent. Commissions earned by the agents from airlines may have to be shared with the corporate customers. A report in the UK-based *Travel Weekly* on 14 October 1998 stated that in the United Kingdom nearly 70 per cent of business travel agents' sales with corporate clients was on a management fee basis. The reduction and capping of commission rates is pushing many travel agents to ask their leisure passengers to also pay booking fees, especially for issuing low-fare tickets. Travel agents feel under pressure and under threat. Their market power is declining most notably in the business travel sector, but with e-commerce their influence in leisure markets will also progressively decline.

Relations with airlines are deteriorating. Is there a danger that airlines, in placing too much emphasis on disintermediation and sales through their own websites and call centres, turn their backs on and even undermine the more traditional distribution methods? Charles McKee, General Manager Global Distribution for Virgin Atlantic, believes airlines are being over-optimistic in their forecasts of sales penetration through the Internet. Between 20 per cent and 30 per cent may be reasonable and achievable for airlines with high density networks such as those in the United States; but the 50 per cent penetration, which British Airways and others are striving for in the next few years, is not. McKee claims that 'These airlines are fooling themselves. It's pie-in-the-sky figures.' (Newton, 1999) Clearly, airlines will need to use a spectrum of distribution channels in the future. In the process of rapidly developing e-commerce and pushing disintermediation, they must be careful not to undervalue or undermine complementary distribution outlets such as the conventional travel agents.

A related issue to that of travel agents is that of the global distribution systems (GDS) which also act as intermediaries. Originally called computerised reservation systems (CRS) they were developed by groups of airlines in order to automate and facilitate reservations and ticketing both by the airlines themselves and travel agents. Five global or very large regional GDSs emerged, selling their services by signing up travel agencies and usually providing them with the necessary computers and IT back-up. Agents could make bookings via their GDS – many agents might be linked to more than one GDS – but the airlines then paid a fee to the GDS provider for each flight sector booked. Airlines using the GDS directly also had to pay the same fees. By switching to the Internet airlines can bypass the GDS and save the GDS fees. The Internet is also producing new and alternative suppliers of search engine technology. For instance, a US company, EDS, has been hosting Continental's reservations system since 1991. GDS providers will suffer loss of business from the process of disintermediation. This will become more severe if virtual online travel agencies also bypass them and book directly with the airlines. Certainly some airlines have foreseen the declining importance of GDS and have sold their shares. They have felt that GDS was a non-core activity and, since by the late 1990s all GDS carried the same unbiased travel information, ownership of a GDS no longer provided airlines with a competitive edge. Moreover, by selling their GDS shares airlines could realise significant profits which were, in some cases, needed to boost flagging airline profits. In 1998–99 both British Airways and KLM, two of the biggest shareholders, sold their shares in Galileo, one of the largest GDS. Other airlines have also divested themselves of some or all of their shares.

Despite the declining interest of airlines in GDS ownership, the latter do have a role to play. The majority of travel agents will continue to make reservations through the GDS. This is especially true of agents in countries where the Internet is not widely used or where personal contact remains an essential part of doing business. They will also continue to be used by some online travel agencies since they provide ideal and powerful search engines. In fact GDS turnover and profits continued to increase in 1999 despite losing their effective monopoly because they spread into new geographical areas, such as the Far East and grew rapidly their car rental, hotel and other non-airline business.

The GDS have been diversifying to ensure their long-term survival. They provide the IT platforms and search engines for many airline websites. The ability of the GDS engines to provide other services such as hotel, car rentals and other booking services makes them potentially very attractive for airlines. Galileo, Sabre and Worldspan, the three largest GDS between them provide the search engines and tools for over 130 airlines. When early in 2000 a group of ten large European airlines announced they would be joining forces to create a new joint website, all four GDS companies, the above three and Amadeus, put in bids. In addition the

GDS are themselves becoming providers of online travel services. Sabre, the GDS owned by American Airlines until it was spun-off in March 2000, has emerged as a major force in direct Internet airline ticket sales through its 70 per cent shareholding in Travelocity. In spring 2000 Travelocity merged with Preview, another online agency, to become the global leader in online airline ticket and travel sales. At more or less the same time, Galileo completed the acquisition of Trip.com in the United States while Amadeus was setting up joint ventures in Europe with online travel providers.

Certainly, the strong technological base of the GDS providers will ensure that they will continue to provide specialist services and support in areas related to the Internet. Or they may provide IT platforms and applications for the global airline alliances. The almost total reliance by airlines on GDS providers for airline reservations is being eroded by the Internet, but GDS companies will continue to provide another channel of distribution as well as the search engines for airline websites. While continuing to develop their own Internet sales, airlines will need to manage this changing relationship with the GDS providers.

7.4 Alternative strategies

A major inhibitor to greater use of e-commerce is the fact that travellers are still unable to find all the data they need on one website in order to make a travel decision. They have to access several sites before they can feel certain that they have identified the best product and price combination that meets their requirements. This is particularly true of many airline websites. For airlines that have a strong brand and/or a very clear market niche or positioning, lack of data on their own site regarding competitors' services and prices may not inhibit users. They will, for instance, access Southwest's or easyJet's website in the clear expectation this where they will find the cheapest fares for the short-haul sectors they are interested in. This is one of the reasons why these airlines' Internet sales have been so high. It is also the case that many airline website visitors, especially business travellers, have already decided on whom they want to travel with. But the greater the choice of airlines one might use for a particular journey and the more additional services one needs, such as car hire or hotels, the less likely it becomes that a single airline website can provide all the necessary information. Yet 'one-stop shopping' is one of the key features driving the long-term development of e-commerce. Conventional airlines must work out their strategic response to this glaring shortcoming in their current electronic distribution systems.

One strategy might be to continue very much as at present. In other words to use all distribution channels available including travel agents, the GDS, direct telephone sales and their own Internet site, but with the latter selling primarily their own services. Customers wishing to book more complex itineraries or travel packages would do so through traditional travel agents or the virtual online agents such as Travelocity or Expedia. The latter would also enable airlines to reduce distribution costs but not by as much as when selling on their own websites because they would still need to pay commissions. However, those are generally US$10 per booking, which is much less than would be paid to high street travel agents. Airlines adopting such a strategy would be effectively opting out of trying to capture for themselves most of their e-commerce sales, arguing that other specialist distributors of travel products could do this more effectively and cheaply. On the other hand they may, like American Airlines, decide to use e-distribution to reinforce the loyalty of customers in their frequent flyer or executive clubs. This airline's website is geared for top-tier customers who are members of their frequent flyer AAvantage club. You cannot book a flight unless you are a member, though you can join online. But potential customers can also book via the Internet using virtual travel agents. Such a low-key e-commerce strategy appears difficult to sustain in the longer term for two reasons. First, because it means losing control over much of one's distribution to other agencies at a time when cost pressures and potential marketing benefits are pushing towards disintermediation. Second, because most of the larger conventional airlines will be members of global alliances and will need to adopt the same strategy on e-commerce as the key members of their own alliance. It is very likely that in most cases the key alliance members will opt for a more active involvement in e-commerce and e-distribution than at present. Other member airlines will inevitably be pulled in the same direction.

The second strategic response is for airlines to become major players in electronic distribution providing a full range of services. This entails developing their websites so as to provide users with more information on, and booking opportunities with, other airlines, possibly competitors. They should also provide seamless access to hotel reservations, car hire, entertainment bookings and so on. They will after all generate some commission revenue by cross-selling while providing an enhanced service to their own customers. In addition they would need to provide corporate customers with the ability to track expenses, monitor travel policies as well as any other services currently offered by travel agents. In other words, they should move towards providing a real 'one-stop shop' for travel. To succeed, they would probably need to team up with a specialist provider of Internet services and develop a strong electronic distribution brand. While it was United States airlines which led the way in adopting e-commerce, in Europe Lufthansa was one of the first to develop a strategy of developing its own powerful website, offering a multitude of services. Unlike the websites of most of its European competitors, it provides an online booking service which embraces most of the world's airlines. In 1999 some 5 per cent of Lufthansa's online ticket sales were for other airlines. Not surprisingly, business travellers are the most frequent users of the Lufthansa website and 40 per cent or so of tickets sold are in Business or First Class (*Financial Times*, 17 February 1999). The site has been developed to provide hotel bookings, tourist information, travel guides, baggage tracing and other travel features. But, like many other airline websites at the start of the new millennium, it was not a truly customer-oriented site. It required a great deal of information from callers before it would allow them to make or even consider making bookings. This was in marked contrast to the easyJet website on which bookings were extremely easy and straightforward. As they entered the new millennium it was not clear how many other European airlines would follow Lufthansa and US airlines such as United down the path of offering a full comprehensive travel service through their own websites.

A real difficulty to overcome is to ensure that an airline website of this kind can be exhaustive enough in its coverage, and whether, if owned by one airline or airline group, customers can be assured that there is no bias in the presentation of information. This was, after all, the problem that beset the computerised global distribution systems in the early days before they became more independent of individual airlines and were forced to adopt codes of practice. One solution is for airlines to combine resources so as to offer a pooled website as they did a decade earlier with the computerised reservation systems. Continental, Delta, Northwest and United decided to set up in 2000 the first joint multi-airline travel portal, even though they belong to different global alliances. It would be independently owned. In Europe, the same thinking pushed ten major airlines to announce in February 2000 that they were joining forces to create their own website though they too were partners in different alliances. This is not an ideal solution. Airlines would clearly prefer to sell direct on their own individual websites both to minimise costs and to maximise the marketing opportunities offered by the Internet. Joint sites are essentially an attempt to undermine, or at least counteract, the growing success of independent online travel sites such as Expedia, Travelocity or ebookers.

A third alternative strategy would be to team up with one of the existing online-only travel distribution companies that have grown rapidly in recent years, especially in the United States. One can combine this strategy with either of the earlier two. At the end of 1998 there were three significant players, Travelocity owned by Sabre and Microsoft's Expedia which each had online sales of about $250 million in that year and Preview, whose sales were lower at $200 million. In 1999 their online sales more or less doubled. A clear indication of the potential for growth. There were in addition several smaller online booking services such as tiss.com or TRIP.com or those of American Express and Rosenbluth International in the United States and Trailfinders and ebookers in the UK, many of them linked to traditional high street travel agencies. Taken together these specialist online agencies were booking almost half the Internet airline business. Inevitably airlines began to show an interest in these online providers. In early 1999 United Airlines acquired BuyTravel.com which it uses to distribute its deeply discounted fares. But it continued to develop its own website as a major online service, cross-selling other products and other airlines' services. Users of BuyTravel can also book with other airlines, make hotel reservations and obtain travel information. Later that year, in September 1999 British Airways bought a 5 per cent stake in Rosenbluth Interactive which had earlier acquired a majority holding in Biztravel.com, which specialises in online sales to smaller businesses. Biztravel was planning to expand into the leisure market since it was already providing hotel and car hire bookings as well as airline tickets. Continental Airlines and Marriott International Hotel group were also shareholders in Biztravel.com. British Airways, like United, was buying into an Internet booking company based on state-of-the-art technology with an established brand name among Internet travel customers. Clearly, the strategy of both these airlines was to widen their e-distribution by buying into a branded online agency while continuing also to sell through their own websites. American Airlines, through its parent company AMR, was already the 83 per cent majority shareholder in Sabre, owner of Travelocity, one of the big three online-only booking services. In September 1999, Travelocity merged with Preview, the smaller of the big three. Sabre was to maintain a 70 per cent shareholding of the merged company. Travelocity's and Preview's joint sales in 1999 were expected to top $1 billion.

Surprisingly, despite their very rapid growth, none of these online virtual travel distributors or agencies was making money by the end of 1999. Their set-up costs were high both because of the need to invest in the latest state-of-the-art technology and because they had to spend heavily on advertising and branding their services and making portal deals. Unlike airlines that already had established brands and direct access to millions of clients through their frequent flyer programmes, these virtual agents had to build up a new client base. This was costly. Yet commissions were being capped by most airlines at US$10 per booking.

The losses incurred by the virtual travel agents should be a warning to airlines but should not inhibit them from developing a strong presence in the electronic marketplace. After all, as described earlier, the advantages of such a strategy are numerous and the potential economic benefits through both cost saving and revenue generation are substantial. Those airlines which can aggressively build up a lead in e-commerce will enjoy additional competitive advantages for some time. The difficulties that traditional booksellers have had to catch up with Amazon.com is evidence of the need to be a leader in e-commerce. Airlines cannot afford to wait to see how this new marketplace will develop.

7.5 Playing by the new rules – customer relations management

Developing and implementing a website strategy is a critical first step but in itself it is not enough. The rules of the game have changed. To fully capitalise on the opportunities offered by e-commerce airlines must change fundamentally their ways of doing business. They must develop and use knowledge of customers' preferences so as to transform what have hitherto been transactions into relationships. This is what customer relation management (CRM) is all about.

Up to now airlines had two sources of information regarding their clients. If they were members of the frequent flyer programme, the airline's database would contain the client's address, credit card details, frequency of travel, destinations travelled most often and possible dietary needs. If not a frequent flyer, the reservations computer booking in the form of the passenger name record (PNR) might contain little more initially than a passenger's name and telephone number. But such data may not provide an adequate passenger profile for effective and highly segmented marketing. Moreover, data from the PNR is not always tied to, or fed in to, the frequent flyer database. Traditionally, passengers making successive bookings through airlines' call centres or websites frequently find that they have to repeat much of their basic information such as their address and telephone numbers.

Customer relations management represents a quantum step in marketing. It has two key facets. First, airlines need to build up customer profiles on their databases that contain not only the traditional data required for ticketing, but also as much information as possible on their customers' travel patterns, both for business and leisure, product and service priorities, age and family structure, lifestyle and so on. Such data should appear automatically every time a customer wishes to make a booking, so as to facilitate and speed up the process. In other retail sectors this is already happening. For instance, Amazon developed and patented an express check-out system called '1-click'. This stores billing and shipping information so that customers are encouraged to make repeat purchases because it is so easy. They do not have to retype their addresses and other details. In fact Amazon in 1999 launched a law suit in Seattle, California, against other book sellers in order to stop them using the same express checkout technology. In the near future information on passenger preferences while flying should also be available to cabin staff through palm-held computers. They could then match the in-flight service to such known preferences, for instance, by providing a passenger with his favourite magazine or drink, or a lighter meal.

The second step is for the airline to use this database for proactive and highly segmented marketing. Products and services offered may need to be customised for individual passenger needs. As the airline product becomes more commoditised, airlines will have to use passenger profiles to identify where they can offer real value added to those potential customers who value particular products or services so as to charge a premium. A relatively small part of most conventional airlines' customer base provides a relatively high proportion of its profits. Airlines need to build a relationship with these customers which entails much more than merely making them members of a frequent flyer or executive club. For instance, in the event of delay or cancellation of a flight these passengers are contacted first and very quickly offered alternative flights or refunds, their hotels are re-booked automatically and their offices warned. At the other end of the market, airlines may need to be proactive in targeting particular market segments to whom they can sell special discounted fares or holiday packages. The Internet enables them to reach thousands of carefully selected and targeted potential passengers worldwide at a cost of a fistful of dollars. The nature of marketing has changed. Increasingly it will be on a one-to-one basis. The Internet makes this possible.

The whole concept of customer relation management is very new. Many airlines are still feeling their way as to how they should implement it. The essence of CRM is not just to sell more but to do this by offering more and better services to the passengers. The software technology is being developed by specialist providers. One of the problems that has to be faced is how to integrate direct sales, through airline call centres or websites, with indirect outlets such as travel agents or GDS, so as to offer the same service standards and to develop similar customer relationships. Another problem is to ensure that customer relation management spans all the airlines in a global alliance so that a passenger flying on an alliance partner which is not his usual airline or airline of choice receives the same high quality of service and treatment.

It is clear that to benefit fully from e-commerce requires a mind-set revolution among airline managers and executives. They must make the jump from seeing e-commerce as just a faster and less costly way of taking bookings and issuing tickets, to appreciating that it is a fundamentally new and more interactive way of doing business. The old functional divisions whereby, for example, sales, airline pricing and yield management, ground handling and in-flight services were in different departments may no longer be suitable or adequate if an airline focuses on e-commerce. The latter requires a much more integrated and co-ordinated approach in servicing passengers (or freight for that matter). This is necessary to ensure that if one is targeting high-yield passengers they receive the same high level of value-added service from the airline at all stages from initial travel inquiry to disembarkation at the destination and are 'recognised' whenever they interface with the airline or its staff. To achieve this, new organisational structures or paradigms may be needed by airlines with customer relations as their focus.

8 State-owned airlines

A dying breed or a suitable case for treatment?

Unjustifiable state aid to flag carriers is the greatest obstacle to the emergence of a viable, competitive airline industry.

(Sir Michael Bishop, Chairman, British Midland Airways)

8.1 Changing attitudes

Until the mid-1980s most international airlines were wholly or majority owned by their national governments. There were exceptions, most notably in the United States, where all airlines were privately owned, and, to a lesser extent, in some Latin American states. It had not always been so. In Europe, most of the early airline ventures in the period up to the mid- or late 1930s were set up by private entrepreneurs, many of them former pilots from the First World War, or private companies, in some cases railway or shipping firms.

Two factors pushed the nascent airline industry into the hands of governments. First, during the 1920s and 1930s there was a growing realisation that air transport was going to be of major significance and importance in economic and social development, as well as trade. Yet in many countries several of the early start-ups were failing financially because the markets were so small. Governments realised that their countries required to have at least one stable international airline. Moreover, the regime of bilateral air services agreements which developed required each state to be in a position to designate an airline controlled by its own nationals to operate on the routes on which traffic rights had been exchanged. Such airlines, or flag carriers, as they came to be known, needed to be stable and project a good image in terms of performance, safety, and so on. Governments needed to ensure that there was at least one strong, well-run and effective airline that could be designated as its country's flag carrier. In many cases this required government involvement and financial support. Second, the Second World War re-emphasised the economic potential and value of air transport, but virtually all European countries emerged from the war with their civil aviation industries in ruins. Many new state-owned airlines were set up in the immediate post-war period. In some cases these new airlines were formed around the nuclei of the pre-war private airlines. This happened in France when air transport was nationalised and the Société Nationale Air France was set up on 1 January 1946. Similarly, the British government set up three State Air Corporations in 1946 when it too nationalised air transport. These were British European Airways (BEA), British South American Airways (BSAA) and the British Overseas Airways Corporation (BOAC), formed around the nucleus of the pre-war Imperial Airways. BOAC and BSAA were merged shortly after, though it was not till 1974 that BEA and BOAC were brought together to form British Airways.

The trend towards state-owned airlines was reinforced in the 1960s and 1970s. As former colonies or protectorates in Africa, the Middle East and Asia became independent they all set up new state airlines or their governments took over majority control of airlines established during the colonial period. Even after this phase, further nationalisations occurred, particularly when privately owned airlines ran into serious financial or organisational problems. Thus, Olympic Airways, the Greek flag carrier, which enjoyed a total monopoly of all air transport within Greece and belonged to the ship-owner Aristotle Onassis, was taken over by the Greek government in 1975. UTA, the second largest French airline, operating long-haul services to Africa and Asia, was not nationalised until 1990 when Air France took over a majority shareholding.

In the mid-1980s the tide turned. The privatisation of state-owned airlines became part of the agenda. Liberalisation of international air transport was gathering pace (as noted in Chapter 2) forcing airlines to abandon old cosy market practices, such as revenue-pooling agreements, and to become more competitive and customer-oriented. Many could not do this effectively if they continued to be run as state enterprises with a government or civil service mentality. At the same time, in Europe especially, there was a growing political view that privatisation of state-owned public utilities, including transport companies, would increase efficiency and service quality while reducing costs to the consumer. This was the political creed of the British Conservative Government under Mrs Thatcher, and it was in Britain that widespread privatisation of state enterprises was pushed forward first and on the widest front.

Other governments in Europe and elsewhere gradually adopted similar policies of reducing state involvement in public utilities and other industries. The collapse of the centralised state economies of Eastern Europe and the Soviet Union in the late 1980s reinforced this trend. In the case of many state airlines there was another reason why privatisation came to be seen as necessary. Nearly all such airlines were heavily undercapitalised. As the airline industry had expanded, their government owners had rarely put additional equity capital into the airlines they owned. Instead, growth and fleet expansion had too often been financed through medium- and long-term debts. After the downturn in the industry's fortunes in 1981–83 (see Chapter 1) many airlines found themselves heavily in debt and poorly positioned to finance the fleet expansion which many of them planned, as demand and traffic growth accelerated after 1984. A case in point was Malaysia. Early in 1984 Malaysia Airlines was finalising its five-year development plan. This required substantial investment in new aircraft. In the absence of additional equity capital from the Malaysian government, the airline would have to raise commercial loans. But it was already heavily in debt and interest charges were likely to be high, so it had to try and self-finance part of its capital needs. The management estimated that to do this it needed to generate a profit of about US$30 million per annum. In 1982/3 its profit was only $3.4 million and, though in 1982/4 it was about $40 million, the $30 million target could not be met every year. Without it, the airline's development programme would be in jeopardy. This was why in 1984 it was decided to inject capital by privatising the airline. Many other governments in the latter 1980s decided to sell off a major part of their state-owned airlines for similar reasons.

In Britain, British Airways was floated on the Stock Exchange through an initial public offer in 1987. In several other European countries and in Latin America, governments reduced their shareholdings in their airlines. For instance, LanChile was sold off in September 1989. The pace towards privatisation quickened in the mid-1990s as international competition became tougher and more acute following deregulation in Europe and the introduction of 'open market' air services agreements in other regions (the third package came into force in January 1993; see Chapter 2). It was also evident that the few non-US airlines which had continued to operate profitably in the bleak years of 1991–93 were nearly all privately owned or operated as if privately owned. These included British Airways, Cathay Pacific, Singapore Airlines and Swissair. The lesson was not lost. The German government privatised a first tranche of Lufthansa in 1994 and completed the full privatisation of its airline in October 1997. Other governments, including those of Argentina, the Netherlands and Finland, also reduced their stakes in their national airlines during this period.

Despite these developments, an astonishingly large number of state airlines were still in existence as the new millennium approached. Over seventy international airlines were majority owned by their governments and of these, about forty were 100 per cent government owned (Table 8.1). There are in addition numerous very small government-owned flag carriers which are not included in Table 8.1, such as Air Botswana or Air Vanuata, as well as many domestic airlines that are effectively government owned or controlled. These include Aviaco in Spain, China United, China Yunan and several other Chinese airlines. Finally, there is a sizeable group of airlines with a minority state shareholding (Table 8.1, part 3).

During 1999 a large number of airlines were in the process of being fully or partially privatised or their government had announced their

Table 8.1 Government shareholding in international airlines, January 2000

1 Fully (100 per cent) government owned

Airline	Airline	Airline
Adria Airways	El Al	Mandarin
Aer Lingus	Emirates	Nigeria Airways
Air Algerie	Ethiopian	Olympic
Air China	Garuda	Royal Brunei
Air India	Ghana Airways	Royal Jordanian
Air Malawi	Gulf Air	Royal Nepal
Air Niugini	Indian Airlines	Saudi Arabian
Air Seychelles	Iran Air	Sudan Airways
Air Tanzania	Iraqi Airways	Syrian Arab
Air Zimbabwe	JAT	TAAG Angola
Bangladesh Biman	Libyan Arabs	TAP – Air Portugal
Croatia Airlines	Kuwait Airways	TAROM
Cubana	LAM (Mozambique)	Vietnam Airlines
Egyptair	Lithuanian	

2 More than 50 per cent government owned

Airline	%	Airline	%	Airline	%
Turkish Airlines	98.2	Air Lanka	74.0	PIA	56.0
Air Malta	96.4	Air Pacific	73.0	Iberia	54.0
Cameroon Airlines	96.4	China Airlines	71.0	SIA	54.0
Thai International	93.0	Air Afrique	70.4	LOT	52.0
Royal Air Maroc	92.7	China Southern	68.1	Austrian	51.9
Air Madagascar	89.6	Alitalia	67.0	Yemenia	51.0
CSA Czech	83.7	Air France	64.0	Aeroflot	51.0
Cyprus Airways	80.5	Malev	63.9	Air Mauritius	51.0
South African	80.0	China Eastern	61.1	SAS	50.0
Air Gabon	80.0	Finnair	59.8		

3 Less than 50 per cent but over 10 per cent government owned

Airline	%	Airline	%	Airline	%
Pluna (Uruguay)	49.0	Sabena	33.8	Kenya Airways	23.0
Lloyd Aereo		BWIA	33.5	Swissair	21.5
Boliviano	48.3	Air Jamaica	25.0	Aeroperu	20.0
Tunis Air	45.2	KLM	25.0	PAL	14.0
Dragonair	43.4	Malaysia Airlines	25.0		
VASP	40.0	Luxair	23.1		

intention to do so. The Italian and Spanish governments had announced their intention to privatise their airlines as early as 1997, though the process was taking a long time. As the economic crisis in East Asia unfolded in the latter part of 1997, growing uncertainty about the future of their airlines pushed many Asian and other governments to announce plans to privatise their state-owned airlines. The Thai, the Indonesian, the Jordanian and

Madagascari governments, among many others, stated that privatisation and a search for strategic partners were the twin pillars of a policy aimed at ending the financial problems faced by their national carriers. It sounded so easy! Privatise, find a foreign airline to become a strategic partner and the airline's problems would be solved.

Unfortunately, it is not as simple as that. To find the right cure in terms of the necessary restructuring one must first identify the symptoms in order to diagnose the nature and severity of the ailment. The vast majority of state-owned airlines suffer from what one might call the 'distressed state airline syndrome'. This is a political and organisational virus which affects most state-owned airlines. One must understand and appreciate the symptoms of this virus in order to ensure that if privatisation is adopted as a cure, it proves successful. What are these symptoms?

8.2 The distressed state airline syndrome

The experiences of Olympic Airways in the period 1994 to 1996 amply illustrate the characteristics of distressed state airline syndrome. Observation around the world suggests that most state-owned airlines, with a very few notable exceptions, manifest many, if not most, of the symptoms described, though to varying degrees.

A key characteristic of distressed state airlines is that they are in *serious financial difficulties*. Most of them have been losing money at least since the economic downturn of 1990 and some for very much longer. Air France accumulated losses of US$3 billion during the six years up to 1995 despite injections of state aid in 1993–94. Olympic Airways, probably more typical of smaller state airlines, posted net losses every year from 1978 to 1994. It produced profits in 1995 and 1996 as a result of a restructuring programme begun in 1994 and involving US$2.3 billion in 'state aid' (see section 8.3).

The real historical losses are in many cases much greater than those shown on paper because many state airlines have received indirect subsidies from their governments which artificially reduced their costs. For instance, state airlines have not paid airport landing fees on domestic sectors and sometimes not even for international flights, as was the case for Olympic Airways or Royal Jordanian in the past. They may not be charged rents for office space, check-in desks or land they use at the national airports. Some have obtained aviation fuel from the government-owned oil company at reduced prices or even free. Invoices presented to the airline from other government agencies for services or goods provided may remain unpaid for years. Government guarantees for loans or aircraft purchases may also have reduced the cost of past borrowing by as much as 0.5 per cent to 1.0 per cent.

State-owned airlines are also invariably *undercapitalised with huge debts* and with debt to equity ratios that are much too high. Olympic, before the 1995 write-off under the agreed state aid package, had long-term debts of over US$2 billion. While the Greek flag carrier frequently made an operating profit, the servicing of its large debt mountain meant that it was pushed into a spiral of annual losses. Alitalia had debts of US$2.3 billion, rising to US$3.1 billion if aircraft lease liabilities were included when, in 1996, it applied for European Commission approval for a capital injection from government sources. In 1998, when its privatisation was announced, Thai International Airways debts were believed to be around US$3.2 billion (*Commercial Aviation Report*, 1 April 1998).

Distressed state airlines are frequently *overpoliticised*. In return for providing direct or indirect support, such as guarantees for loans to buy aircraft or to cover annual deficits, governments and taxpayers expect to be able both to influence the airline's management and to impose numerous obligations on the airline. To achieve these twin aims governments change the airlines' managements frequently and often without apparent reason.

Between 1975 and 1999 Olympic Airways had some twenty-nine chairmen, with an average job expectancy of ten months. One chairman lasted for forty-two days but was called back a second time and stayed eleven months! At the end of 1997 a newly appointed chairman resigned after only four days, claiming lack of political support. Board members may also be changed frequently. During the author's fourteen months as chairman and CEO between February 1995 and April 1996, Olympic Airways' board of directors was changed three times. Though appointed as chairman by the same government, his views on whether to change the board or on who should be appointed were not sought. Board members of state-owned airlines are frequently appointed to achieve government political or internal objectives or to pay off political debts rather than to ensure the commercial success of the airline.

Owner governments interfere indirectly, as well as directly, in management decisions. Examples abound. As a result of a 1976 agreement with the Greek newspaper publishers and distributors, Olympic agreed to charge GRD5 (barely 2 US cents) per kilo for transporting newspapers on its domestic flights. Because successive governments were unwilling to upset the newspaper proprietors, the airline was permitted to raise this tariff only very marginally during the next twenty years to around GRD7 (2.5 US cents). By contrast foreign newspapers air-freighted within Greece in 1996 paid the IATA-based tariff, which was around 32 US cents per kilo, or more than ten times as much. It is estimated that Olympic lost close to US$6.5 million a year in revenue as a result. Its costs were also pushed up by the need to operate early morning flights just to carry newspapers. For instance, for many years Olympic was forced to operate an Airbus A300 at 5.30 or so every morning from Athens to Salonika to carry each day's bulky Athens newspapers. This flight was a major loss-maker since few passengers were prepared to travel so early.

It is common in many countries for governments to impose very low cargo tariffs to facilitate the export of particular commodities or to refuse domestic fare increases for long periods in order to facilitate domestic air travel and national cohesion. In the case of agricultural products, low tariffs may stimulate traffic and generate revenue. But in some cases yields may be so low that they do not cover their directly attributable costs. Domestic fares that are kept too low may have a doubly adverse impact. They may make certain routes unprofitable. At the same time they may generate high demand and high load factors because of the artificially low fares. The airline then finds itself under political pressure to add more flights on such routes because demand is not being met, even though each additional flight increases the overall losses.

Interference also manifests itself in the expectation of many governments that their national carrier will fly scheduled services to certain foreign or domestic points, irrespective of whether such services are profitable. They are deemed to be necessary by the government concerned to achieve certain domestic, social or economic objectives or, in the case of foreign routes, in order to 'show the flag'. When new regional airports were opened or existing ones upgraded airlines such as Iberia, Olympic or PAL found they were required to serve them with scheduled services whether or not such flights were commercially viable. Many such domestic and international routes are a millstone around the airlines' neck producing losses year after year but airlines find it impossible to withdraw despite the commercial sense and necessity of doing so.

Distressed state airlines, in Europe at least, are characterised by very *powerful unions*, and often by a multiplicity of different unions. Their power stems from the ability of almost every specialised group of workers to bring an airline to a halt. The union leaders have traditionally used their power and the threat of strike action to influence management decisions at every level. Traditionally union power has been used to hold up change and innovation unless the employees received some financial compensation. Early in 1996 Olympic Airways' union leaders torpedoed the introduction of sleeper seats in business class on Olympics long-haul B747s even though this was an essential part of a strategy to improve the product. In many state airlines measures to reduce costs or improve service quality have frequently been held up.

In some state airlines, union leaders interfere directly in management decisions in areas which should not be the concern of unions, such as fleet planning or internal promotions. In Olympic Airways' case, unions expected to have a say in every promotion or appointment so as to place their own supporters into key posts. Union leaders were outraged when anyone was promoted to a middle or junior manager's post whom they had not approved, and asked for such decisions to be reversed, even threatening strike action.

Union leaders change less frequently than the senior management, and are therefore likely to be better informed and more knowledgeable than the relatively new chairmen or chief executives especially if they come from outside the airline industry. This gives the unions a distinct edge when negotiating with management or the government.

In countries, many of them in the developing world, where unions are not strong, there may be other *cultural constraints* on airline managements arising from each country's particular social ethics and customs. It may, for instance, be socially and politically unacceptable to make large-scale redundancies or staff cuts or even to reduce wages. Thus, whether because of strong unions or because of social custom airline managements may find themselves severely constrained.

One direct consequence of being both overpoliticised and over-unionised is that distressed state airlines are also *overstaffed*. The unions have used their power over many years to negotiate working conditions which drastically reduce labour productivity and force the airline to take on extra staff to fill the gaps. Managements find it difficult to take back concessions granted by their predecessors and to renegotiate improved work practices.

Similarly, governments may use airlines as a way of disbursing patronage and favours to their supporters by offering them jobs or promotions to those that are already employed. Traditionally in Greece, in the 1970s and 1980s when a new party came to power not only did it change Olympic's board of directors and chairman but these, once appointed, then filled the top thirty to forty managerial posts with their own party's supporters from within the airline. The new appointees in turn changed personnel lower down. The previous occupant of a post was pushed sideways, often to a non-existent job for which they were still paid. Even a change of transport minister within the same government may lead to many 'inexplicable' changes at the top of an airline.

Distressed state airlines *rarely have a clear and explicit development strategy*. This is not surprising, given the lack of management continuity as senior executives are changed too frequently. But it is also due in part to government intervention which confuses the management by imposing political or other constraints on the airline. Governments will frequently veto any attempt to cut routes even though they may be hugely unprofitable. Without a coherent long-term strategy airline executives flounder from one strategic mistake to the next. An example was Iberia's disastrous foray in the early 1990s into buying shares in three unprofitable Latin American airlines, Aerolineas Argentinas, VIASA and Ladeco. In the period 1991 to 1995 Iberia lost over US$1 billion from its Latin American investments (de Irala, 1998). State airlines end up with inappropriate and over-extended networks which bear little relevance to present-day commercial requirements.

One major result of the poor financial performance of distressed state airlines is that re-equipment is delayed. This usually means that they have ageing fleets and aircraft which may not be the most appropriate for the routes operated. Often, given the small number of aircraft, there will be *too many different aircraft types* in the fleet, resulting in much higher maintenance and crewing costs. Predictably, within the EU the oldest aircraft tended to be found in the state airlines of southern Europe. For instance, the last Boeing 727s in Europe in 1998 were being flown by Iberia, Olympic and JAT, the Yugoslav airline. At the beginning of 1998 Olympic Airways, with a jet fleet of only thirty-four aircraft, had six totally different aircraft types, including only two Airbus A300-600 aircraft. In 1999 it added two Airbus A-340s to make a seventh type. In the smaller state-owned airlines of Africa and the Pacific it is not unusual to find very small aircraft fleets made up of too many different types. Thus, in 1998 Air Madagascar had a total of twelve aircraft in its fleet but of six different types, while Air Gabon had a fleet of six aircraft, each one of a different type! In many airlines fleets need to be both rationalised and modernised.

Too many state-owned airlines are characterised by *bureaucratic and overcentralised management.* Overstaffing, frequent management changes and constant political interference breed a culture in which managers are afraid to take decisions and bureaucracy stifles initiative. Decision-making becomes increasingly concentrated at the top of a sharply pyramidal management structure. The one or two decision-makers at the top are swamped by paperwork and by the number of decisions they must take. Many decisions are delayed. Memos, seeking decisions, are passed slowly up the pyramid, gathering signatures on the way. At Olympic it was not uncommon for the CEO to receive memos asking for some authorisation but already bearing four, five or more signatures. Centralised management may have been acceptable in the era of airline regulation. It is totally inappropriate in today's deregulated and highly competitive environment where decisions have to be taken quickly by the person most closely involved.

Finally, most distressed state airlines offer relatively *poor service quality* both in the air and on the ground. This is usually due to a combination of factors, both cultural and institutional, such as the inability to replace inadequate staff, poor management and strong unions. Unions may be unwilling to relax outdated work rules and conditions in order to improve customer services. Even existing rules are frequently flouted with impunity. It may also be a function of the total absence of a service culture within the airline. Too many state airline employees are not customer oriented. But management too are at fault, since they have been slow to adopt new ideas and new practices.

The symptoms of distressed state airline syndrome are summarised in Table 8.2. The symptoms will manifest themselves to differing degrees in different airlines. Any airline which is suffering badly from several of the symptoms is in serious trouble and in danger of becoming extinct in tomorrow's increasingly deregulated and competitive world unless corrective action is taken urgently.

Table 8.2 Symptoms of distressed state airline syndrome

Symptom	Details
Substantial losses	• Indirect subsidies hide real losses, • large accumulated debts, • undercapitalised.
Overpoliticised	• Frequent management changes, • excessive government interference.
Strong unions	• Delay innovation and change, • influence many decisions.
Overstaffed and low labour productivity	• A significant drain on resources.
No clear development strategy	• Over-extended historical network, • inappropriate and ageing fleet, • too many aircraft types.
Bureaucratic management	• Pyramidal management structure, • fear of taking decisions.
Poor service quality	• Outdated processes, • culture not customer-oriented.

8.3 Preparing for privatisation

Privatisation does appear to be one way of tackling the symptoms of the distressed state airline. It is consistent with changing attitudes world-wide and with the current trend of reducing direct government involvement in most industrial sectors. Privatisation may also facilitate the injection of the new capital which is needed not only to reduce debts and interest payments but also to support fleet rationalisation and modernisation. But privatisation by itself is not enough. It should be accompanied by a fundamental restructuring of every aspect of each airline's activities aimed at reducing costs and improving the quality of the products and services offered. If privatisation is to succeed it needs to be part of a wider process of recovery and change involving action in several key areas.

A fundamental prerequisite for successful privatisations is a *change of culture and of expectations* at all levels. The employees must appreciate that privatisation means that the government is no longer there to protect and support the airline financially when it dips into losses. Success or failure, employment or unemployment will depend on the joint efforts of employees and management. They must see themselves as partners, not opponents. Confrontation is out. Co-operation and reconciliation of differences is the only way forward. Yet in airlines approaching privatisation in 1997 and 1998, such as Air France or Iberia, one saw bitter and very costly industrial disputes. Union leaders seemed unable to face up to a new reality, that their members' jobs might no longer be guaranteed by the state. This may be partly the fault of governments and politicians. They too must change their attitudes. They must accept they can no longer interfere in the management of the national airline in order to use it to increase their political or popular support. The governments must make it clear to the public at large and to the airline employees that they have no further role other than that, possibly, of a minority shareholder. Even if they remain majority shareholders, governments must deal with their airlines at arm's length without imposing upon them any particular obligations.

Prior to privatisation, government have one last key role to play. With the help of external advisers they must put in place stable professional management with clearly defined business aims, free from any form of political interference. New managers, with experience of the commercial world, may need to be brought in. The management must become less bureaucratic with responsibility and decision-making devolved to senior and middle managers who must not be afraid to take decisions. The short-term priorities for such managements are not to embark on a multiplicity of alliances but rather to reduce costs, improve labour productivity, and make their staff and the airline as a whole more customer-oriented. This can be done only with the support and co-operation of the workforce. But many of the necessary actions will upset those union leaders who fail to grasp that change is the prerequisite for survival. Thus, winning over employees and union leaders to the process and necessity of change will be another management objective.

The larger the airline the more essential it becomes to set in motion a change of culture and attitudes at the earliest possible stage. This is both because changing management and employee culture is a long, slow process and because the larger the airline the more difficult it is for a new owner or strategic partner effectively and quickly to implement cultural change. If culture and attitudes do not change a privatised airline will not survive in a more competitive world.

An equally urgent requirement in virtually all cases is *financial restructuring*. This should be aimed primarily at clearing the balance sheet of large accumulated debts, especially those that in effect are unlikely ever to be repaid. Many of these will be to state-owned banks. In many cases there will also be a need to inject new capital into the airline. In the process of financial restructuring the state-owned airlines of southern Europe required huge amounts of 'state aid' to be pumped into them by their respective governments (see Table 8.5). This had to be approved by the European Commission. Approval was forthcoming only after very detailed examination by the Commission to ensure that the state aid was part of a detailed recovery plan whose prime purpose was to turn the airline round and enable it to be financially self-supporting without any further government help. (See section 8.5 for detailed discussion of state aid.)

The European Commission rightly saw that any debt write-off or capital injection would only be effective in the longer term if it was part of a *detailed recovery plan.* This must be so. In the case of Olympic Airways the approved recovery plan had three key elements (Table 8.3). First, US$1.8 billion of medium- and long-term debts were written off, that is, to say they were taken over by the government who, in any case, had been the guarantor. A further US$270 million of government loans were converted to equity. In addition, the government was to inject a further US$230 million as working capital in three annual tranches. The second part of the recovery plan involved a major effort to reduce labour costs by a cut-back in staff numbers of about 15 per cent through voluntary retirement (encouraged by high redundancy compensation payments) and by a two-year wage freeze. The wage freeze was especially harsh in a country where inflation was around 9–10 per cent per annum. Over the two years, it meant a loss of real income of close to 20 per cent. At the same time, work practices and conditions were revised to ensure further gains in labour productivity. Finally, the plan involved a shrinking of the network as certain routes, such as the Athens–Tokyo service, were abandoned. The network changes in turn allowed Olympic to return two Airbus A300-B4 aircraft to the lessor. This should have been the first step in the rationalisation and modernisation of the fleet. However, cutting routes, especially if it involves reducing the fleet size, is very difficult for airline managers and employees to accept. The Olympic Airways case is interesting because it highlights the three most fundamental requirements of any recovery plan for most distressed state airlines, namely, capital restructuring, cost-cutting primarily through reduced staff numbers and higher

Table 8.3 Olympic Airways three-pronged recovery programme, 1994–97

End	Means
Financial restructuring	• Debts of US$1.8 billion written off. • Government loans of US$270 million converted to equity. • Capital injection of US$230 million in three annual tranches.
Cost reduction	• Early retirement of 1050 staff in 1995 out of a total of 11,000. • Staff reduction of over 15 per cent by end 1996. • Wage levels frozen for 1994 and 1995. • Revised work practices. • Organisational restructuring to reduce number of management levels.
Network/fleet rationalisation	• Tokyo route closed. • North Atlantic services cut back. • Two Airbus A300-B4 returned to lessor in 1994. • Fleet expansion delayed.

labour productivity, and a revised and probably slimmed down route network accompanied by fleet rationalisation.

Other state airlines adopted restructuring measures that were very similar in terms of fundamental objectives. Thus, in implementing its viability plan in 1994–96, Iberia first restructured its finances by reducing its debt burden from US$1,366 million to $476 million by 1997. It was helped in this by a capital injection of nearly $600 million in 1995, though, in a controversial decision, this was deemed not to be 'state aid' by the European Commission on the grounds that it met the commercial requirements of a private market investor. Of this capital about 57 per cent was used to write off accumulated debts. The balance was used to encourage early retirement of staff. Staff numbers were cut by 7 per cent between the end of 1993 and December 1996, while total traffic increased by 15 per cent. As in Olympic there was a salary freeze which in Iberia's case lasted for three years from 1994 to 1996. As a result of these measures and further cost-cutting, overall costs were slashed each year and in 1996 Iberia made a profit of $28 million, its first of the decade. Network re-organisation and fleet rationalisation and renewal were part of the 1997–99 'Director Plan' aimed at preparing Iberia for privatisation (de Irala, 1998).

The final requirement is to audit and *clarify the airline's accounts and to identify any explicit or hidden subsidies* provided by government or government enterprises. As previously mentioned these may include non-payment of airport charges or of rents for the use of airport or other facilities, reduced fuel prices, a preferential tax regime and so on. All potential buyers, especially if they are another airline, will want to assess the true value and potential of the airline being privatised. They can only do this if past subsidies are identified and quantified. Privatisation should entail withdrawal of all subsidies except those with very specific objectives, for instance financial support for air services to isolated communities. Such subsidies, if they are to continue, should be explicit and transparent. Some subsidies, such as non-payment of airport charges, are in any case contrary to the Chicago Convention of which virtually all states are signatories. Governments may be tempted to make their airlines appear more attractive to potential buyers by continuing certain direct or indirect subsidies, such as lower fuel prices or non-payments of rent for airport facilities or guarantees for the airline's loans. However, such a policy is double-edged. It may make the airline appear more viable, but it creates great uncertainty in that buyers will inevitably fear that a current direct or indirect subsidy will be arbitrarily removed by some future government. Uncertainty and risk reduces the potential value of the airline and therefore the price at which its shares can be sold.

Since the airline will no longer receive direct or hidden subsidies it should not be required to undertake any non-commercial activities such as operating routes just to 'show the flag' or provide free flights/tickets for ministers or officials. It should be treated by government as a stand alone commercial enterprise even if the state continues to be a share-holder. Any obligations placed upon the airline which impose a loss should ideally be paid for by central or local government.

Governments find it difficult to understand that in the new liberalised and more competitive markets, airlines will only survive if they are freed from both government intervention and any obligations to the state. Employees and unions encourage this blinkered view. They see government involvement as a safeguard. They fear that breaking the direct links between government and airline will lead to greater staff cuts, changes in work practices and a shrinking of the airline's network. They particularly fear privatisation.

8.4 Resolving privatisation issues

Unless the actions outlined above are implemented or at least set in motion newly privatised airlines are unlikely to survive long, especially if there is a cyclical downturn. The collapse of Philippine Airlines in September 1998, privatised only two years previously, is ample evidence of this. While Philippine Airlines was financially restructured, the recovery plan was largely cosmetic and did not cut deeply enough into labour costs or eliminate sufficient unprofitable routes. Nor was there a fundamental change of culture among managers or other staff. It is the cultural change which is the most difficult to implement. Olympic Airways has also failed in this respect. The potential benefits of the recovery plan detailed above were dissipated during 1996 and 1997 by the failure to change the traditional attitudes of management, employees, unions and government.

Various airline privatisation models are available from the simple and straightforward stock market flotation of 100 per cent of shares to more complex models involving sales of different proportions of share to particular investors. An example of the latter was the privatisation plan for Iberia finalised in December 1999. It involved acquisition of 9 per cent of its shares by British Airways and 1 per cent by American Airlines, with the purchase of a further 30 per cent by five domestic Spanish institutions. About 6 per cent was to be held by employees. The remaining 54 per cent was due to be floated in the second half of 2000.

In deciding to raise finance through partial or total privatisation, governments will normally be trying to achieve several objectives. Maximising proceeds for the public exchequer will only be one of these. They will also be aiming to reduce the airline's debts and provide new capital for route development, fleet modernisation or other investments such as IT. Privatisation may in turn make it easier for the airline to raise capital on the money markets. The government may wish to limit its own involvement in the airline so as to accelerate the decision-making processes within the airline and to make it more commercially oriented. Or the priority may be to facilitate the airline's restructuring by bringing in another airline or strategic investor as a major shareholder. The government may also wish to ensure wider share ownership among the population at large as well as among employees. The prioritisation of these different objectives will very much determine the form and sequencing of the privatisation process.

The best approach in each case will depend on the financial strength of the airline being privatised, the government's objectives in pursuing privatisation, and the prioritisation of those objectives, as well as the strength of the local capital markets and of the stock exchange. Thus, an appropriate model will very much depend on the specific local circumstances. It is the role of the banking advisers to recommend the best approach. But in identifying that model, governments, airlines and bank advisers would need to resolve a number of key issues.

First, should all the airline's shares be sold or only some proportion? If the latter, does the government retain less than 50 per cent, or does it keep a majority of the issued shares? When the government does not keep a majority share it must ensure that there are enough local shareholders (including itself) to meet the nationality and control requirements of the bilateral air services agreements. But if the government is no longer a majority shareholder, should it create a 'golden' share to enable it to take back effective control in the event of some specified crisis such as war or threat of a hostile takeover of the airline?

The risk in keeping a majority shareholding or a 'golden' share is that potential investors may feel that the risk of future government intervention reduces the value of any investment and, therefore, the price of the shares. Investors' response depends very much on the track record of each particular government in relation to other privatisations and to the economy in general. If it is perceived to be an interventionist government, then maintaining a controlling share will adversely affect the initial selling price of the shares. If governments are deemed to be unlikely to intervene, the current and future prices of the share will not be adversely affected by maintenance of a majority stake or golden shares. This is the case with Singapore Airlines' shares even though the Singapore government has always, in theory, kept a controlling interest.

The second issue to resolve is whether the shares should be sold through an initial public offering (IPO) on the stock exchange or through direct sale to one or more major investors or some combination of the two. The key question here is whether one wishes to encourage or even invite one or more major strategic investors to buy a significant shareholding of at least 10 per cent but possibly up to 50 per cent or more. If this is the preferred approach, governments must also decide whether the key strategic investor should be a non-aviation company or an airline. The advantage of strategic investors, who are not airlines, is that they may have greater financial resources to inject into the privatised airline to help it through difficult periods. Thus, in 1994, when Iberia, Spain's state-owned airline, faced mounting labour problems and losses in VIASA, the Venezuelan airline in which it had bought a 45 per cent share, it decided enough was enough and refused to provide more support. VIASA closed down. However, the more recent experience of Philippine Airlines in 1998 is that additional financial resources may not necessarily be forthcoming from a non-airline investor.

If the strategic investor is to be an airline, then choosing the preferred airline becomes a sensitive task. Should one choose the bidder offering the highest price or should the choice be made on the basis of some clear and explicit alliance strategy. If being part of a wider airline alliance is the aim, how does one evaluate and balance the potential benefits and disadvantages of different alliance partners (see Chapter 9, section 9.4)? An airline buying a strategic stake will want to include as part of the purchase deal further agreements on co-operation at many levels between the two airlines. This makes the sale more complex than if one is selling to a non-airline investor. There is a further risk that if there is only one airline interested in purchasing a strategic share, that airline may be able to squeeze all sorts of costly concessions through the alliance negotiations. In several cases, where airlines have become strategic investors in state-owned airlines, the partnership has not worked. The Alitalia 30 per cent investment in Malev or Air France's in CSA Czech Airlines, both made in the early 1990s, effectively failed and the larger airlines subsequently pulled out.

When it privatised Qantas the Australian Government chose a two-stage process. As a first step in 1993 it asked for bids from airline investors for 25 per cent of Qantas shares. British Airways was chosen as the strategic investor. This was followed in 1995 by a public flotation, in which the existence of the BA shareholding undoubtedly increased the share price, which was heavily oversubscribed. The government also allowed up to 49 per cent foreign share ownership in order to access international capital markets and further push up the price. Another government objective, wider share ownership, was also achieved with over 100,000 separate shareholders. In 1999, 38,000 of these held less than 1,000 shares each.

A third issue in any privatisation is whether the government should reserve some proportion of the shares for local investors or companies from its own country? This may in any case be required under the ownership and nationality articles of the existing bilateral air services agreements. It may also be politically attractive in suggesting that ownership of the national airline is not being surrendered entirely to foreign interests. High local shareholding can be ensured by reserving an agreed proportion of the shares for large local investors, such as banks, through direct sales or by placing nationality restrictions in the event of a public offering. The former tactic was adopted for the privatisation of Iberia, as described earlier.

A related issue is the degree to which, if any, shares should be reserved for employees and whether such shares should be sold to employees on preferential terms or even given free of charge. Employee shareholding may be politically attractive. It has two further and more important advantages. First, share ownership can be offered to employees in exchange for those concessions, discussed earlier, deemed necessary to reduce wage costs and increase labour productivity. For instance, the French government, in anticipation of the imminent public share offering of Air France in 1999, was prepared to grant shares to the latter's pilots in exchange for an equivalent value in salary concessions. This was as a reaction to the pilots' strike in the summer of 1998. The bartering of share options in return for salary and other concessions has been discussed earlier (Chapter 5, section 5.7).

Second, share ownership by staff should help in changing the culture within the airline and reducing confrontational attitudes. In fact, in most airline privatisations, when shares have been offered to staff, the main objective has been to involve employees in the fortunes and success of the airline and thereby to change the culture. It has not been as a trade-off for concessions. The schemes have been more or less generous. One of the earliest was that of Singapore Airlines. When it was privatised in 1985, employees were offered shares using a complex formula. The number of shares each could buy depended on seniority or grade and years of service. The formula ensured that long-standing employees, such as senior pilots, could buy large numbers of shares. To facilitate the share purchase, employees could borrow 95 per cent of the purchase price of their shares from the airline at a fixed 6 per cent interest and repay it over eight years or earlier if they left the airline. In other words, employees only had to find 5 per cent of the purchase cost of the shares they were entitled to. The scheme was very attractive even though there were no free shares. It has proved successful in ensuring staff loyalty and involvement with the airline. A different scheme, which included free shares, was that of British Airways. When it was floated in January 1987 each employee was offered 76 free shares. Then for each share, up to a maximum of 120, for which he or she paid the full offer price, they were given an additional 2 free shares. Finally, employees could apply for up to 1,600 shares through the public applications at a discount of 10 pence on the £1.25 public offer price. The fact that most employees became shareholders greatly facilitated the management of change within BA after 1987 and its transformation from a state corporation to a commercially oriented business with a strong service culture. In 1995 Qantas too offered some free shares to employees when it was privatised – again, with favourable results.

A final issue to resolve is who benefits from the sale of shares. If the government sells its own shares it can use the revenue to cover past airline losses it has financed or debts which it may have to take over as part of any financial restructuring. But it is crucially important for the airline itself to raise finance for its own use. This can be done by issuing new shares which are sold off by the airline itself. Many distressed state airlines need injections of working capital for fleet renewal or to provide for early retirement of surplus staff as well as a reduction of their accumulated debts. Therefore, governments opting for share sales should ensure that during the privatisation process adequate funds are also injected back into the airline. The partial privatisation of LOT, the Polish airline, early in 2000 is a good example of a balanced and sound approach. Swissair, after being chosen as the strategic investor, bought 10 per cent of the government's airline shares. The funds went to the government. New shares were then issued by the airline and Swissair bought sufficient to raise its overall shareholding to 37.6 per cent. In total Swissair paid US$120 million of which the bulk went to the airline. The government kept 52 per cent of the shares, which were scheduled to be floated later in 2000 or 2001, and employees held 10.4 per cent.

In conclusion, there are two crucial ideas that need to be emphasised. First, for most airlines needing an injection of new capital, the additional capital cannot ensure their long-term viability unless it is accompanied by cultural change at all levels and explicit financial and operational restructuring based on a clear recovery plan. Second, for state-owned airlines re-financing which involves partial or full privatisation is in itself much more likely to produce the cultural changes and restructuring necessary for longer-term success.

8.5 State aid and the single European market

Within the European Union, state-owned airlines have gone through a two-stage process. Following large losses in the early and mid-1990s, their governments pumped in huge funds to enable their airlines to carry out both the financial restructuring mentioned above and to implement a recovery plan. The assumption, in some cases only implicit, was that this was the first step in moving towards privatisation. Given that this so-called 'state aid' was highly controversial and has been heavily criticised by Europe's private airlines, it is worth considering whether such government aid was and is justified and whether it has distorted airline competition in Europe.

In the period 1991–94 the airline industry experienced the worst financial crisis in its history. Collectively the world's airlines lost US$15 billion in four years (see Chapter 1). During that period, most European airlines experienced heavy losses. Whether state- or privately-owned, many required major capital injections. In the case of seven state-owned airlines within the European Union such capital injections came in the form of state aid which required approval by the European Commission. Its purpose was to enable them to restructure and survive after a period of large losses. The sums involved were very substantial, high profile and controversial, totalling over ecu11 billion or over US$12 billion (Table 8.4).

Table 8.4 State aid and capital injections to airlines of the European Union, 1990–97

Airline	Capital injection (US$ millions)
State-owned	
Commission-approved state aid	
Sabena (1991)	1,800
Iberia (1992)	830
Aer Lingus (1993)	240
TAP (1994)	1,965
Air France (1994)	3,300
Olympic (1994)	2,245
Alitalia (1997)	1,708
Not classified as state aid	
Air France (1991)	338
Sabena (1995)	267
AOM (1995)	49
Iberia (1995)	593
Private sector	
British Airways (1993)	690
KLM (1994)	620
Lufthansa* (1994)	710
Finnair (1992/4/5)	175

Note
* German government also contributed DM1.55 billion (about ecu 800 million) to the Lufthansa pension fund in 1995.

In addition, over ecu1 billion (US$1.1 billion) of capital was injected into these airlines, but was not classified as state aid. The Commission had deemed that these smaller capital injections were consistent with the 'market economy investor' principle. In other words, the Commission judged that a private investor would have considered it a commercially viable investment to inject these sums into the airlines at that particular time.

But even those privatised airlines, which were relatively more profitable, required new capital from shareholders through rights issues or other means (such as conversion of bonds). British Airways ($665m), Lufthansa ($730m) and KLM ($480m) were among these. It should also not be forgotten that some of these airlines had themselves received direct or indirect government financial support in the past.

Inevitably, the huge amounts granted by some governments to their national carriers in the form of 'state aid' created reaction and opposition from those airlines which had not received any aid and which had been largely dependent on raising capital from private or commercial sources. They and others have argued repeatedly that 'state aid' leads to a distortion of the competitive working of the free market and is contrary to consumers' interests. In a 1996 paper Sir Michael Bishop, Chairman of Airlines of Britain, parent company of British Midland, stated bluntly that: 'Unjustifiable state aid to flag-carriers is the greatest obstacle to the emergence of a viable, competitive airline industry.'

Implicit in this statement, and similar statements by other airline chairmen or executives, is the view that most, if not all, state aid is *unjustifiable*. Yet it is frequently forgotten that the Treaty of Rome specifically allows 'state aids' provided they are 'exemptible'. This means, provided that their advantages in terms of European interest can be demonstrated to outweigh any restrictions to competition which may result. While the general rule, enshrined in Article 88(1) of the Treaty, is that state aids in whatever form are prohibited, the Treaty also provides for both mandatory and discretionary exceptions to this general rule.

Mandatory exemptions (Article 88(2)) allow state aid if it has a social character; to make good damage from natural disasters; and to compensate for the economic disadvantages caused by the division of Germany.

Discretionary exemptions (Article 88(3)) allow the Commission to approve state aid in a variety of cases. In the case of air transport it is Article 88(3c) which is most frequently invoked and accepted by the Commission. This allows: 'aid to facilitate the development of certain economic activities or economic areas, where such aid does not adversely affect trading conditions to an extent contrary to the common interest . . .'

Clearly 'state aid' for airlines can be granted discretionary exemption within the Treaty of Rome, but two questions follow: first, is 'state aid' justifiable in economic terms? Second, if 'state aid' is approved under Article 88(3c), can the Commission ensure that it achieves its agreed objectives; that it is not misspent, and that it does not unnecessarily distort competition within the single market? One can answer these two questions with reference to the experiences of Olympic Airways in relation to state aid. The Olympic story parallels to greater or lesser extent the experiences of other 'distressed state airlines' such as Aer Lingus or TAP that received state aid in the mid-1990s.

Is state aid justifiable?

Strong arguments can be put forward to show that state aid to government airlines suffering the distressed airline syndrome is justifiable. First, that in most cases state aid has not been just a free handout of cash from taxpayers to loss-making airlines. Rather, it should be considered as *partial or even full compensation* for past or present costs and penalties imposed on state airlines by government actions. In return for providing direct or indirect support, such as government guarantees for loans to buy aircraft or for bank overdrafts, governments and their taxpayers expected to be able to impose numerous obligations on their airlines and to interfere directly in management. That was the quid pro quo. Political backing and support from the state in return for 'favours' from the airline.

Over time, the numerous obligations imposed on many state airlines sapped their strength and undermined their economic well-being since such obligations were uneconomic and costly. In the case of Olympic Airways, it suffered over many years in numerous ways from government controls and interference. As mentioned above (section 8.2) the obligations imposed on the airline included the operation of uneconomic domestic and international routes, the imposition of cargo or passenger tariffs that were too low, pressure to take on unnecessary additional staff, and so on. At Olympic, as at many state airlines, government interference over many years in these and many other ways, resulted in losses and an inability to compete effectively, to modernise and rationalise the fleet or to become customer oriented.

Among those privately-owned European airlines who have clamoured for state aid not to be granted were several who had themselves benefited from state aid in some form or other prior to their own privatisation. In many cases such aid was seen explicitly as compensation to offset earlier costly obligations imposed on the airlines. For instance, in 1980 the British government wrote off £160 million, or 47 per cent of the capital it had invested in British Airways because of the exceptional costs associated with the supersonic Concorde aircraft which the airline had been more or less forced to buy. The government had also guaranteed British Airways overseas loans, thereby reducing the interest charges. Furthermore, the UK Treasury, while encouraging British Airways to borrow foreign exchange, itself covered the gain or loss on exchange rate fluctuations on certain US dollar loans under the Treasury Exchange Cover Scheme (British Airways, 1984). More recently, the German government, in anticipation of Lufthansa's 1997 flotation, contributed DM1.55 billion to the Lufthansa pension fund in 1995. This was to enable Lufthansa and its subsidiaries to break away from the more costly public sector supplementary retirement benefit scheme UBL which they had previously been obliged to be part of (Lufthansa, 1995).

The second justification for state aid is that most state airlines have been grossly undercapitalised. This occurred because of the unwillingness or inability of most European governments to inject fresh shareholders' capital into their state-owned airlines as they grew and expanded. For example, Aer Lingus in 1993 with a turnover of close to £1 billion, had an equity base of only £65 million. If and when airlines have been making reasonable profits undercapitalisation was not a critical problem. But where, as in the case of Olympic and others, several years of losses, as well as aircraft purchases, had to be financed by loans, then airlines were caught in a spiral. Increasing interest payments on short- or medium-term loans induced net losses even in year of operating profits. These required further medium- or short-term borrowing, creating a growing debt burden. This further increased the following year's interest payments. In Olympic's case, losses were largely financed by medium-term loans from state institutions and banks at interest rates of 16–18 per cent per annum. When Olympic was unable to repay the loans on the due date, interest levels shot up to a punitive 30–35 per cent per annum.

The inability of state-owned airlines to raise capital through injections of equity, has seriously undermined their financial performance. If 'state aid' is used primarily for capital restructuring of an airline and, in particular, for the writing off of accumulated debts, then it appears justifiable. It is correcting an imbalance between state-owned and privatised airlines which have had access to equity capital. It should not be forgotten that British Airways since privatisation has had two major capital injections from its shareholders through rights issues.

In so far as much state aid has involved writing off large airline debts to government banks and other institutions, governments are merely acknowledging and doing what any private investor would do. Namely, accepting that these debts are unlikely ever to be repaid. Examples abound. Most of our major banks have at some time written off large Third World debts. British Airways itself in 1996–97 wrote down its investment in USAir while early in 1997 Swissair decided to write off its $180m investment in Sabena.

Finally, one should consider that the alternatives to state aid may be worse. A private investor running a company with huge and mounting debts might well consider putting the company into liquidation and starting again, possibly using the same assets. Thus the 'owners' of Olympic or Air Portugal say might have considered allowing these airlines to cease trading in order then to set up a new company, buy the former airline's assets cheaply and take on staff with new and better terms and conditions of employment.

This could be done. It was done successfully by the Israeli government in the 1980s with El Al. It was considered by the Greek government in 1994 as an alternative to seeking European Commission approval for state aid. For the government, the financial implications would have been largely the same as formal state aid. Namely, it would have had to take over all the airline's debts which it had guaranteed. Of course there can be little doubt that such a course of action would be politically and socially very difficult. But *in extremis* it is an alternative. From the point of view of the single European market, the 'El Al' solution would surely have distorted competition much more than state aid. It should also be borne in mind that if there was no mechanism within the Treaty of Rome to allow for state aids subject to approval, transparency and control by the Commission, then governments might well find other uncontrolled and non-transparent ways of supporting their ailing industries.

Another key question is whether state aid can achieve the stated objectives. In the early days the European Commission did not have a clear-cut policy on the issue of state aid. However, in 1993 the European Commissioner for Transport appointed a group of experts, the so-called 'wise men' or Comité des Sages, to reflect and advise on the future of aviation in Europe. In their January 1994 report, they urged the European Commission to enforce strictly the state aids provisions in the Treaty of Rome, but accepted that: 'Support for the transition of an air carrier to commercial viability may be in the Community's interest if the position of competitors is safeguarded.' The 'wise men' outlined a number of conditions for approving such support. These included a requirement for a restructuring plan leading to economic viability within a specified timescale and creating in the longer term an airline potentially attractive to the private sector and a clear 'one time last time' proviso (Comité des Sages, 1994).

As a result of the Comité's report and intensive lobbying and campaigning from Aer Lingus' competitors in 1993, when the Irish Government submitted its state aid proposal for Aer Lingus, the European Commission modified its position on state aids. Up to 1993 the Commission's decisions on applications for state aids for airlines had been taken without close reference to the general terms of the Treaty of Rome or any specific principles arising from decisions in non-transport cases.

In November 1994 the Commission approved guidelines for the evaluation of proposals for state aid for airlines (*Official Journal*, 1994). These mirrored to a considerable extent the recommendations of the Comité des Sages. The guidelines suggested that in approving proposals for state aid to airlines the Commission might impose the following conditions:

- The aid must be part of a comprehensive restructuring programme which can ensure viable operations for the airline within a reasonably short period.
- No additional aid should be required in the future.
- The aid should not be used to increase the capacity of the airline concerned to the detriment of its direct EU competitors. Nor should its capacity on offer within the EU market area increase faster than the overall growth of traffic in this area.
- If the restoration of financial viability requires capacity reductions, these should be included in the programme.
- The government providing the aid must not interfere in the airline's management for reasons other than those stemming from its ownership rights and must allow it to be run according to commercial principles.
- Aid must be used only for restructuring and the recipient must not acquire shareholdings in other airlines.
- The aid must not be used for increased direct competition with other EU carriers.
- The grant of aid must be transparent and controllable.

In the case of Olympic, as with other airlines receiving state aid, the Commission imposed a large number of very specific conditions arising from the above guidelines when it approved the Greek government's state aid proposal in October 1994. Moreover, the Greek government, like other governments concerned, explicitly accepted the conditions imposed and agreed to implement them. Commission approval was required for each annual tranche and was dependent on each government and its respective airline convincing consultants sent by the Commission and ultimately the Commission itself that they had met fully the agreed conditions and targets. Thus, in theory state aid conditions are enforceable.

The crucial question is to what extent have the conditions imposed on Olympic, Aer Lingus, Air France, TAP or Iberia achieved the Commission's three primary objectives? Namely:

- to ensure the restructuring plan enabled the airline concerned to operate successfully in the single European market without further state aid;
- to ensure that the aid has not been used to intensify or strengthen the recipient's competition with other EU airlines; and
- to allow the restructured airline to operate on a commercial basis free of government interference.

The Commission has generally been more successful in achieving the first two objectives than the third. Most of the airlines receiving state aid were able to restructure and move into profit, though in one or two cases, profitability took longer to achieve than anticipated. Nor has the state aid been used directly to strengthen the recipients' competitive position, since strict conditions imposed by the Commission on capacity and pricing ensured that this did not happen. However, it proved more difficult to eliminate or even reduce continued government interference in the airlines' management and operations. In the case of Olympic Airways, the initial success of the restructuring made possible through state aid was destroyed by the Greek government's inability to stop meddling in the airline's affairs.

8.6 The Olympic Airways case

After the first restructuring plan proposed in 1993 by the Greek government for Olympic was rejected by the Commission, a significantly improved plan was approved in 1994. The difficulties in obtaining Commission approval played a key part in persuading union leaders to accept significant sacrifices on the part of their members as their contribution to saving the airline. The key elements of the restructuring plan were implemented during 1995, its first year (see Table 8.3). The plan focused on three key action areas: financial restructuring, cost reduction, primarily through reducing labour costs, and network revision.

Actions on these three areas, together with very strict cost control during 1995, dramatically improved labour productivity and financial performance. In the financial year 1995 the airline's operating surplus jumped to US$56.5 million compared to US$21.3m in the previous year. More significantly, an annual loss in 1994 of US$129.4m after interest and capital charges and before extraordinary items was transformed into a profit of US$59.3m. This was due in no small measure to the elimination of interest payments of $150 million as a result of the write-off of most of Olympic's accumulated debts. Olympic's restructuring plan appeared to be achieving its financial and cost objectives during the first two years.

However, when, early in 1996, the Commission was due to approve payment by the Greek government of the second tranche of state aid, in the form of a cash payment of US$98 million, it failed to do so. In its decision published on 19 June 1996, the Commission stated that 'while on the one hand Olympic Airways seems to be making a very satisfactory recovery in conformity with the plan on which the decision is based, it appears on the other hand that several of the commitments and conditions set out in Article 1 of the (1994) Decision have not been met by the Greek government' (*Official Journal*, 1996a). The Commission listed at length the numerous ways in which various conditions had not been met. But these effectively focused around two issues. The first was the continued interference by the Greek government in the management of the airline in a variety of ways such as frequent changes in the board of directors, the maintenance of civil service procedures in staff recruitment, failure to settle debts owed to the airline and so on. The second related to US$47 million which had been voted by the Greek parliament in December 1994 to assist Olympic in paying for voluntary redundancies and which had not been included in the original state aid package.

While the Greek government during the spring of 1996 was trying to convince the European Commission that it no longer interfered with the management of Olympic, it shot itself in the foot by summarily dismissing the then Chairman and CEO in March 1996 without explanation. Moreover, this happened the day after the Chairman announced Olympic's successful results for 1995 when it produced the first bottom line profit for 18 years. In removing the Chairman, a new Minister of Transport was giving way to pressure from some of Olympic's trade unions. The Minister then appointed a new Chairman and a team of senior executives approved by the union leadership. The latter had effectively captured the airline. Inevitably, decisions taken by the new union-approved management during the next year and a half, often with government support, undermined much of the progress and success achieved in 1995. For instance, substantial wage increases averaging over 20 per cent were granted in 1997, yet at the same time the management took no steps to implement any kind of recovery plan. Profits evaporated and by the end of 1997 the airline was facing substantial losses again. A new Minister of Transport changed the management twice more in rapid succession as one chairman resigned after four days.

Meanwhile, the issue of government interference in Olympic's operations held up payment of the second cash injection for two years. It was not till early 1998, and after the submission of yet another revised recovery plan, that the Commission was convinced that the Greek government would in future deal with Olympic strictly at arm's length as a shareholder, rather than as a public authority. Regrettably, repeated changes in management in the period 1997 to 2000 led to further losses and deviations from the recovery plan. A British Airways subsidiary, Speedwing, brought in to manage Olympic on 1 July 1999 appeared unable to reverse this trend. By summer 2000 the European Commission had still not approved the final tranche of the capital injection originally agreed in 1994.

The Olympic case shows that it is in relation to its third objective, that of ensuring that governments deal with their airlines entirely at arm's length as a normal shareholder, that the Commission has had less success. This is partly because government pressures and involvement are not always transparent and partly because a 'hands off' approach requires a fundamental change of attitude and culture by politicians, civil servants, taxpayers and airline managers. In many countries this is difficult to achieve in a short period of time.

Despite their commitments to the Commission not to interfere, governments have in most cases found it difficult to avoid doing so. In Greece, successive transport ministers continued to treat Olympic and its management as their predecessors had done before the restructuring, that is, as an appendage of government. What is worse is that when there is a juxtaposition of strong unions opposed to the restructuring plans and governments that are politically weak, for instance if elections are imminent, then governments have tended to withdraw their support from the chairmen and managers put in to implement the restructuring. One saw this happen with Bernard Attali, Chairman of Air France in 1993, and early in 1996 it happened with Renato Riverso of Alitalia and Pierre Godfroid, Chairman of Sabena and also in Olympic.

If state aid and government support to European airlines or to distressed state airlines elsewhere in the world fails to ensure long-term financial viability for such airlines, the most likely cause is likely to be continued government interference in the management of the airlines. If the major injections of state aid have failed to ensure the transformation of the 'distressed state airlines' into efficient competitors then this is most likely to be due not to poor management, or insufficient state aid, but to a lack of political will and a failure to provide political support for the managers put in to restructure these airlines. Further state aid will not solve this political problem.

9 Strategies for the twenty-first century

9.1 A period of uncertainty

A major question mark hanging over airlines at the start of the new millennium has been whether the early years will be marked by a cyclical downturn of the industry's fortunes as happened in each of the three preceding decades. The signs were not good. In 1998 the financial results of the world's international scheduled airlines began to worsen following the very good years of the mid-1990s (see Chapter 1, Figures 1.1–1.2). In 1999 profits for these airlines dropped to US$1.9 billion from $3.1 billion a year earlier. Significantly higher fuel prices, growing overcapacity in key markets and falling yields appeared to be the root causes of the deteriorating financial performance. Unless at least one of these three trends can be reversed a further deterioration in the early years of the new decade is inevitable. It remains to be seen whether the downturn, if it worsens, will be as severe and painful as that of 1990 to 1993. But whatever the economic outcome, the preceding chapters have highlighted the numerous problems and the uncertainty which the international airline business will face in the coming years.

The regulatory environment, as it moves from 'open skies' to 'clear skies', will be one cause of uncertainty. Deregulation will spread to regions of the world hitherto untouched, while Europe and North America will try to move in gradual steps towards the creation of a Transatlantic Common Aviation Area. The ownership rule requiring airlines to be substantially owned and effectively controlled by nationals of their country of registration will be under pressure and is likely to be progressively abandoned. In Europe, the expansion of the European Common Aviation Area to encompass an additional ten or eleven states will create new opportunities but also threats for many of Europe's airlines. The airlines, of the new member states, largely government-owned, will be facing the full force of open and free competition domestically and internationally for the first time. During 2000 and 2001 they will be looking to partial or full privatisation and strategic alliances to help them meet the challenges of the single European market.

While the regulatory environment is changing, the structure of the airline industry will also be going through a period of flux. There will be further industry concentration both through the continued enlargement of some alliances and the strengthening of others, as they move from being largely commercial in character to being more truly strategic. This will be done through the creation of joint operating companies and other joint ventures. When the ownership rules begin to be relaxed, a new period of instability and change will occur as cross-border acquisitions and even mergers begin to replace the more traditional alliance agreements. Old partners may be abandoned and new partnerships created. Moreover, the gradual and further privatisation of the seventy or so international airlines which in 2000 were still majority-owned by their governments will also bring these airlines into play. The better ones will also become acquisition targets. A few will not survive for long. The industry will move from an era of concentration to a period of consolidation.

On medium- and long-haul routes, competition will increasingly be between alliances and their hubs rather than between individual airlines. On short-haul routes of up to three or four hours, the low-cost carriers of North America and Europe will capture an increasing share of the market by growing more rapidly than the conventional scheduled and charter airlines. New low-cost carriers will also emerge in other regions such as East Asia and South America. Not all the new entrant low-cost carriers will survive. Some of the European and other low-cost carriers operating at the beginning of 2000 will no longer be flying two or three years later. This too is an unstable sector. Nevertheless its impact on the conventional airlines will continue to be substantial. Airlines such as Southwest in the US or Ryanair and easyJet in Europe will force the conventional operators to reduce fares where they compete head on, but also to constantly re-examine their cost structures. There is little doubt that the latter airlines still have much to learn from the former.

Not only is the structure of the airline industry entering a period of change and uncertainty but markets too will become more unstable. This is an inevitable result of the further liberalisation as the US negotiates more 'open skies' bilaterals, as the European single market spreads eastwards to encompass the central European states, and as different parts of the world move to set up regional open aviation areas. Freer market access will result in more new entrant carriers coming in to compete against the established airlines. The latter will themselves be competing more aggressively as regulations are relaxed by adding more frequencies and building up their own and their alliance partners' hubs. Periodic overcapacity in most markets will be endemic. Downward pressure on fares and yields is almost certain to continue. On shorter sectors such pressures will be made worse from the incursion of low-cost carriers. The accelerating switch to e-commerce and online ticket sales will also create market instability. The Internet will give consumers instantaneous and easy access to airline price and service data thereby enhancing consumers' market power. This will aggravate the downward pressure on tariffs and fares. There is a risk that the airline product will be commoditised. If this happens, price will emerge as the crucial, perhaps the only, competitive variable. Branding and product differentiation will become increasingly necessary for airlines but at the same time progressively more difficult and costly. The switch to online selling will particularly favour the low-cost carriers because search engines will enable consumers to identify and select their low fares even when online travel intermediaries may not list them.

9.2 Clarifying the corporate mission

In a climate of continuous change and uncertainty airlines in the coming years will face critical problems and serious challenges. Many of these have been outlined in the earlier chapters. As a first step in the difficult years ahead, airlines will need to identify and clarify their own corporate mission. What kind of airline do they wish to be?

The key issue which needs to be resolved is whether the airline is to be a global network carrier or a niche player. A global carrier would aim to provide a world-wide network of routes and destinations. It can do this by linking its own wide route network with that of a handful of alliance partners through their respective hubs to create a truly global system. British Airways, Lufthansa, Singapore Airlines, American, Delta and several others clearly aim to be global airlines. The alternative is to be a niche carrier. The niche to focus on may be either geographical or a particular type of service. A geographical niche may take various forms. Some airlines see their corporate objective as providing only domestic services within a particular country. In a large country, a domestic niche carrier may have a very extensive network or may focus on a particular region within that country. Alaskan Airlines in the United States or Regional Airlines in France are niche carriers of this kind. Another niche strategy is to focus on being the scheduled international airline serving a particular country or a particular region. Many national airlines are of this kind. They have no pretensions to be global carriers. Their corporate mission is to provide high-quality services to and from their own country or the particular region they are serving. Cyprus Airways and Tunis Air are examples of the former while Gulf Air and Emirates have a more regional niche. To be successful and profitable geographical niche airlines must ensure that they are so strong in the markets they serve that it is difficult and costly for other airlines or new entrants to challenge them effectively. Many niche carriers will reinforce their market position by entering into route-specific alliances or even becoming regional partners of larger network carriers. Smaller domestic or international carriers may also decide to become franchisees of larger airlines operating part or all of their services in the colours and livery of the franchiser. Several small UK domestic airlines have done this as a result of franchisee agreements with British Airways.

Very large or relatively small airlines should have little difficulty in clarifying their corporate mission. The greatest difficulty is faced by medium-sized international airlines, such as Finnair, LOT Polish Airlines, Olympic, Pakistan International or Mexicana. They may be too small to be global players but too big to reconcile themselves to the role of a niche airline. But unless they can identify the long-term role that is most realistic and feasible for them, they will have difficulty in taking the right strategic decisions to achieve their corporate mission since the mission itself will be unclear. Lack of a cohesive, long-term strategy will endanger their survival in the more competitive world of the future.

There are in addition several market niches which are not geographical in nature but are linked to the type of air services being offered. One niche is that of the specialist charter or non-scheduled carrier. On the passenger side, this sector of the industry is most developed in Europe with several large airlines such as Britannia Airways and Condor. There are of course separate niche airlines, such as Cargolux, focusing exclusively on scheduled and/or non-scheduled freight traffic. Another niche, discussed earlier at some length, is that of the low-cost carrier. Finally, we have the integrated or express carriers such as Federal Express, DHL or UPS, who offer door-to-door high-speed services for parcels and 'small' freight.

Clarifying the corporate mission is crucial for two reasons. It facilitates the identification of the correct strategies for long-term success and survival. But, in the short term, it helps to ensure that current management decisions are consistent with achieving the corporate mission and objectives. Unclear, confused or incompatible corporate objectives lead to poor and often contradictory commercial and operating decisions. The sudden collapse in 1999 of Debonair, one of the first European low-cost carriers, was due in no small measure to confused corporate objectives. It was trying to operate as a low-cost low-fare carrier but offering frills, such as a business class or more leg room, which inevitably pushed up the costs (see Chapter 6, section 6.6). At the start of 2000, Virgin Express, the Brussels-based low-cost carrier, also appeared to suffer from confused corporate objectives. Was this a danger signal?

9.3 New paradigms for the airline business?

Airlines need to have a clear, unambiguous corporate mission. One key aspect of that mission must be to decide whether the airline is in the airline or the aviation business. Because of the way the airline business has grown, the traditional airline itself provided in-house most of the services and functions it required. Its departmental structure reflected this. There were and still are, in most airlines, separate departments dealing with engineering and overhaul, in-flight catering, ground handling, cargo, reservations and ticketing, sales, management information systems and informatics, and so on. All these functions were considered so important and critical for the efficient running of the business that airline managements have felt they had to control them directly. As a result, most medium-sized and large airlines are self-sufficient in these areas. Some work is contracted out to other carriers or suppliers but usually in locations away from an airline's home base. For instance, ground handling or catering is often provided by others at distant airports. Several airlines contract out some of the more difficult engine or airframe overhauls to specialist maintenance organisations or other carriers with more advanced facilities. The overall aim has been self-sufficiency in most areas with only limited contracting out. As a result, most airlines look very similar in their method of operation and their management structures. This was, and for most airlines still is, what the airline business is about.

During the 1990s two alternative and different business models have emerged. British Airways epitomises the one and Lufthansa and Swissair the other. In the mid-1990s as a reaction to the crisis years of 1990 to 1993 and the need to reduce costs, senior managers at British Airways, among others, launched the notion of the 'virtual airline'. The concept was simple. An airline should focus on its core competences, which is operating a network of air services and outsource to others as many non-core activities and functions as possible. By doing this, it could significantly reduce its own costs, especially in areas where traditionally it was over-staffed, and at the same time achieve low future costs by putting out the functions concerned to competitive bidding from alternative suppliers (Figure 9.1, part 2). In the years that followed, British Airways, as mentioned earlier, outsourced its ground transport services at Heathrow and Gatwick to a US company Ryder, it sold off its in-flight catering at Heathrow to Swissair's Gate Gourmet and also sold off its heavy engine maintenance facility in South Wales (Chapter 5, section 5.6). The airline abandoned the provision of third-party terminal and ramp handling to other carriers at Heathrow's terminals 1 and 2. In other words it more or less withdrew from the provision of ground handling services to third parties.

BA would have gone further in its outsourcing strategy but for union opposition. While outsourcing worsened industrial relations, British Airways failed to make significant inroads in its staff numbers. It was still employing 56,000 staff at the beginning of 1999, about 8,000 more than five years earlier. The virtual airline strategy appears much more effective for new start-up airlines that are not encumbered with existing facilities and staff. By outsourcing most functions they can get the best and lowest cost deals and they can start flying very quickly. Some of the low-cost airlines, such as easyJet and Go, BA's subsidiary, are close to being virtual airlines. In fact when easyJet started in 1995 it even outsourced the aircraft provision and the flying.

The alternative model is one that suggests that airlines are not just in the core *airline* business, but that they are in a wider *aviation* business (Figure 9.1, part 3). The latter consists of much more than flying. In-flight catering, aircraft maintenance, ground handling, air-transport-related informatics and other activities or functions are all parts of the aviation business. Many airlines are too small to provide all of these services economically in-house and are now looking for outside suppliers. Even larger airlines may wish to outsource some of these functions, for instance, ground handling, when and where it can be done more cheaply. Some of these services can also be supplied to non-airline customers. Thus, there is a whole host of services and activities that are separate business activities in their own right. Traditionally, as mentioned earlier, most scheduled and charter airlines had these activities provided in-house by their own relevant departments and considered them as part of their core business. Increasingly, however, a few airlines have seen the potential value of these activities as profit generators and businesses in their own right. They have set about transforming what were previously internal departments into separate specialist companies. In Europe, Swissair and Lufthansa have led the way in this. In Asia, it has been Singapore Airlines.

Lufthansa has identified seven separate business segments. These are (i) the 'Passenger Business', which covers the core passenger airlines of which there are two, Lufthansa and Lufthansa Cityline, but also subsidiaries Lauda Air (20 per cent shareholding) and Luxair (13 per cent Lufthansa stake); (ii) a 'Maintenance, Repair and Overhaul' organisation; (iii) 'Catering', both in-flight and on the ground; (iv) 'Ground Services' both in Germany and world-wide; (v) 'Leisure Travel' which encompasses Lufthansa's charter airline Condor; (vi) 'IT Services'; and (vii) 'Logistics', a separate business which includes Lufthansa Cargo and effectively all Lufthansa's cargo carrying activities (Lufthansa, 1998). By setting these up as separate businesses with their own accountable managements it became easier to achieve more effective cost control and to make each of them much more customer-focused. As a result marked increases in turnover were achieved in most areas in 1998 and 1999. The Lufthansa Group board was able to set a tough corporate objective for each business segment, namely, for each to become one of the top three providers in the world in its own particular business area. By the end of 2000 most of the businesses had achieved this! The Swissair approach has been very similar, though there are only five separate business areas. It is clear that today Lufthansa and Swissair see their corporate mission as being in the aviation business. British Airways remains primarily an airline. Which is the correct strategy to follow?

While there is a logic in the BA approach of moving towards a virtual airline in terms of reducing costs through outsourcing, it does carry a major risk. The airline business is very cyclical. Concentrating purely on the core activities and abandoning the provision of peripheral services makes an airline more susceptible to any sustained economic downturn.

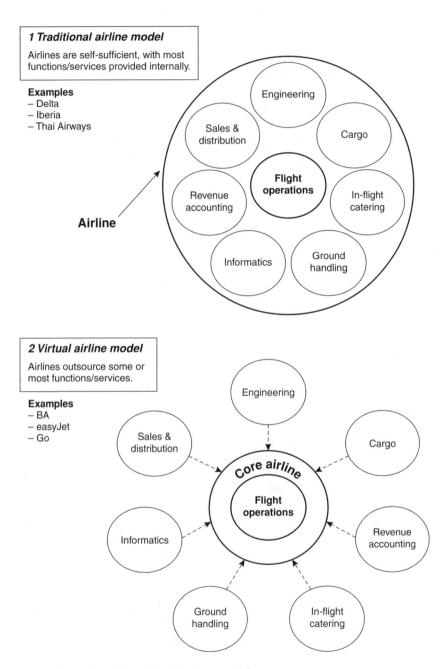

Figure 9.1 Alternative airline business models

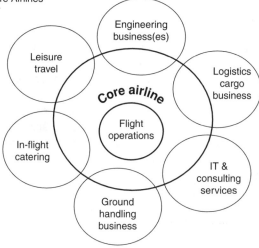

3 Aviation business model

Airlines have separate business units that support the passenger core, but generate most revenue from external clients.

Examples
– Lufthansa
– Singapore Airlines
– Swissair

Figure 9.1 (continued)

If passenger growth falls off or if yields decline and revenues go down there are no countervailing sources of revenue, from, say, catering or ground handling services, to offset the revenue fall. Revenues from these areas may also be adversely affected by a cyclical downturn, but much less so than the core airline revenues. After all, other airlines' aircraft, as well as one's own, still have to be handled or maintained, and passengers continue to require in-flight meals and catering. In 1999 it was the absence of any countervailing revenues from other sources that led to the dramatic drop in BA's profits. This poor performance and the collapsing share price ultimately lead to the resignation of the chief executive, Robert Ayling, in March 2000, one of the chief proponents of the virtual airline strategy. Airlines such as Lufthansa or Swissair also saw profits from their airline business decline that year. Like BA they too were affected by higher fuel prices, overcapacity in key markets and falling yields. But revenue in their ancillary businesses held up better and helped cushion the shortfall in airline revenues. Their chief executives did not have to resign!

The Lufthansa-Swissair paradigm also involves some risks. If, as seems most likely, the core airline business is required to buy all the services it needs, such as catering or maintenance, from its own non-core business units, can one be certain that it is always obtaining the best and cheapest deal possible? On the other hand it could be argued that because these specialist business units are likely to be large they will enjoy economies of scale, and since they are constantly in competitive bidding for external third-party work they are likely to be more efficient than an airline's internal supplier who does not face real competition. There is an added risk that, in the longer term, the non-core businesses may prove consistently profitable while the airline business itself is marginal. Does one then abandon or sell off the latter and keep the former?

In the coming years airlines will have three business models to choose from. There is the traditional model of the self-sufficient airline which provides in-house most of the necessary ancillary support services. This may be more expensive than contracting out but the management feels it is in control of its destiny. Some contracting out is undertaken but usually in specialist areas or for services away from its home base(s). Work may also be contracted in from other airlines. Such work is always welcome but not seen as a major revenue source in its own right, rather as a way of optimising the utilisation of existing staff and facilities. Second, there is the virtual airline model partially adopted by British Airways. But perhaps the best examples are some of the European low-cost carriers such as easyJet. Cost minimisation is the priority. If any service or function can be provided more cheaply by an external supplier then it should be outsourced. This is of course much easier to do for new start-up airlines than for airlines trying to move from the traditional self-sufficiency model to a more virtual model, since they are encumbered with existing staff and facilities. They inevitably face considerable employee and union opposition. Finally, there is the aviation business model. This sees each of the ancillary activities related to the core provision of air services as separate and potentially profitable businesses in their own right. Moreover, such businesses aim to capture a customer base which is much larger and wider than their own host airline. To date, the most successful proponents of this model are Lufthansa and Swissair and to some extent Singapore Airlines. Surprisingly, no North American airlines have yet gone down this road.

Airline executives and their boards will have to choose which of the three business models to adopt and develop as part of their long-term corporate strategy. *A priori*, the third option, the aviation business model, appears to be the most attractive. However, not all airlines are large enough or have sufficient resources to adopt this model.

9.4 Developing an alliance strategy

It was suggested in the earlier chapter on alliances that there are strong economic forces driving the airline industry towards increased concentra-

tion and globalisation. In turn it is the existing regulatory regime which
has forced such concentration to be achieved through alliances of various
kinds rather than through cross-border acquisitions and mergers. The
alliance frenzy will continue. New partnerships will be forged and some
old ones will break up. For all airline executives, but especially those of
medium-sized and smaller airlines, this is a major area of uncertainty and
concern. They understand the clear rationale in favour of alliances, but
also perceive that alliances pose a real threat, especially as they evolve
from being largely commercial to being more strategic and binding. Many
are worried that by entering into an alliance with a larger carrier or group
of carriers they will lose effective control over their own destiny in matters
such as route development, pricing, branding, customer service standards,
and so on. They fear that decisions will be made by the two or three
dominant carriers and that junior partners will have to follow along. There
is also great concern as to how airlines should choose between possible
partners when alternative alliances are available. To overcome such
concerns airlines need to develop a clear and coherent alliance strategy.

The economic pressures pushing the airlines into alliances are real since
the benefits from joining alliances can be very substantial. This is particularly so in terms of the marketing advantages of larger scale and scope.
This, however, does not mean that alliances are an end in themselves.
They should only be seen as a means to an end, which is to improve an
airline's operating and marketing efficiency and its financial returns. This
means that each alliance proposal should be examined on its merits. Some,
perhaps many, may need to be rejected after careful evaluation. Evaluating
and developing alliance tactics and strategy requires three clear steps.

The first is for an airline to identify and clarify its own objectives and
aims in seeking a particular alliance with another carrier or group of
airlines. Is the focus on increasing market spread through serving more
destinations? In other words is it on revenue generation? Or is the initial
focus on reducing costs in particular markets or individual routes through
a joint sales force, shared sales offices, mutual ground handling, and so
on? In many cases both revenue generation and cost reduction will be
primary objectives. But to what extent is the avoidance or reduction in
competition between the prospective partners an objective? In some cases,
especially on route-specific alliances, this may be the primary aim with
cost reduction taking second place. For those airlines seeking a strategic
investor, as part of a privatisation process, the need to attract and inject
new capital may be the most important consideration in choosing an
alliance partner. One needs not only to identify the objectives to be
achieved in entering partnership but also to prioritise them.

The second step is to determine what kind of alliance best meets the
objectives identified. If the objectives relate primarily to a particular route
then the airline will most likely wish to enter a route-specific alliance. It
could, as many airlines do, have separate alliances involving code-share

or other agreements, for different routes on its network. A smaller airline with a domestic or regional network may feel that its objectives can best be met by entering into a regional alliance with a larger carrier. This would involve linking a significant part or even its whole network into the larger partner's route system. This could be done through simple code sharing on several routes and joint marketing and possibly joint selling. Or, at the other end of the spectrum (as illustrated earlier in Figure 4.1), the smaller carrier could operate as a franchisee of its larger partners, adopting its livery, brand and service standards. The latter would be a truly strategic alliance. Alternatively, an airline might feel that its longer-term objectives could best be satisfied by joining a truly global world-wide alliance. This would be the case if it gave priority to achieving the widest network spread possible. If it decides to follow this strategy, then there is a further choice to be made. Should it join a global alliance that is marketing oriented such as Oneworld, or should it seek a more strategic alliance such as the Swissair-Sabena grouping which is likely to involve greater co-mingling of assets.

The final step in developing an alliance strategy is to assess and quantify the benefits and costs of different potential partners. Many related issues need to be considered and, where possible, quantified. The starting point should be to ensure that, *a priori*, there are potential benefits to all partners and that such benefits are broadly in balance. If one partner feels it is getting much less out of the alliance than the other partner(s), then the alliance is inherently unstable. To assess both the balance of benefits and an individual airline's advantages in moving into a partnership, a very detailed route-by-route assessment is required. This will forecast the traffic gains, in terms of additional passengers or cargo, as a result of the link-up with the other carrier, and the marketing improvements which are created. Traffic and revenue gains may also result from reduced competition on routes where the alliance partners were previously competing head on. These traffic gains will need to be converted into increased revenue projections. Any increased operating costs resulting from higher traffic levels would need to be offset against the revenue improvements. It would also be crucial to assess any revenue reductions on routes not directly part of the alliance agreement if the latter leads to a redirection of passengers to a new hub. For instance, Aer Lingus's decision early in 2000 to join the Oneworld alliance may mean that Aer Lingus passengers previously hubbing through Amsterdam to fly to long-haul destinations would be switched to London to transfer onto British Airways. Aer Lingus revenue from a Dublin–London passenger transferring in London would almost certainly be less than from a Dublin–Amsterdam passenger doing the same in Amsterdam. On the cost side, the level of cost reduction through joint activities and synergies of any kind will very much depend on the nature of the agreement between the partners. An alliance may of course result in some increased costs from a variety of sources such as the need to advertise the alliance or from some rebranding and service improvements. All the potential benefits and costs arising from alternative partnerships must be evaluated in detail. In turn these will reflect the degree to which a partner's network is complementary in scope and destinations served rather than one which merely duplicates one's own network. In traffic generation terms the former is likely to be more attractive. For smaller airlines linking with a larger carrier, the attractiveness and efficiency of the latter's hub(s) is an important consideration. But this too should be reflected in the amount of new traffic generated.

There are also non-quantifiable factors that need to be considered. Often they may be the most critical in choosing an alliance partner. Do the partners have a common long-term vision of where they want the alliance to go? Do they have shared objectives? A failure to share and work towards common goals will eventually destroy the alliance. This is what happened with the British Airways-US Airways alliance and also with the earliest global alliance, that between SIA, Swissair and Delta. Apart from common objectives, partners should also have a similar culture in terms of service standards and ideally similar management styles. The latter may be less critical than the former. Another important consideration, especially for smaller airlines, is whether the alliance partner demands exclusivity. That means, would the smaller carrier be excluded from making marketing or commercial agreements with other carriers, say, on routes not directly affected by the alliance? Exclusivity may be required if a smaller regional airline has a choice of hubs through which it can interline its long-haul passengers. Even large carriers joining global alliances may be concerned about exclusivity. Thus, early in 2000 Japan Airlines was still hesitating in joining the Oneworld alliance for fear of jeopardising existing bilateral agreements with non-alliance carriers (*Flight International*, 28 March–3 April 2000). The final issue to examine is whether there are strings attached to the alliance agreement. Thus, when Air Mauritius entered into an alliance with Air France in 1998 it was required to use Air France for its in-flight catering, for its aircraft maintenance and other bought-in services. In some such cases the new supplier of these services may turn out to be more expensive than the airline's former supplier. Such impacts, whether adverse or beneficial, would also have to be costed.

It is clear that each alliance proposal and potential partner would have to be assessed in detail on a case-by-case basis. The issues raised above provide a starting point for such an evaluation. But two things should be borne in mind. First, as previously mentioned, alliances are not an end in themselves. They must be used to achieve clearly defined objectives. Second, what Michael Porter stated in relation to industrial alliances in general appears equally true of airline alliances. Namely, that 'Alliances are a tool for extending or reinforcing competitive advantage, but rarely a sustainable means for creating it!' (Porter, 1990).

9.5 Cost reduction as a long-term necessity

In the past, the airlines' response to the cyclical downturn that occurred near the start of each decade was a determined effort to reduce costs by whatever means possible. Staff numbers were reduced, seasonal staff were not taken on, advertising and training budgets were cut, fleet renewal was delayed, a few unprofitable routes were cut, and so on. As the economic climate improved and as airline losses gave way to profits, airline managements tended to relax their vigilance. The downward pressure on unit costs lessened. Instead of falling further, unit costs in real terms tended to flatten out and in the case of some airlines they actually rose. At least until the next cyclical downturn when a new bout of cost control and, where possible, cost reduction began. Drastic cost cutting and control was seen very much as a short-term measure to face imminent crises.

Over the last ten years or so the nature of the airline industry has changed. Progressive international liberalisation, as shown in Chapters 2 and 3, has made overcapacity endemic to many markets. The disappearance of most controls on passenger fares and cargo tariffs has made both the latter more volatile. Pricing freedom wherever it is combined with overcapacity leads inevitably to downward pressure on average yields. This problem will be increasingly exacerbated by the impact of electronic commerce which will shift the balance of market power from the suppliers, the airlines, to the consumers, that is, passengers and freight shippers. Where low-cost, no-frills airlines enter new markets they too will induce further tariff cuts among conventional airlines. In markets where liberalisation has not yet caught up or where there are infrastructural constraints on airline frequencies, as at slot-constrained airports, capacity may be under- rather than overprovided, and it will be possible to ensure that yields hold up. But such markets will be in a minority. The expectation is that during the present decade the overall trend in airline fares and yields in most markets will continue to be downward.

Whether the cyclical downturn evident in 1999 continues and worsens in 2000 and 2001 or not the reality is that falling real yields are certain to be a long-term phenomenon. Any short-term increases which may occur when airlines collectively try to reverse the trend are likely to be short-lived. In the circumstances attitudes to cost control must change. Cost reduction is no longer a short-term response to declining yields or falling load factors. It is a continuous and permanent requirement if airlines are to be profitable. Many airline executives are clearly already aware of this necessity. But how can airline unit costs be contained and reduced?

Improvements in aircraft technology can play a part. The further penetration of new generation jet aircraft, as older aircraft fleets are renewed, the switch from smaller to larger aircraft, where runway capacities have been used up or where traffic has grown sufficiently to justify upsizing, and the wider use of regional jets will all help to reduce unit costs.

However, the impact will not be as great as occurred for instance when wide-bodied aircraft were introduced, because more recent improvements in engine and airframe technology are not so radical. Therefore the focus of cost control strategies must be elsewhere.

The continuous battle to contain and, where possible, to reduce costs will need to be fought on three fronts. It has been argued earlier in this book that labour represents the largest single cost item for airlines and that staff costs per employee vary significantly between airlines, especially between those in different countries. For these two reasons, labour will inevitably be the first key area for cost containment. Airlines will need to contain if not reduce the unit cost of labour and at the same time improve the productivity of that labour. An earlier chapter suggested ways in which this might be done (Chapter 5). The second area on which to focus is that of sales, ticketing and distribution which, taken together, account for 15 to 20 per cent of most airlines' total costs. The key to success here clearly lies in the rapid introduction of e-commerce and online sales as well as more widespread use of automation for ticketing, check-in and so on (Chapter 7). Finally, costs can be reduced through operational and service changes. Here, conventional airlines have much to learn from their low-cost competitors (Chapter 6). They must explore the ways in which, and the degree to which, they can emulate any of the operational or other improvements and product changes introduced by the latter so as to reduce their own costs further. In all the areas mentioned above, it is evident that costs could be reduced through outsourcing. The degree to which airlines are prepared to follow this path to lower costs may be dependent on the business model they have adopted (see section 9.3). Whatever strategies each airline adopts the underlying requirement is clear. Cost reduction must be seen as a continuous and long-term prerequisite for financial survival.

9.6 Marketing focused on yield improvement

The airline business is dynamic and potentially unstable. The interplay of three key factors determines whether an airline is profitable or not. These are the unit costs, the unit revenues or yields, and the load factors achieved. Low yields can be compensated for by higher load factors so that total revenues generated exceed the costs. Conversely, if load factors are falling average yields need to be pushed up in order to continue generating the same total revenue as before. It has been suggested throughout this book that the long-term trend in average yields is likely to be downward because of further liberalisation and overcapacity in some markets, because of the impact of low-cost carriers and the growing commoditisation of the airline product as distribution becomes more dependent on Internet sales. As discussed above, one crucial response to such a trend must be to focus on cost reduction as a continuous priority. Though industry yields may be moving downwards, each individual airline must try to push up its own yields while maintaining or increasing load factors. Marketing strategies must focus on yield improvement.

This is self-evident and easy to say. The difficulty lies in effectively implementing marketing strategies which can achieve higher yields in markets which are inherently unstable. Airlines need to focus on three areas. First, they must identify the market segments they wish to target both in their passenger and cargo markets. This means clarifying the characteristics of each segment, its product requirements and the degree to which it generates profitable business for the airline. An example of the approach needed was the exercise undertaken by British Airways in the second half of 1999 in response to falling passenger yields and disappearing profits. The study identified that economy class traffic transferring through its London hubs between two short-haul routes was the most unprofitable market segment, followed by short-haul to long-haul economy transfer passengers and economy passengers on short-haul European routes. The airline decided to reduce its exposure in these market segments by reducing the seating capacity available for them. But within each of these market segments it was possible to identify sub-segments which could be targeted. At the other extreme the most profitable segments overall were the direct short-haul and long-haul point-to-point premium passengers, that is, those paying business, full economy or first-class fares. These were the markets BA decided to grow and defend. There were some traffics which were more marginal such as long-haul to long-haul economy transfer passengers, where BA's response was to try and improve the fare mix so as to push up average yields. Different airlines will undertake the process of market segmentation in different ways. But the aim is the same, to identify the characteristics and potential profitability of the various market segments as a prerequisite for effective marketing and pricing policies. In addition to internal economic analysis, market segmentation also requires detailed and frequent market research and customer surveys to establish the wants and needs of the different market segments.

The second step is to constantly improve every aspect of the product and service offered or at least those aspects identified as being important in the market research. This applies equally to the passenger and cargo services offered. The aim of such improvements for each airline must be to try and differentiate its product from that of its competitors. This makes it easier for the airline to brand its product and counter the trend towards commoditisation which electronic commerce will accelerate. Effective branding and product differentiation should in turn make it possible to charge a premium on the prevailing market tariff and thereby push up yields. Since any product improvement can be matched within a year or two by competitors, it is important to be innovative and constantly searching for ways to upgrade the service offered on the ground or in the air. On medium- and long-haul routes it is easier to differentiate one's product or service because passengers spend a much longer time in the aircraft. When towards the end of 1996 British Airways was the first to introduce seats that converted into fully flat beds in first class, it generated new demand for this service and diverted passengers from other airlines. It enjoyed a major competitive advantage. BA was even able on some routes to charge a premium over the normal first-class fare for a couple of years or so until competitors caught up. The airline was hoping to repeat its success in 2000 by introducing sleeper beds in business class. Some years earlier Virgin Atlantic had identified a market segment poorly served in terms of value for money. These were the passengers who paid full economy fares on long-haul sectors and travelled in the crowded and often tightly packed economy cabin with passengers who had paid much less. Virgin set up a mid-class cabin for them and provided improved in-flight services. British Airways also recently identified this market segment as being important. As from August 2000 it was introducing a separate cabin on long-haul flights for such passengers with wider seats, more legroom, and other improvements.

On short-haul sectors differentiation is more difficult because airlines have fewer critical product features to juggle with, since journey times are so short. They tend to focus on flight frequency as a competitive tool, on check-in procedures, on seating density, on in-flight catering and so on. Product innovation is particularly difficult. Conventional scheduled airlines have been very poor at innovation on short sectors compared to the low-cost carriers. There are several areas where further improvements could be made to speed up elapsed travel times or on-board comfort and convenience. For instance, more automated check-in, or more on-board space for hand luggage and coats. Better service features may mean higher costs. So a balance must be maintained between what is desirable and what is feasible in terms of additional revenue generated through attracting more passengers, improving the traffic mix or higher yields.

The third aspect of marketing strategy must be to ensure that an airline and everyone working within it and for it is customer focused. This means not only being aware, as a result of the market research and surveys recommended earlier, of what customers require, but also making sure that their expectations are met in a way which encourages them both to become loyal repeat customers and where possible to pay a premium. The ability to achieve this is partly related to the product and service quality being offered and partly to staff attitudes and culture. From first enquiry about service availability and fares to baggage collection at the end of a flight, passengers will have around a dozen or more separate contacts with airline employees. If any one of those turns unpleasant or is unsatisfactory for the passenger it can sour his or her view of the airline. The quality of personal contacts is of key importance in a service industry. Online selling and automation will reduce the number of personal, one-to-one contacts, but will re-emphasise how important the remaining contacts are. Too many airlines still do not have a sufficiently strong service culture. This is particularly true of many state-owned airlines and a few of the older privatised airlines (see Chapter 8, section 8.2). Even when airlines have developed a high-quality service culture they may begin to lose it through poor and inadequate management, as happened with British Airways in the late 1990s. Thus, in the coming years, airlines must undertake massive and constant training and retraining of staff in all departments to ensure a high level of interpersonal skills and a culture of service.

The ultimate aim is to attract new customers and capture the loyalty of existing ones. Several different tools are used, apart from the quality of service provided in all areas, to ensure customer loyalty and repeat business. A key one is an airline's frequent flyer programme (FFP). But since frequent flyers, who are often the high-yield premium passengers, tend to belong to several airlines' FFPs the latter are becoming less significant in choice of airline. As part of a strategy both of product differentiation and being customer focused, airlines must move rapidly to customer relations management. They must use the opportunities offered by electronic commerce and informatics to develop one-to-one relations with their customers, tailoring service provision to each customer's individual and known requirements (see Chapter 7, section 7.5). The airlines who will succeed at maximising the opportunities offered by electronic commerce are likely to be those that adopt and use e-commerce the quickest and in the most wholehearted way.

Too often, airline managements place too much emphasis on improving market share as an end in itself. They tend to add frequencies and reduce fares to fill the additional seats in the pursuit of higher market shares. It appears attractive as a strategy. More passengers support even higher frequencies, which in turn provide a competitive advantage and attract yet more passengers. Higher frequencies and more passengers mean lower costs per passenger. If the routes involved are from a hub, the attraction of that hub airport is reinforced. But if one is capturing higher market share primarily through more aggressive and lower tariffs, there is a real risk that average yields fall more rapidly than costs. Or that passenger load factors do not rise sufficiently to compensate for and offset the fall in yields. It is the near obsession with increasing market share that has driven and continues to drive many airlines towards the brink of disaster, especially when overall market conditions worsen.

In the more uncertain and unstable years ahead airline marketing should be refocused to give priority on increasing yield. This can be done only through a better understanding of the requirements of different market segments, through constantly improved and innovative products and services to reflect those requirements, and through the more effective use of customer relations management.

Appendices

Appendix A: Freedoms of the Air

Negotiated in bilateral air services agreements

First Freedom The right to fly over another country without landing.

Second Freedom The right to make a landing for technical reasons (e.g. refuelling) in another country without picking up/setting down revenue traffic.

Third Freedom The right to carry revenue traffic from your own country (A) to the country (B) of your treaty partner.

Fourth Freedom The right to carry traffic from country B back to your own country A.

Fifth Freedom The right of an airline from country A to carry revenue traffic between country B and other countries such as C or D on services starting or ending in its home country A. (This freedom cannot be used unless countries C or D also agree.)

Supplementary rights

Sixth 'Freedom' The use by an airline of country A of two sets of Third and Fourth Freedom rights to carry traffic between two other countries but using its base at A as a transit point.

Seventh 'Freedom' The right of an airline to carry revenue traffic between points in two countries on services which lie entirely outside its own home country.

Eighth 'Freedom' or cabotage rights The right for an airline to pick up and set down passengers or freight between two domestic points in another country on a service originating in its own home country.

Sixth Freedom rights are rarely dealt with explicitly in air services agreements but may be referred to implicitly in memoranda of understanding attached to the agreement. In the application of many bilaterals there is also de facto acceptance of such rights.

Seventh and Eighth Freedom rights are granted only in very rare cases.

Appendix B: definitions of common air transport terms

Aircraft kilometres are the distances flown by aircraft. An aircraft's total flying is obtained by multiplying the number of flights performed on each flight stage by the stage distance.

Aircraft utilisation is the average number of block hours that each aircraft is in use. This is generally measured on a daily or annual basis.

Available seat-kilometres (ASKs) are obtained by multiplying the number of seats available for sale on each flight stage by flight stage distance.

Available tonne-kilometres (ATKs) are obtained by multiplying the number of tonnes of capacity available for carriage of passengers and cargo on each sector of a flight by the stage distance.

Average aircraft capacity is obtained by dividing an airline's total available tonne-kilometres (ATKs) by aircraft kilometres flown.

Average stage length is obtained by dividing an airline's total aircraft kilometres flown in a year by number of aircraft departures; it is the weighted average of stage/sector lengths flown by an airline.

Block time (hours) is the time for each flight stage or sector, measured from when the aircraft leaves the airport gate or stand (chocks off) to when it arrives on the gate or stand at the destination airport (chocks on). It can also be calculated from the moment an aircraft moves under its own power until it comes to rest at its destination.

Break-even load factor (per cent) is the load factor required to equate total traffic revenue with operating costs.

Cabin crew refers to stewards and stewardesses.

Code sharing is when two or more airlines use their own flight codes or a common code on a flight operated by one of them.

Flight or cockpit crew refers to the pilot, co-pilot and flight engineer (if any).

Freight tonne-kilometres (FTKs) are obtained by multiplying the tonnes of freight uplifted by the sector distances over which they have been flown. They are a measure of an airline's cargo traffic.

Freight yields are obtained by dividing total revenue from scheduled freight by the freight tonne kilometres (FTKs) produced (often expressed in US cents per FTK).

Grandfather rights is the convention by which airlines retain the right to use particular take-off and landing slot times at an airports because they have done so previously, and continuously.

Interlining is the acceptance by one airline of travel documents issued by another airline for carriage on the services of the first airline. An interline passenger is one using a through fare for a journey involving two or more separate airlines.

Online passenger is one who transfers from one flight to another but on the same airline.

Operating costs per ATK is a measure obtained by dividing total operating costs by total ATKs. Operating costs excludes interest payments, taxes and extraordinary items. They can also be measured per RTK.

Operating ratio (per cent) is the operating revenue expressed as a percentage of operating costs. Sometimes referred to as the Revex Ratio.

Passenger-kilometres or Revenue passenger-kilometres (RPKs) are obtained by multiplying the number of fare paying passengers on each flight stage by flight stage distance. They are a measure of an airline's passenger traffic.

Passenger load factor (per cent) is passenger-kilometres (RPKs) expressed as a percentage of available seat kilometres (ASKs) (on a single sector, this is simplified to the number of passengers carried as a percentage of seats available for sale).

Revenue tonne-kilometres (RTKs) measure the output actually sold. They are obtained by multiplying the total number of tonnes of passengers and cargo carried on each flight stage by flight stage distance (Revenue Passenger Kms are normally converted to revenue tonne-kms on a standard basis of 90 kg average weight, including free and excess baggage, although this has been increased recently by some airlines, e.g. British Airways have increased the average weight from 90 kg to 95 kg, as a result of a CAA directive.

Seat factor or passenger load factor on a single sector is obtained by expressing the passengers carried as a percentage of the seats available for sale; on a network of routes it is obtained by expressing the total passenger-kms (RPKs) as a percentage of the total seat-kms available (ASKs).

Seat pitch is the standard way of measuring seat density on an aircraft. It is the distance between the back of one seat and the same point on the back of the seat in front.

Scheduled passenger yields is the average revenue per passenger kilometre and is obtained by dividing the total passenger revenue by the total passenger kilometres. This can be done by flight route or for the network.

Slot at an airport is the right to operate one take-off or landing at that airport within a fixed time period.

Stage or sector distance should be the air route or flying distance between two airports. In practice many airlines use the great circle distance which is shorter.

Weight load factor measures the proportion of available capacity actually sold. It is the revenue tonne kilometres performed expressed as percentage of available tonne kilometres (also called overall load factor).

Wide-bodied aircraft are civil aircraft which have two passenger aisles (Boeing 767); narrow-bodied aircraft, such as the Airbus A320 have only one aisle.

Bibliography

AEA (1999a) *Airline Alliances and Competition in Transatlantic Markets*, Brussels: Association of European Airlines.

AEA (1999b) *Towards a Transatlantic Common Aviation Area*, AEA Policy Statement, September 1999, Brussels: Association of European Airlines.

Airbus (1999) *Global Market Forecast 1999–2018*, Toulouse: Airbus Industrie, May.

Airline Monitor (1999) *The Airline Monitor*, August, Florida: ESG Aviation Services.

Alamdari, F. and Morrell, P. (1997) 'Airline labour cost reduction: post-liberalisation experience in the USA and Europe', *Journal of Air Transport Management*, Vol. 3, No. 2, April.

Aviation Strategy (1999) 'KLM and Alitalia: One big ticket', *Aviation Strategy*, No. 23, September (London).

Aviation Strategy (2000) 'US low-cost carriers reassert themselves', *Aviation Strategy*, No. 29, March (London).

Avmark (1988) *Avmark Aviation Economist*, October, London.

Balfour, J. (1995a) 'The EC Commission's policy on state aids for airline restructuring: is the bonfire alight?' *Air and Space Law*, Vol XX, No. 2, April.

Balfour, J. (1995b) 'State aid to airlines – a question of law or politics', *Yearbook of European Law*, No. 15.

Bonnassies, O. (1999) 'Debonair: recovered pan-European pioneer?', *Avmark Aviation Economist*, Vol. 15, No. 9, November (London).

British Airways (1984) *Annual Report and Account 1983–84*, London.

Brown, M. (1998) 'Manufacturing aircraft for the 21st century – the challenges ahead', *The 12th Annual Financial Times World Aerospace and Air Transport Conference*, September, London.

Brueckner, J. and Whalen, W.T. (1998) *The Price Effects of International Airline Alliances*, University of Illinois, November.

Bruggisser, P. (1997) 'Controlling costs: Third International Airline Conference', London: UBS, February.

CAA (1998) *The Single European Aviation Market: The First Five Years*, CAP 685, London: Civil Aviation Authority, June.

CAA (1999) *UK Airlines Annual Operating, Traffic and Financial Statistics 1998*, London: Civil Aviation Authority, May.

Callison, J. W. (1992) 'Globalisation of the world's air transport industry : the North American, North Atlantic and EC Markets', *Airports and Aviation Educational Conference*, Washington, DC, May.

Cassani, B. (1999) 'Go', *Warburg Dillon Read Transport Conference*, London, October.

CEC (1987a) *Council Directive of 14 December 1987* on fares for scheduled air services between Member States (87/601/EEC). *Council Decision of 14 December 1987* on the sharing of passenger capacity on scheduled air services between Member States (87/602/EEC). Brussels: Commission of the European Communities.

CEC (1987b) *Council Regulations (EEC) No. 3975/87 and No. 2976/87 of 14 December 1987* on the application of rules of competition in the air transport sector. Brussels: Commission of the European Communities.

CEC (1988) *Commission Regulation (EEC) No. 2671/88 of July 1988.* Brussels: Commission of the European Communities.

CEC (1992) *Council Regulation No. 2407/92* on licensing of air carriers; *Council Regulation No. 2408/92* on access for community air carriers to intra community air routes, and *Council Regulation No. 2409/92* on fares and rates for air services. *Official Journal*, 24 August, Brussels: Commission of the European Communities.

Cheong, C.K. (1998) 'Alliance realities', *Aerospace Journal*, August, London: Royal Aeronautical Society.

Comité des Sages (1994) *Expanding Horizons*, a report by the Comité des Sages for Air Transport to the European Commission, Brussels: European Commission, January.

Commission (1999) *The European Airline Industry: From Single Market to Worldwide Challenges*, Communication from the Commission. COM (1999) 182 Final. Commission of the European Communities, Brussels, 20–05. 1999.

Corbin, P. (1999) 'The journey of an airline within an airline', *Low-cost Airlines Conference*, Amsterdam (September).

Cranfield (1998) *User Costs at Airports in Europe, S E Asia and the USA, 1997–98.* Research Report No. 6, Air Transport Group, College of Aeronautics, Cranfield University, UK (January).

Cranfield (2000) *Measures of Strategic Success: The Evidence Over Ten Years.* Research Report No. 8, Air Transport Group, College of Aeronautics, Cranfield University, UK (February).

de Irala, X. (1998) 'The transformation of Iberia', *Third Annual Transport Conference*, Warburg Dillon Read, London (September).

de Palacio, L. (1999) Speech to *Beyond Open Skies Conference*, Chicago, December. Brussels: European Commission.

Debonair (1998) *Annual Report and Accounts 1998*, Debonair Holdings plc, London.

Doganis, R. (1991) *Flying Off Course: The Economics of International Airlines*, London: Routledge.

Doganis, R. (1994) 'The impact of liberalisation on European airline strategies and operations', *Journal of Air Transport Management,* Vol. 1 (1).

Ebbinghaus, D. (1999) *The Impact of E-business and E-commerce in the Air Transport Industry*, IATA Airline Financial Forum, Hong Kong (September).

European Commission (1994) *Official Journal 1994 C350/5*, Commission guidelines on state aid to airlines.

European Commission (1999a) *The European Airline Industry: From a Single Market to a World-wide Challenge*, Brussels (June).

European Commission (1999b) *The European Airline Industry: From Single Market to Worldwide Challenges*, Commission of the European Communities. COM (1999) 182 Final. Brussels (May).

Freiberg, K. and Freiberg, J. (1996) *Nuts: Southwest Airlines' Crazy Recipe for Business and Personal Success*, Austin, TX: Bard Press.

GAO (1995) *International Aviation: Airline Alliances Produce Benefits but Effect on Competition is Uncertain*, Washington, DC: US General Accounting Office.

Godfrey, B. (1999) 'Virgin Express, "A different approach" ', *Nordic Aviation Conference*, Den Danske Bank, Copenhagen (June).

Guillebaud, D. (1999) 'The needs of innovation in managing a range of distribution channels', *IBM Travel and Transportation Executive Conference*, Vancouver (February).

Hanlon, P. (1996) *Global Airlines: Competition in a Transnational Industry*, London: Heinemann.

Holiday Which (1999) *Holiday Which*, London: Consumers Association.

IATA (1996) *Distribution Costs Study*, Hounslow, UK: International Air Transport Association (April).

IBM (1999) *World Airlines Benchmark Report*, Feltham, UK: IBM United Kingdom Limited.

ICAO (1996) *Civil Aviation Statistics of the World 1995*, Montreal: International Civil Aviation Organisation.

Kasper, D.M. (1994) 'The US Airline Commission: an insider's perspective' *Journal of Air Transport Management*, Vol. 1, No. 1, March.

Kropp, T. (1999) 'The rationale of alliances: the perspective of Lufthansa', *Seminar on Alliances*, European Aviation Club, 30 March, Brussels.

Lobbenberg, A. (1999) 'Strategic alliances', *Air Transport Management Seminar*, College of Aeronautics, Cranfield University, November (unpublished).

Lufthansa (1995) *Annual Report 1995*, Cologne.

Lufthansa (1998) *Annual Report 1998*, Cologne.

Merrill Lynch (1999) *Global Airline Alliances*, New York (June).

Newton, G. (1999) 'Distribution – changing channels', *Airlines International*, Oct.–Nov. (London).

Nuutinen, H. (1998) 'Southwest now appearing in the east', *Aviation Strategy*, No. 6, April (London).

Official Journal (1994) Application of Articles 92 and 93 of the EC Treaty and Article 61 of the EEA Agreement to State Aid in the Aviation Sector, *Official Journal of the European Communities*, 10 December 1994 (No. C350/5), Brussels.

Official Journal (1996) *Lufthansa/SAS*. Official Journal of the European Communities No. L54/28.

Official Journal (1996a) Commission Communication Pursuant to Article 93(2) of the EC Treaty Addressed to the Other Member States and Interested Parties Concerning Aid Granted to Olympic Airways, *Official Journal of the European Communities*, 19 June 1996, No. C176/5. Brussels.

Official Journal (1998) Commission Notice Concerning the Alliance Between Lufthansa, SAS and United Airlines. Commission Notice Concerning the Alliance Between British Airways and American Airlines, *Official Journal of the European Communities*, 30 July. Brussels.

O'Leary, M. (1999) 'Ryanair: the Low Fares Airline', *Fourth Annual Transport Conference*, Warburg Dillon Read, London (October).

Pena, F. (1995) *Statement of the Secretary of Transportation. International Air Transportation Policy*, Washington, DC: US Department of Transportation (April).

Porter, M. (1990) *The Competitive Advantage of Nations*, New York: Free Press.

Presidential Documents (1978) *Weekly Compilation of Presidential Documents*, Vol. 14, No. 34, August (Washington, DC).

Reitan, G. (1999) 'The impact of alliances on traffic patterns and the competitive climate', *Nordic Aviation Conference*, June, Copenhagen.

Ryanair (1997) *Ryanair Holdings plc. Combined Offering of 54,167,596 Ordinary Shares of IR4p each*. Prospectus. Dublin.

Salomon Smith Barney (1999) 'From the jetage to the netage', *European Airline Review: A New Dawn for 2000?* London: Salomon Smith Barney, Global Equity Research (November).

Samuel, M. (1992) *Presentation to World-Wide Air Transport Colloquium*, 6–12 April, International Civil Aviation Organisation, Montreal.

Scard, L. (1998) 'Franchising: paper to air transport marketing seminar', Cranfield College of Aeronautics, May (unpublished).

Schorderet, G. (1999) 'SAir Group strategy, alliances, key financial', *Nordic Aviation Conference* June, Copenhagen.

Shane, J.N. (1992) *Presentation to World-Wide Air Transport Colloquium*, 6–12 April. International Civil Aviation Organisation, Montreal.

Soames, T. (1999) *The Application of EU Competition Rules to Aviation and Alliances*, Brussels: Norton Rose.

Soames, T. (2000) 'Harmonisation of competition rules', *IATA Legal Symposium 2000*, San Diego, California, 6–8 February.

Soames, T. and Ryan, A. (1995) 'State aid and air transport', *European Community Law Review*, No. 5.

US government (1995) *International Air Transportation Policy*, Washington, DC: US Department of Transportation (April).

Index

Note: numbers in **bold** type refer to figures (diagrams) and numbers in *italics* refer to tables